World Wisdom
The Library of Perennial Philosophy

The Library of Perennial Philosophy is dedicated to the exposition of the timeless Truth underlying the diverse religions. This Truth, often referred to as the *Sophia Perennis*—or Perennial Wisdom—finds its expression in the revealed Scriptures as well as in the writings of the great sages and the artistic creations of the traditional worlds.

A Spirit of Tolerance: The Inspiring Life of Tierno Bokar appears as one of our selections in the Spiritual Masters: East and West series.

Spiritual Masters: East & West Series

This series presents the writings of great spiritual masters of the past and present from both East and West. Carefully selected essential writings of these sages are combined with biographical information, glossaries of technical terms, historical maps, and pictorial and photographic art in order to communicate a sense of their respective spiritual climates.

Cover: The Great Mosque of Djenné, Mali

A Spirit of Tolerance
The Inspiring Life of
Tierno Bokar

by

AMADOU HAMPATÉ BÂ

Edited by
Roger Gaetani

Introduction by
Louis Brenner

World Wisdom

A Spirit of Tolerance:
The Inspiring Life of Tierno Bokar
by Amadou Hampaté Bâ
© 2008 World Wisdom, Inc.

This book is a complete translation, by
Fatima Jane Casewit, of
Vie et enseignement de Tierno Bokar:
Le Sage de Bandiagara (Éditions du Seuil, 1980).

Most recent printing indicated by last digit below:
10 9 8 7 6 5 4 3 2

Library of Congress Cataloging-in-Publication Data

Bâ, Amadou Hampaté.
  [Vie et enseignement de Tierno Bokar. English]
  A spirit of tolerance : the inspiring life of Tierno Bokar / by Amadou Hampaté Bâ ;
edited by Roger Gaetani ; introduction by Louis Brenner.
       p. cm. -- (The library of perenniel philosophy. Spiritual masters--East & West
series)
  Includes bibliographical references and index.
  ISBN 978-1-933316-47-5 (pbk. : alk. paper) 1. Cerno Bokar Saalif Taal. 2. Tijaniyah
members--Mali--Biography. 3. Sufism--Mali. I. Gaetani, Roger, 1954- II. Title.
  BP80.T54.B313 2008
  297.4092--dc22
  [B]
                                                                              2007044694

Printed on acid-free paper in the United States of America.

For information address World Wisdom, Inc.
P.O. Box 2682, Bloomington, Indiana 47402-2682
www.worldwisdom.com

CONTENTS

PREFACE

The story of remarkable individuals should belong to the world, as well as to a specific time and place. In a world where religious faiths are often at odds with each other, where fundamentalisms fight for dominance, and where tolerance too often lacks the foundation of clear intelligence needed to communicate and sustain it, the story of Tierno Bokar should be shared.

Tierno Bokar (1875-1939) was an African mystic and a Muslim spiritual teacher of the early twentieth century. He was a man immersed in the pursuit of proximity to God, but besides this he made it his mission to share selflessly what he knew inwardly with others around him, if they also sincerely aspired to proximity with God. He was born and died in the desert country of Mali during the period of French occupation. Such forced "modernizations" and the influx of foreign rulers always cause upheaval, and tribal or sectarian differences become magnified. This was the environment that surrounded Tierno Bokar his entire life, and it made his free pursuit of spiritual growth very difficult. Yet, despite all this, as we read the pages on his life and teachings that follow, we find in them no trace of sectarian divisiveness, but instead we sense a pervasive peace and calm, love and charity, a clearly communicated and accessible spiritual wisdom, and a saintly tolerance toward others. This is a teacher whose words deserve close attention.

This is the first full English translation of the book *Vie et enseignement de Tierno Bokar: Le Sage de Bandiagara*, which was written by his student, the well-known writer on African life and spirituality, Amadou Hampaté Bâ (c. 1900-1991). It is our hope that the gift given to the French-speaking world by Bâ through this extraordinary story will now be extended to the English-speaking public through the publication of this English translation.

Tierno (pronounced "Chair-no") Bokar was a relatively obscure figure in the history of African and Muslim spirituality. This was by his own design. He did not want to be known as a spiritual master, though as this book will reveal he surely was one; he preferred to humble himself before another master whom he considered to be greater. He never sought power, though people of his learning and magnetism often exploit these traits for personal gain; instead, he sought to bring light to the hearts and minds of his devoted students. He did not call special attention to doctrinal points that distanced his spiritual teachings from those of others, though this sectarian impulse seems to be a universal human affliction; rather, his instinct towards brotherhood with all those who sincerely seek God's Presence resulted in a life and in teachings that serve as wonderful examples of religious tolerance. Tierno Bokar's tolerance, too, was exemplary because it was based not on some vague sentimentality but on profound understanding of spiritual realities and on vast love and charity towards others.

These are the qualities that attracted us to this book and why World Wisdom has undertaken the considerable effort required to present this book to you now. Catherine Schuon, the widow of the great twentieth-century perennialist and writer on traditional spirituality, Frithjof Schuon (1907-1998), brought this book to our attention. Her late husband had read the book and liked it very much, and even "highly recommended" it to others. We can safely assume that he, like so many others, must have been attracted to the person and thought of Tierno Bokar due to the indisputable virtue and intelligence of the man. It is our hope that this volume will join the very select company of inspiring books on important contemporary Muslim mystics, such as Martin Lings' *A Sufi Saint of the Twentieth Century: Shaikh Ahmad Al-Alawi, His Spiritual Heritage and Legacy.*

Virtue is not a subject often discussed in contemporary writings on religion. Yet, it is certainly the most accessible bridge over which we can cross to understand, appreciate, and even to love someone of another time, place, and tradition. For example, Westerners came to honor Saladin for his chivalry, Gandhi for his courage, the Dalai Lama for his gentle wisdom, and so on. It usually is not the specific ideas or doctrines of these people that first attract those outside their traditions—it is their virtue. Part One of this book, on the life of Tierno Bokar, gives a detailed biographical sketch, to be sure, but more than this it communicates to us the virtue of this great soul which, though cruelly tried by the petty stupidities, jealousies, and ambitions of men, transmits to us unfaltering love, intelligence, and the glow of a never-diminished communion with God.

Intelligence that can see through the glaring differences in religious forms to the universal celestial principles that underlie and, in a sense, unite them all is rare. It is particularly rare when one's environment is charged with sectarianism, political intrigue, and fundamentalism, as was the case for Tierno Bokar. It is all the more remarkable that he arrived at his ideas on the validity of different faiths and sects largely on his own, with his own intelligence and heart his primary source. He had, certainly, read some of the most esoteric writings of classical Sufism, and these may have assisted in opening his mind to the possibility of what Frithjof Schuon called "the transcendent unity of religions." Still, in the discourses of Part Two of this book, "His Words," we sense that it was just as much Tierno's expansive heart that would not permit him to accept any one religion's exclusivist claims to God's acceptance and Love. Tierno's great personal virtue and his love for all creation combined with and guided his piercing intelligence, permitting him to penetrate beyond worldly appearances to celestial realities. Sufis and other mystics would explain this as the result of his having achieved a spiritual state in which one's full being becomes suffused with the Truth, a state in which only a perfected soul (i.e. a completely virtuous soul) can perceive the perfect Light that shines beyond all particular forms. The parables and discourses of Part Two, though very much grounded in the culture of West Africa, are surprising in their capacity to speak to us despite our distance from that culture. Somehow, we all can find some light for our own paths in these words that are reflected to us through the illuminated and pure soul of a Muslim and Sufi from many years ago in Africa.

Tierno Bokar's greatest gift was his ability to live inwardly, contemplatively, and to achieve a spiritual realization that most of us will never know. His presence and quiet magnetism made a powerful impression on and gave a clear example to those who knew him. One need only read his student Amadou Hampaté Bâ's words to see the proof of this. However, Tierno Bokar's greatest bequest to those around him was his teaching, an endowment which we can also share through this book. He was, above all, a master teacher. He had an unusual ability and inclination to tailor his teachings to common people. In his school in Bandiagara, he taught difficult texts of theology and metaphysics, and he delighted in discussions about esoteric topics, but Tierno Bokar's mission always was to communicate to any sincere seeker, farmer or scholar, various ways to approach God. The discourses in Part Two can speak to anyone of any level of education or from any religious background or culture, if that person seeks God.

As a measure of this saintly teacher and communicator, we might ask ourselves, "Can there be any greater purpose and merit of learning and communication than to accomplish the goal of bringing people closer to God?"

Part Three, "His Teachings," shows another side of Tierno Bokar: his role as a Sufi instructor. Tierno Bokar was a Sufi in the Tijani brotherhood, an initiatic order widespread in that part of Africa. Tierno was very learned in Sufi symbolism, metaphysics, and practice. He was a representative of his spiritual master and a teacher of doctrine and practice. As was mentioned above, he was a master teacher, and so his skill was turned to teaching the doctrine and method of his Sufi order. This is what we find in Part Three: a system for conveying Tijani doctrine. It is not as accessible to Western or non-Muslim readers as the preceding sections, but gives us a more detailed understanding of his own beliefs and how he conceived a way to convey them to others. Although the message here is more focused on those learning about one form of esoteric Islam, the mark of the master teacher is still apparent.

In the appendices, readers will find various Tijani litanies and some additional background on Sufism.

For readers who are interested in learning more about the life and teachings of Tierno Bokar, we highly recommend *West African Sufi: The Religious Heritage and Spiritual Search of Cerno Bokar Saalif Taal* (1984; paperback edition 2005) by Dr. Louis Brenner. This detailed study can supply readers with an abundance of helpful historical, religious, and cultural context to understand Tierno Bokar and his teachings. *West African Sufi* also includes additional discourses of Tierno Bokar and information that Dr. Brenner gleaned from personal interviews with Amadou Hampaté Bâ.

A few words about conventions we have adopted in this book: In most cases, we have followed French spelling of the names of people. This is simply to aid readers who may want to further their research, since more research on this area is available in French than in English, as well as the fact that many who have written in English have also followed the French spellings. We have corrected many transliterations of Arabic terms from the original, but have chosen to use only a partial set of special characters and not the full set. This was done to make the text less distracting for non-specialist readers, but we think that the terms will still be easy to find in other books used for further study. We have added a number of editor's notes, clearly marked, to the original text of Amadou Hampaté Bâ, but we have done this with some reluctance. We only hope that readers will find them helpful in understanding the text.

This, then, is the story and the message of a remarkable man of God. We, too, though distant in time, space, and culture, can become students of this master teacher if we can in our readings absorb and retain something of his virtue and wisdom. Amadou Hampaté Bâ gave this book to the world for that very purpose.

Roger Gaetani, editor

At a time when most information circulating about the African continent is often limited to distressing reports about widespread poverty, disease, and economic woes, it is unfortunate that the inspiring works of the Malian author Amadou Hampaté Bâ, who won the prestigious Grand Prix Littéraire de l'Afrique Noire award, are not better known in the English-speaking world. Bâ devoted his life to recording, collecting, and preserving the wisdom of sub-Saharan Africa: the myths, sayings, anecdotes, and oral teachings of the peoples of the French "Soudan" (present-day Mali, "Upper Volta," and present-day Burkina Faso). He has contributed immeasurably to preserving the heritage of the Fulani (Peul), Bambara, Dogon, Hausa, Tukolor, and other ethnic groups whose traditions, teachings, and cultures are rapidly being eroded by the mesmerizing intrusion of radio, television, and other mass media.

Bâ was born into the last generation of West Africans who lived in a purely traditional African cultural setting, a milieu that had only relatively recently been penetrated by the nobility of Islamic virtues. During Bâ's lifetime, the Western values and mindset being imposed by the French colonizers were still largely being kept at bay in most regions, but were rapidly and insidiously penetrating and influencing the mindset of the growing number of young Africans who were being educated in French schools. As Bâ grew up, Providence led him to a French education and a long career in the French Colonial Administration. Our author instinctively realized that the ancient African wisdom, as well as Islamic knowledge, were gradually being eroded and were throwing African societies into tumult. Intuitively understanding the dangers threatening the survival of Islam and traditional African culture under the French colonial occupation, Amadou Hampaté Bâ not only devoted his life to preserving the great "jewels" of African civilization, but also became a scholar of Islamic sciences in his own right and took charge of his own soul by attaching himself to a spiritual guide, Tierno Bokar. He spent his adult life striving to perfect his soul through the spiritual teachings and practices that were transmitted to him by this erudite and wise master.

Their two families being linked from Bâ's childhood, Tierno Bokar was the most influential figure in Amadou Hampaté Bâ's life. Tierno Bokar (Tierno meaning "master" in Fulani) personified the finest fruit of the harmonization and adaptation of Islam to this vast West African land, the great periphery of the Muslim world. Like most West Africans untouched by Western education, Tierno Bokar absorbed and retained much of the wisdom and oral teachings of his native ethnic group, the Fulani-speaking Tukolor, whilst being born into and integrating himself fully into the Islamic perspective. He became a learned scholar of the Koran and Koranic exegesis, Islamic jurisprudence, the Prophetic traditions, as well as the writings of the great Sufi scholars. This vast learning served as a backdrop to the master's profound metaphysical knowledge and spiritual intuition. He transmitted metaphysical truths, wisdom, and Islamic teachings to his students and disciples through very simple, direct language as well as through anecdotes and similes, in the same manner as African traditions and values had been transmitted throughout the ages. Amadou Hampaté Bâ's mastery of the French language and his literary skill not only capture the spirit of Tierno Bokar's teachings, but also the latter's physical presence which is at times almost tangible as the reader moves through this inspiring work.

Tierno Bokar's final days and tragic departure from this worldly realm are a testimony to the potential pettiness and cruelty of human nature which all Sufi and spiritual masters of other traditions have warned their adepts against. Tierno Bokar and others have given us the tools with which to combat these lower tendencies of the soul. Towards the end of the biographical section, the reader will be able to draw his or her own spiritual lessons and inspiration through Bâ's thorough explanation of the infamous "eleven- versus twelve-bead dispute" and how it led ironically to the clouding of the discernment of even the most devout members of the Tijaniyya brotherhood at that time. Tragically, the dispute eventually led to Tierno Bokar being betrayed and abandoned by all except his closest family and friends during a prolonged period of agonizing illness at the end of his life.

During the course of working on this translation I had the privilege of visiting Bandiagara. There I discovered that Tierno Bokar's spirit lives on in the presence of his last living *talibé* (student/disciple) Ahmed Baydi Dia and his learned and wise son Marabout Madani Baydi Dia. Marabout Madani received us warmly in his simple dwelling in the center of Bandiagara and introduced us to his bed-ridden father, whose silent but radiant presence moved us all. Whilst writing this preface in Ramadan/September 2006, I received a message from Bandiagara that Marabout Ahmed had passed into the next world.

During the visit with the Madani family, we were joined by the *imām* of the mosque of Bandiagara, which we later discovered, with its wooden pillars and sand-covered floor, remains in the very pure, pristine state that it was in during Tierno Bokar's days. Being in the company of these noble men and praying in the mosque of Bandiagara mentioned so frequently in this book, I felt that I had been granted a taste of the traditional Islamic spirit of West Africa. It is this spirit which is brilliantly transmitted by Amadou Hampaté Bâ through telling the forgotten story of this twentieth-century African saint, Tierno Bokar.

Fatima Jane Casewit, translator

We would like to acknowledge the following for their assistance in this project: We thank Dr. Louis Brenner for his detailed and extensive comments, suggestions, and changes to this text. He has freely shared his expertise and love of this subject with us, and we are very grateful. We thank Aftab Ahmed who has been very generous with his time and careful eye. World Wisdom has been very supportive and patient as we painstakingly translated and assembled this manuscript. Their attention to production values is evident, and we appreciate their efforts. We thank our families for their support. Finally, we acknowledge those selfless teachers who have guided us, through their examples and their words, to so many diverse lessons of the Spirit, which, like a Saharan desert wind, "blows wherever it pleases" throughout the great spiritual traditions of the world. To those teachers, our endless thanks.

INTRODUCTION

Amadou Hampaté Bâ's biography of Tierno Bokar is in many ways an exceptional book. It is an unusually intimate portrait of a Muslim teacher and Sufi master, written by a man who grew up under his direct influence. Hampaté Bâ repeatedly expressed his gratitude for what he had received from Tierno Bokar: "Everything that I am, I owe to him." It is difficult to imagine a more generous or humble tribute that one human being might offer another. Tierno, he said, "'opened my eyes'; . . . he taught me how to read the great book of nature, of men, and of life, by relating everything to a primordial Unity. I am indebted to him for my [moral] education, my way of thinking, my social mores, and for teaching me how 'to listen to others', which is perhaps his most cherished legacy".[1] This book is a further expression of that gratitude, the culmination of many years of effort to bring Tierno Bokar's life story and teachings to the attention of a wider public.

Tierno Bokar himself never sought to spread his ideas beyond those of his immediate acquaintance. He lived all his adult life in the small town of Bandiagara in eastern Mali. He was a simple and self-effacing teacher, a devout and contemplative Muslim who passed much of his day in prayer and reflection. He was also exceptionally humble and compassionate. He refused to be addressed by any titles, even teacher. He is reported to have said, "We are all teachers and we are all students". If someone called him master, he responded by calling them master; he refused to be considered the "master" of anyone. He referred to all his students as "brother".[2]

His tolerance and humility was combined with a resolute commitment to his own convictions and beliefs, a quality that, in the final years of his life, drew him into the midst of a religious conflict that ended with his becoming the victim of severe political persecution. He was forced to live the final months of his life under virtual house

---

[1] Amadou Hampaté Bâ, *Oui mon commandant!* (Paris: Actes Sud, 1994), p. 386.

[2] Interview with Amadou Hampaté Bâ, 3 May 1978.

arrest; he was banned from the mosque in Bandiagara, his religious school was forcibly closed, and his students and followers were dispersed and prohibited from visiting him. He died in February 1940, ill and impoverished and isolated from the Bandiagara community that he had served for many years.

We would know virtually nothing about Tierno Bokar, and certainly nothing of his religious ideas and teachings, had it not been for Amadou Hampaté Bâ. Tierno's teaching was entirely oral. Although an accomplished scholar, literate in the Arabic language, he never authored any text, and it is only through Hampaté Bâ's prodigious memory and his decision to commit Tierno's words to writing that they are available to us today. Through these words, we hear a voice of Islam of a kind that has been almost totally obscured by the anger and militancy of many contemporary Muslims. But even if the reflections of Tierno Bokar are the thoughts of only one single individual, spoken over a half century ago in a small town in West Africa, his words nonetheless represent an authentic voice of Islam.

Hampaté Bâ wrote in his preface that "There is a story behind this book" ("Ce livre a une histoire"). The book does indeed have a history, and one that is much longer, more complex, and more engaging than Hampaté Bâ relates in his preface, where he acknowledged the role of Marcel Cardaire in making possible in 1957 the publication of *Le Sage de Bandiagara*, the first published version of the life and teachings of Tierno Bokar, and of which this book is an extensively revised edition.[3] This introduction is intended to share with the reader something more of this "story".

*
*   *

Amadou Hampaté Bâ is considered by many to have been one of Mali's most renowned "men of letters". He published extensively in the French language, contributing to many fields of knowledge: history, ethnography, culture, religion and religious thought, biography and his own autobiography (three volumes of memoirs, of which one

---

[3] Amadou Hampaté Bâ and Marcel Cardaire, *Tierno Bokar, le sage de Bandiagara* (Paris: Présence Africaine, 1957).

still remains unpublished),[4] and the translation and re-presentation of many traditional texts. All these publications were based primarily on material he gathered orally or on events that he experienced himself.

He also wrote in Fulfulde, his mother tongue, the language of the Peul or Fulani peoples of West Africa. His Fulfulde writings are in the form of verse, much of which is based on the teachings of Tierno Bokar and remains unpublished. According to Christiane Seydou, a French scholar of the Fulfulde language and a long-time collaborator of Hampaté Bâ, this is the most original aspect of his oeuvre, written in his own unique style and designed to communicate "traditional" knowledge to a wider African audience.[5]

The most prominent theme that runs through his extensive and diverse range of publications is the valuation he placed on Africa's oral traditions, and of the wisdom and riches to be found in them. It was he who coined the now memorable phrase that "In Africa, when an old person dies, it is as if a library has burned down."

In sum, Amadou Hampaté Bâ has made an extraordinary contribution to our knowledge of Africa and African culture. Again, according to Christiane Seydou, his talent, and the appeal of his work, emanated from the quality of his powers of observation: his ability to observe African culture both from the inside with insights drawn from his own life experience, and from the outside with a kind of objectivity that arose both from his naturally curious and inquiring mind and from his contact with a variety of different cultures, both African and European.

All these qualities can be recognized in *A Spirit of Tolerance: The Inspiring Life of Tierno Bokar*, which is an invaluable contribution to our understanding of the Islamic religious culture of West Africa. It is a highly personal book, as much autobiographical as biographical. The religious and spiritual teachings recounted here are those that Hampaté Bâ received from Tierno Bokar; his descriptions of Tierno's gentle yet direct manner of teaching are drawn from his own experience as student and disciple. These portrayals of Tierno as teacher and

---

[4] The first two volumes are *Amkullel, l'enfant peul* (Paris: Actes Sud, 1991), and *Oui mon commandant!*

[5] Christiane Seydou, "L'oeuvre littéraire de Amadou Hampaté Bâ", *Journal des africanistes*, 63 (2) 1993, pp. 57-60.

spiritual guide are juxtaposed with the story of his spiritual search and the terrible persecutions that he suffered at the hands of those who refused to allow him to follow his own conscience in submitting to Shaykh Hamallah. Hampaté Bâ's unswerving loyalty to Tierno in this crisis also made him an object of political harassment, but he never desisted from his efforts to defend his "teacher" and to seek to clarify the spiritual reasons for his submission to Shaykh Hamallah. The publication of *Le Sage de Bandiagara* was central to these efforts.

*
*   *

Tierno Bokar's influence pervaded Hampaté Bâ's life from his childhood. When he was about seven years old, his parents placed him in Tierno's Qur'anic school, shortly after which he was "conscripted" into the local French school. French policy at the time set enrolment quotas for the number of children required to attend the French school, a policy that many Muslim parents fiercely resisted, fearing the experience would indoctrinate their children away from Islam. Or, as Hampaté Bâ so vividly put it, they felt that French schooling was a road that led "straight to hell".[6] Hampaté Bâ's mother was of this view, and she hoped to "ransom" him from the school authorities. But Tierno counseled otherwise: "Don't place yourself between Amadou and his God. Leave him in the hands of God, and allow God to make of him what He wills".[7]

This decision dramatically affected the course of Hampaté Bâ's life. French schooling provided him with the knowledge and skills upon which he would build his future career, not least his fluency in the French language. Unusually, Tierno Bokar did not think that Hampaté Bâ's integration into the newly emerging social milieu of colonial Soudan would necessarily detract from his living his life as a good Muslim, although neither did he leave the matter to chance! Tierno shocked Hampaté Bâ when, having completed his twelve years of French schooling and about to depart for his first posting as a junior functionary in the African section of the colonial service, he asked him

---

[6] *Amkullel*, p. 239.

[7] *Ibid.*, p. 261; interview with Amadou Hampaté Bâ, 4 May 1978.

to convert to Islam! Perplexed, Hampaté Bâ insisted that he already was a Muslim. No, Tierno retorted; he had been born a Muslim, but now as an adult he must decide whether he would live his life as a Muslim; he must make a conscious commitment. And so, in his early twenties, he "converted" to Islam in the presence of Tierno Bokar.[8]

From this moment, Tierno took the decision to make Hampaté Bâ the repository of his teachings.[9] But it was not until 1933, when granted an extended leave from his administrative duties, that Hampaté Bâ went to Bandiagara in order to pursue a course of intense religious and spiritual instruction from Tierno, which began with the "teaching" that is presented in the third part of this book. Tierno had developed this "teaching" as a kind of catechism for instructing local Muslims in the basic principles of Islam. It is divided into three "lessons", the first two of which contain the principles of doctrine and dogma that every Muslim should know. The third lesson is an "esoteric" interpretation of the content of the first two lessons and was transmitted to those Muslims who had become adherents of the Tijaniyya Sufi order. Hampaté Bâ rarely spoke or wrote about his personal Sufi activities, but he probably was first 'initiated' into the Tijaniyya order not long after his "conversion" in the early 1920s; he later renewed his initiation with Tierno Bokar.[10] During his sojourn in Bandiagara, he also received instruction from Tierno in the "esoteric" science of numerology.[11]

The words "initiation" and "esoteric" require some explanation.[12] Hampaté Bâ occasionally used the word initiation simply to mean instruction, or the transmission of knowledge. "From the day you

---

[8] *Oui mon commandant!*, pp. 63-4.

[9] *Ibid.*

[10] For a discussion of Hampaté Bâ's adherence to the Tijaniyya, see L. Brenner, "Amadou Hampaté Bâ, Tijani francophone", in J-L Triaud and D. Robinson (eds.), *La Tijâniyya. Une confrérie musulmane à la conquête de l'Afrique* (Paris: Karthala, 2000), pp. 289-326.

[11] Hampaté Bâ's interest in numerology is best illustrated in his, *Jésus vu par un musulman* (Abidjan: Les Nouvelles Éditions Africaines, 1976), pp. 45ff.

[12] For a more extensive discussion of these themes, see L. Brenner, *West African Sufi: The Religious Heritage and Spiritual Search of Cerno Bokar Saalif Taal* (London: C. Hurst, 1985; second impression 2005), *passim.*

pronounce the *shahāda*[13] and become a Muslim," he said, "you begin your initiation, because initiation is teaching someone what they do not know about their religion".[14] But more often, he spoke of initiation in a much more precise sense, as a process through which one deepens one's knowledge and understanding of religion through continued study and practice. For him, initiation is the process through which one internalizes one's religion, which begins for everyone with the acquisition of religious knowledge through the faculties of the intellect, and which can progress, for some, to the acquisition of "higher" knowledge through direct experience. These degrees of knowledge are discussed in this book, both in the somewhat technical language of Islamic scholarship[15] as well as in the more evocative imagery that Tierno Bokar employed when he spoke about the three ways in which one can know a river. The first is the man who hears about the river from others, the second is the man who journeys to the river in order to see it for himself, and the third is the man who throws himself into the river so that he "becomes one with it".[16]

"Becoming one" with God is the highest ambition of the Sufi quest. The "direct knowledge" that comes with such an experience is acquired through a process that is said to transcend the intellect; Sufis liken it to the "knowing" that one acquires through "tasting". This kind of higher knowledge cannot be transmitted from one person to another; not even the most accomplished Sufi master can transmit it to his disciples, and it is an indication of Tierno's humility that he denied ever having "tasted" it.[17]

The Sufi quest is a spiritual preparation for the possibility that one might receive this higher knowledge, and the Sufi master directs and supports his disciples in preparing for this possibility. Such preparation consists primarily of devotional practices in the form of special prayers and spiritual exercises. When first entering a Sufi order, adherents

---

[13] The Muslim creed: "There is no god but God, and Muhammad is the Prophet of God".

[14] Interview with Amadou Hampaté Bâ, 4 May 1978.

[15] p. 192.

[16] p. 199.

[17] p. 118.

are authorized to recite the prayers that constitute the liturgy of that order, the *wird*.[18] As they advance along the spiritual path, disciples may be authorized to engage in additional devotional exercises, which are often referred to as "secrets".

In the past, these kinds of secrets, including prayers, spiritual practices, and various esoteric sciences, such as numerology, were integral to West African Islamic religious culture. In principle, esoteric knowledge and practice was transmitted only to persons considered capable of understanding and of making proper use of it. Hampaté Bâ tells us that Tierno Bokar was initiated into the secrets of the Tijaniyya Sufi order by one Amadou Tafsir Bâ.[19] He was also initiated into the esoteric sciences of Muslim numerology, which explores how the mathematical relationships among numbers can be interpreted to demonstrate the Oneness of God and the Unity of His creation. Although referred to only occasionally in this book, Tierno was deeply immersed in the practice of Muslim numerology.[20] And Tierno, in turn, initiated Hampaté Bâ into many of the secrets that he himself had received.

Although initiation, as instruction, is grounded in the formal transmission of specific, often esoteric, knowledge and practice, its ultimate aim is the internalization of one's religion, a process that evolves in the context of a close relationship between master and disciple. As Hampaté Bâ explained, "One must try to live these ideas. Otherwise, they are only theories that serve no purpose at all. It's like someone who has a large supply of seeds, but doesn't sow them. If you don't plant them, they won't grow!"[21]

---

[18] For the content of the Tijani *wird*, see p. 201ff. Significantly, perhaps, Hampaté Bâ never refers to initiation as *al-bay'ah*, the formal rite so common in classical Sufi orders in which the disciple pledges his personal allegiance to his *shaykh*. In West Africa more generally, Sufis speak of "taking" or "receiving" the Order, which refers to being authorized to recite the *wird* of that Order, and the rite that accompanies this event can be very informal and without the implications of the more formal *al-bay'ah*. One reason for this difference may be that historically, Sufism in West Africa focused much more on the power of the Sufi prayers themselves rather than on those who authorized their recitation.

[19] pp. 20-21.

[20] See *West African Sufi*, pp. 91ff. and *passim*.

[21] Interview with Amadou Hampaté Bâ, 12 May 1978.

This process of internalization demands nothing less than a reordering of one's thoughts and behavior, which is not something that can be taught directly; nor can it be easily described in writing. For Hampaté Bâ, the process was nurtured through his personal relationship with Tierno, who was for many a living model of what it could mean to be a Muslim. Perhaps the greatest contribution of this book is that it records so much of what Tierno actually said, sometimes in gatherings of students or fellow scholars and more often in informal conversations with friends and neighbors. When one considers the content of Tierno's words together with the contexts in which they were spoken, it becomes more possible to understand what it was like to be in his presence. For Tierno, every event, every situation, every aspect of the natural world contained a religious message for those who could perceive it. This is what Hampaté Bâ meant when he said that Tierno taught him how "to read the great book of nature, of men, and of life". Teaching by metaphor and analogy was an informal and more public extension of the esoteric knowledge that he had received: the teaching of hidden realities that exist beyond the visible world.

*

*   *

Following his sojourn in Bandiagara with Tierno Bokar, Hampaté Bâ was posted to Bamako where he took up a new position in the colonial service. He had been authorized by Tierno to transmit the teachings that he had received as he felt appropriate, but the contexts in which he would do so would be very different from that in which he had learned them. Very soon he took the decision to publish the teachings in French, but neither the translation nor the transformation of an oral teaching into a written form was a simple matter. He found he required a lot of support to bring his plan to fruition, and the persons who helped him most were not Muslims, but French-speaking Europeans.

As early as 1938, Hampaté Bâ was seeking assistance to publish what he called "a brief esoteric Tijani text", which was in fact his first effort to translate part of Tierno's oral catechism. This was at the height of the crisis that marked the final years of Tierno's life following his submission to the spiritual authority of Shaykh Hamallah. Hampaté Bâ had begun to correspond with Théodore Monod, the man who probably did more than any other to encourage and support him in his wish to transmit the teachings of Tierno Bokar through the medium of the French language. Monod, renowned natural historian and much-published author, was director of the Institut Français d'Afrique Noire (Ifan), the French research institute in Dakar.

Although the text was not published until it appeared in *Le Sage de Bandiagara* in 1957, the intervening years were critical and formative both for the evolution of Hampaté Bâ's personal career and for the manner in which he would eventually present Tierno Bokar to a French-reading public. Monod's influence was profoundly significant in both domains. From 1938, the two men engaged in a sustained correspondence that led to a close personal friendship. Both men were deeply religious, Monod a Protestant Christian and Hampaté Bâ a Muslim, and each expressed a sincere interest and respect for the religion of the other that emerged from a shared ecumenical understanding of religion: that all monotheistic religions, although they differ in outward form, are the same in their relationship to God.[22] Hampaté Bâ's ecumenical approach to religion was derived directly from the teachings of Tierno Bokar, which are fully elaborated in this book.

The friendship between these two men had numerous significant ramifications. It was Monod who arranged, in 1942, for Hampaté Bâ's transfer from the Colonial Administration in Bamako to the research institute at Ifan, where he was encouraged to begin his formation as a researcher and writer; this was yet another absolutely critical turning point for the course that his future life and career would follow.

Even more significantly, with respect to the present book, it was primarily through Monod's influence that Hampaté Bâ began to rethink and reformulate the manner in which he would present Tierno Bokar's teachings to a French-reading public. The text of the oral catechism was redrafted, following in part suggestions from Louis Massignon, the renowned French scholar of Sufism. And in 1947, while on leave from Ifan and apparently in response to a direct request from Monod, Hampaté Bâ also began to commit to writing Tierno's informal teachings, most of which are presented in Part 2 of this book in the section entitled "His Words", where they are described as

---

[22] For a discussion of the relationship between Monod and Hampaté Bâ, see "Amadou Hampaté Bâ, Tijani francophone".

"teachings" or "anecdotes". Although Hampaté Bâ may have collected some of these "teachings" from others who were close to Tierno Bokar, most of the texts were spoken in his own presence. And it is worth noting that apart from relatively minor changes, the substantive content of the texts as recorded in the original handwritten manuscript has never been modified in any subsequent publication.[23]

More significantly, the texts were committed to writing with the specific intention of communicating Tierno's teachings to Europeans. As Hampaté Bâ wrote to Monod, these texts "seem to me to be the best echoes of the teaching of my Master that might be presented to a European audience".[24] And it was Monod who, in 1950, first published an article about Tierno Bokar in which a selection of these texts appears.[25] Perhaps it was Monod's intention to write this article that encouraged Hampaté Bâ to commit the texts to writing when he did.

Whatever the case, there seems little doubt that Hampaté Bâ's relationship with Monod was profoundly influential in shaping the form in which the ideas and teachings of Tierno would eventually be presented in the French language. These texts constituted a large part of the documentation that Hampaté Bâ shared with Marcel Cardaire in the early 1950s, and which led him to encourage Hampaté Bâ to write a book on the life and teachings of Tierno.[26]

But whereas Monod's interest in Tierno Bokar's ideas was primarily religious, Cardaire's interests were largely political. By the 1950s, the French administration in Soudan was much more concerned about the possible political threat of Wahhabism in West Africa than the Hamalliyya, the branch of the Tijani Sufi order to which Tierno Bokar adhered towards the end of his life. Shaykh Hamallah had died in exile

[23] The original manuscript is contained in the Fonds Monod; see "Amadou Hampaté Bâ, Tijani francophone".

[24] ". . . ce qui me semble être les meilleurs échos de l'enseignement de mon maître, à l'intention des Européens". Letter from Amadou Hampaté Bâ to Théodore Monod, 22 July 1947; see "Amadou Hampaté Bâ, Tijani francophone", p. 295.

[25] T. Monod, "Un Homme de Dieu: Tierno Bokar," *Présence Africaine*, 8-9 (1950), pp. 149-57. Reference to Tierno Bokar was also made in an earlier article by Monod, "Dans l'Islam noir: un mystique soudanais", in *Almanach des missions* (Montpellier, 1943) pp. 19-25.

[26] p. xxxi.

in 1943, Tierno Bokar had died three years earlier, and the Hamallist movement had lost much of its driving force. Hampaté Bâ had become the object of numerous hostile intrigues in Bamako, because he had followed Tierno Bokar in taking the "eleven beads" of the Hamalliyya, but it seems likely that Cardaire had contacted Hampaté Bâ in order to seek his cooperation in the struggle against Wahhabi influence rather than to pursue an investigation of the Hamallists.[27]

Wahhabism is an Islamist movement that doctrinally espouses a return to the origins of Islam as recorded in the Qur'an and in the traditions of the Prophet as the basis for all aspects of Muslim life. Wahhabis consider all Muslim practices that were introduced in subsequent generations to be religious innovations and as such are to be condemned. For this reason, and others, Wahhabis are firmly opposed to Sufism in all its forms. Hampaté Bâ was one of the most active local opponents of Wahhabi activities, especially their efforts to reform local Muslim schooling. They opened Muslim schools in which they taught Wahhabi doctrine and in which they employed Arabic as the language of instruction. Hampaté Bâ was the architect of what came to be known in Soudan as the movement of "counter-reform".[28] With the support of the French administration, the counter-reform movement founded its own Muslim schools in which local African languages, rather than either French or Arabic, were the languages of instruction, and in which the curriculum was infused with the ideas of Tierno Bokar: that is, these schools were meant to teach an ecumenical, open, and tolerant form of Islam of the sort that Hampaté Bâ had received from Tierno.

The implementation of the "counter-reform" programme, which opened its first school in 1953, would not have been possible without the agreement of Marcel Cardaire and the Office of Muslim Affairs, whose interest in stifling Wahhabi influence was clearly served by this project. From the perspective of the Office of Muslim Affairs, the publication of *Le Sage de Bandiagara* could serve similar ends: the promulgation of a "sympathetic" version of Islam. Théodore Monod

---

[27] pp. xxx-xxxi.

[28] For further information on the "counter-reform" movement, see L. Brenner, *Controlling Knowledge: Religion, Power, and Schooling in a West African Muslim Society* (London: C. Hurst & Co.; Bloomington: Indiana University Press, 2000), especially ch. 3.

advised Hampaté Bâ against accepting assistance from the Colonial Administration, warning that this might tarnish the spiritual message contained in Tierno Bokar's teachings. But Hampaté Bâ was insistent; he felt he must take advantage of any opportunity that presented itself to disseminate the ideas of Tierno.[29] And so, *Le Sage de Bandiagara* was co-authored by Marcel Cardaire and published with his support.

*

* *

Hampaté Bâ's association with Cardaire has indeed been interpreted by some as a nefarious form of collaboration with the colonial powers. Some have even doubted the authenticity of the texts that he recorded, suspecting that he had modified their content, or perhaps even composed them himself with the intention of portraying local African Islam in a manner that was particularly sympathetic to European, and especially to Christian, sensibilities.

It is true that Hampaté Bâ had committed the texts to writing in the form that they now appear with the intention of presenting them to Europeans, and that he had been encouraged to do so by Monod, a devout Christian. But this project to record Tierno's oral religious teachings was completed in the mid-1940s, some years before the French administration had become concerned about the Wahhabi movement in West Africa. It is also true that Hampaté Bâ subsequently became deeply embroiled in the politics of "counter-reform" and that colonial support for the publication of *Le Sage de Bandiagara* was part of the French response to increasing Wahhabi activity. But readers of this book should not allow this fact to obscure their appreciation or their understanding of the teachings that Tierno Bokar brought to those among whom he lived, which in my view Hampaté Bâ has preserved as faithfully as he could. Although *A Spirit of Tolerance: The Inspiring Life of Tierno Bokar* is an extensively revised edition of *Le Sage de Bandiagara* that was intended to correct certain minor errors in the first edition,[30] nothing of the substance and content of Tierno's teachings has been changed.

[29] See "Amadou Hampaté Bâ, Tijani francophone", pp. 298-300.

[30] p. xxxi.

In *West African Sufi*, I have traced the historical antecedents of Tierno's teachings and religious practices as recorded by Hampaté Bâ, and I have demonstrated that they are entirely compatible with those that prevailed in West Africa in the late nineteenth and early twentieth centuries. Tierno was a product of his religious and cultural milieu, but he was also an exceptional representative of it. Or perhaps he only seems to be exceptional because the life stories and spoken words of other "sages" have not been recorded.

That we have his story and his spoken words is due entirely to the persistence and commitment of Hampaté Bâ to make them known to us. And yet, as Hampaté Bâ himself warns us, one cannot encapsulate a man like Tierno Bokar in a book, ". . . his words, his deeds, his every gesture, even his silences" were integral to his teaching.[31] No book can capture the whole of such a teaching, but Amadou Hampaté Bâ, who sincerely tried to live what he had received from Tierno, has come as close as anyone to achieving such an elusive aim.

Louis Brenner

[31] p. xxxii.

AUTHOR'S PREFACE
to the 1980 edition of
Tierno Bokar, le Sage de Bandiagara

There is a story behind this book. It may be useful to recall it briefly, for no other reason than to pay homage to the memory of the man who allowed me to publish a first version of the life of Tierno Bokar. I am speaking of Marcel Cardaire, the co-author of the book *Tierno Bokar, le Sage de Bandiagara* (*Tierno Bokar, the Sage of Bandiagara*) published in 1957 by Éditions Présence Africaine.

It was thanks to Marcel Cardaire's stubborn courage, patience, and above all his spirit of justice that this book could be published. This French officer of [the Bureau of] Muslim Affairs was necessarily obliged to serve the interests and prestige of his country, but he intended to do it while respecting truth and fairness.

Marcel Cardaire was a student of the great ethnologist Marcel Griaule.[1] He had learnt from his teacher how to approach Africans, especially, the "Sudanese," the Malians of today, and, through trust, to obtain from them that which neither force nor fortune can produce.

But here are the facts:

Around 1905–1906 a religious dispute broke out in Nioro in the Sahel (Mali) between different branches of the Tijani order regarding ways of reciting a certain prayer. From 1917 the conflict took on such proportions that the Colonial Administration was forced to resolve the question. They opened a dossier entitled "Hamallism," a label taken from the name of Shaykh Sharīf Hamallah, head of one of the two Tijani branches in question. The present book discusses the Hamallists in depth. Their followers received the name of "Hamallists" and their enemies the name of "Umarians" because the latter were adherents of the Tijani branch of the great leader al-Hajj Umar.

My teacher and spiritual father, Tierno Bokar, himself a *shaykh* (master) of the Tijani order of the Umarian branch, belonged to the

---

[1] Editor's note: Marcel Griaule (1898-1956) was a French anthropologist and Africanist.

family of al-Hajj Umar. However, in 1937, disregarding the troubles that threatened to plague him, Tierno Bokar recognized the spiritual eminence of Sharīf Hamallah and placed himself under his authority. I followed him on this path.

From that time on, Tierno Bokar's Umarian cousins struggled violently against him. Amongst them were very influential members of the federal government of the AOF,[2] who succeeded in bringing about the intervention of the Colonial Administration by presenting the affair, which was only a local religious conflict, as having an anti-French bias.

At that time, my administrative duties in the District of Bamako permitted me to defend Sharīf Hamallah and Tierno Bokar with the Administration by putting the facts into perspective and by breaking up several intrigues that were intended to discredit Tierno Bokar, Sharīf Hamallah, and the Hamallists. In this way, for the enemies of Tierno Bokar, I became a major obstacle that they needed to be rid of. The campaign directed against me became so intense that the Colonial Administration of the time (it was the Vichy period) decided to proceed with an investigation. Two lieutenants of the Office of Muslim Affairs were sent to the Soudan (the former name of present-day Mali) on successive tours with instructions to find fault with my professional duties. But they were unable to find anything against me, and for good reasons.

It was then that Captain Marcel Cardaire, because of his shrewdness and his experience in Africa, was sent to the French Soudan to take charge of Muslim issues and to investigate me.

Upon the urging of Professor Griaule, Captain Cardaire met with me directly, listening only to his conscience and to his moral duty to inform his government in total objectivity. He visited me mornings and evenings and frequently invited me to his home. For an entire year, we had a very close relationship. Through my intervention, he was able to enter without difficulty all the Hamallist *zāwiyas*[3] of the

---

[2] Editor's note: Afrique Occidentale Française (AOF), or French West Africa, was the federation of territories under French colonial rule until 1960, including what is now Mali.

[3] *Zāwiya*: a place for meeting and prayer for members of a Sufi brotherhood.

Soudan, Senegal, Upper Volta, Ivory Coast, Niger, and his final destination, Nigeria.

All during the year that we were together on a daily basis, I answered all of his questions about African traditions, local religions, Islam, the Tijani way, and in particular the Tijani practice called "the eleven beads"[4] which had been at the root of the conflict. I also gave Captain Cardaire voluminous written documents, part of which were the teachings and words of Tierno Bokar that I had collected.

After meticulously studying all of these notes, Marcel Cardaire came to find me and said, "It would be a crime against knowledge and against the spirit not to publish the teachings of Tierno Bokar. These teachings truly contain an important message."

"But you know very well," I answered, "that a Hamallist would never be able to get published!"

"Well," replied Cardaire, "put the life of Tierno Bokar and his teaching into writing and I will add my personal comments and we will be co-authors. I will take personal responsibility for getting the book published."

So I wrote a draft of the life and teachings of Tierno Bokar and gave the manuscript to Marcel Cardaire, entrusting him to make judicious use of it.

The book was published by Éditions Présence Africaine in 1957 without my being able to revise the final text. A few errors had slipped in (very understandable given the complexity of the events that were reported upon), but these took nothing away from the merit of Marcel Cardaire and the usefulness of his work. As a Pullo proverb says: "Error does not erase the value of the effort accomplished."

In any case, I decided to undertake a complete recasting of the original work, but have done this while still preserving its original structure.

Therefore, in the first part of this book the reader will find an account of Tierno Bokar's life as well as a survey of the historical events that marked the society into which he was born. In fact, these events are linked to the passions that in part determined his destiny and the ordeals he had to face at the end of his life.

[4] Beads refer to the beads of a rosary used to recite certain devotional litanies.

In the second part, I have gathered the sayings of Tierno Bokar which I collected day by day at his side in Bandiagara in the courtyard of his modest home where he led the simplest possible life, dividing his time between teaching and prayer. These are words imbued with love, of tolerance and infinite goodness toward all men; words opposed to all violence and oppression, whatever the source may be; words surprisingly timely, as well as universal.

For Tierno Bokar, Love and Charity are the two inseparable sides of Faith. The love of God cannot be understood without the love of man. "Faith is like a piece of hot iron," he said. "In cooling down, it reduces in volume and becomes difficult to shape. It is therefore necessary to heat it in the hottest furnace of Love and Charity. We must plunge our souls into the vivifying element of Love and keep on guard to leave the doors of our souls open to Charity. It is thus that our thoughts will orient themselves towards meditation."

The bases of the schematic teaching that Tierno Bokar imparted to his students are found in the third part of the book. A detailed in-depth study of this teaching will hopefully be the subject of a future work.

In the appendix we have added a short chapter on Sufism and Muslim brotherhoods for readers who are not familiar with this subject.

It is certain that a man like Tierno Bokar cannot be encompassed in a book. To divide his life, sayings, and teachings into distinct chapters is necessarily an artificial and imperfect undertaking, because such a man was a whole. Teaching was everything for him: his words, his deeds, his every gesture, even his peaceful silences that we loved to share were also part of his teachings.

I will also be happy if this work permits readers to discover African spirituality and perhaps to love this old master who felt sincere and warm love for all men.

And now let us go to the heart of black Africa, in the east of Mali, in the region of Masina where, at the beginning of the twentieth century the light of God shone upon a man, Tierno Bokar, who was known as the Sage of Bandiagara.

Amadou Hampaté Bâ

Part 1

His Life

ROOTS

At the beginning of the nineteenth century, the Muslim Fulbe Empire of Masina was erected upon the ancient substratum of the local religions. A certain Sekou Amadou, a man of genius, established a structure that provided a political, economic, and social framework for different peoples who had been accustomed to living side by side with each other while jealously preserving their various ethnicities and characteristics. Peasants, herdsmen, craftsmen, and fishermen were all united by their religious bonds, the mythical origins of which go back to the beginning of time. Sekou Amadou is given credit for founding the Fulbe Empire of Masina in 1818, codifying all of the outward manifestations of these social bonds, and building a state.

As nothing in black Africa can be built without the breath of the Spirit, the religious Spirit, the theocratic kingdom of Masina was established by followers of the Kunta Sufi brotherhood. To this kingdom the "Kunta"[1] contributed the chain of transmission of their brotherhood, the King donated his organizational genius, and the remnants of the native religions bequeathed their traditional structures. Out of all of these contributions a state was born.

When al-Hajj Umar,[2] the great Master of the Tijani order,[3] appeared in Masina in 1862, he became the leader of the Masina Empire, an empire that had already begun to disintegrate spiritually under the reign of Amadou Amadou (or "Amadou III"), the grandson of the founder, Sekou Amadou.

The rise of the "Umarian tide" caused the Soudan[4] to enter into a new period of perhaps one of the most violent upheavals of her his-

---

[1] "Kunta" is the name of a very ancient family of Arab origin that gave birth in Africa to the religious brotherhood of the Kunta. [Editor's note: This is a branch of the Qadiri Sufi order.]

[2] Editor's note: The term "Hajj" is an honorific title that refers to someone who has performed the pilgrimage to Mecca.

[3] For more on the Sufi brotherhoods, see Appendix II.

[4] Editor's note: As it is used in this book, "Soudan" refers to the portion of Western Africa called "French Sudan" that was administered by the French colonial power.

tory. Like many conquests, this one did not merely end in an enslavement of peoples by their conquerors. With its often unexpected developments, history seems to teach us that a military conquest generally follows a peaceful period. During the peaceful periods, the occupying forces are in turn absorbed by the conquered peoples. This process is undoubtedly a positive one. In cases when this phenomenon does not occur, the conqueror rapidly finds himself isolated, marginalized from the system, as if enclosed in a cyst, and thus reduced to living in an ivory tower from which he can no longer see anything and consequently ceases to be a leader.

During the invasion of Masina by the Tukolor,[5] these two phenomena undoubtedly played themselves out simultaneously.

The Tijaniyya, the religious brotherhood of the Tukolor, imposed itself on the right bank of the Niger River, whereas the Kunta brotherhood maintained their influence throughout Masina.

The Spirit often bursts forth like a spark at the clash of two swords. It is impossible to focus on the spiritual life of Masina during the first part of this century if one ignores the wars that had ravaged it during the preceding century. In the same way, it would be impossible for an historian to ignore the European struggles, the Mediterranean conquests, and finally the wars that took place within Italy itself during the time when the Renaissance was still gestating within her. Can one understand Francis of Assisi if one ignores the struggles against the Perugians that he lived through during his youth and all the other bloody battles of that period? Therefore, it is not possible to understand the character of Tierno Bokar Salif Taal without keeping in mind the first eighteen years of his life, during which conquests and uprisings, victories and defeats were the sole burning issues of conversation heard around him outside of his immediate family. One must also not forget that half of his blood made this child a prince, a Tukolor prince, a conquering prince.

Although the area of the administrative entity changed from time to time, it consisted primarily of what is today the Republic of Mali.

[5] Tukolor: A people of West Africa, living mainly in present-day Senegal and in Guinea (the ancient kingdom of Futa Toro). The Tukolor are not an ethnic group but a fairly homogeneous cultural group (Islamized and speaking Fulfulde). Led by al-Hajj Umar, they went all the way to the "loop of the Niger" where in 1862 they conquered the Fulani Empire of Masina.

On March 10, 1861, al-Hajj Umar entered Segou, the capital of the Bambara kingdom. A year later he left for the north to conquer the Fulani Empire of Masina. Before leaving Segou, he entrusted the administrative and military command of the city to his eldest son, Amadou Sekou, while entrusting the "spiritual supervision" to a certain al-Hajj Tierno Seydou Hann for whom he felt boundless affection.

Who was this man who was to become the grandfather of Tierno Bokar and who was to transmit to him a solid tradition of peace and tolerance as well as eminent spiritual qualities?

Al-Hajj Umar had met al-Hajj Tierno Seydou Hann in the Court of Sokoto (in the northwest of present-day Nigeria) where Umar had stopped upon his return from his pilgrimage to Mecca. Al-Hajj Umar became attached to this man of great quality. He was certainly one of al-Hajj Umar's most noteworthy "spiritual conquests."

Al-Hajj Tierno Seydou Hann's family was of Tukolor origin and lived amongst the Hausa.[6] He was a pious man if there ever was one and he kept his distance from the political wars of the Sokoto Empire. He had a very deep knowledge of Sufi esoterism. Al-Hajj Seydou Hann was a man of prayer and meditation who possessed the gift of clairvoyance, and his predictions, which were often proven true, very much impressed al-Hajj Umar on several occasions.

Al-Hajj Seydou Hann's meeting with al-Hajj Umar was the determining event in the former's life. Although al-Hajj Seydou Hann belonged to the Qadiri Sufi brotherhood, he did not hesitate to submit to the authority of al-Hajj Umar, and he entered the Tijani order enveloped in the aura of al-Hajj Umar's vast knowledge of religious texts and in the power of his inner life. When al-Hajj Umar set off again, al-Hajj Seydou Hann broke off from all of his past life, abandoned Sokoto and, accompanied by his immediate family, followed his new spiritual master. By virtue of his gifts and his knowledge, al-Hajj Seydou Hann was certainly one of those who contributed to the religious luster of al-Hajj Umar's wars.

Al-Hajj Seydou Hann thus entered Segou with his wife and daughters as part of the entourage of the Taal family of al-Hajj Umar.

---

[6] An important ethnic group in the Sokoto region.

Since the beginning of time, Segou had been the "lazy" city, lying on the right bank of the river. Cooled by the eastern winds of January, scorched under the May sun or drenched under the rains of August, it always remained Segou, the ancient capital, on the old river. Paddlers of dugout canoes, their black skin as smooth as marble, like those in the era of Biton Coulibaly[7] and like those of today, glided along the banks in long, hollowed-out skiffs balanced as precariously as if they were on ice skates. It was a city where the people clustered around a Bambara center, a city of ancient religions born from the "river-god," a town of the Bambara mystique that had also enlightened and vivified the empire. It was a town of tolerance where the local mythical characters rubbed shoulders with those of the Fulbe[8] both Islamized and not, with those of the Bozo, the Somono, or the Soninke. It was a town of joy for the sweetness of life, a town of subtleness of spirit and of wit of which Fily Dabo Sissoko, the first deputy of the Soudan once said, "If you ask a favor of the people of Segou and they want to refuse it, they will do so with so much intelligence and courtesy that you will find yourself obliged to thank them."

With the arrival of al-Hajj Umar, Segou officially became a Muslim town, but her soul certainly had not changed—she remained the Segou of long ago.

Once in Segou, al-Hajj Seydou Hann settled there with his family, not altering anything about his simple lifestyle. He opened a school and offered religious and scholarly teaching. Al-Hajj Umar entrusted "the spirit of the town," that is, the spiritual and moral administration, to al-Hajj Seydou Hann.

Seydou Hann increased the family prestige by taking as a second wife a descendant of the Prophet, a *sharīfa*. An amusing anecdote told about this young *sharīfa* better illustrates the behavior of the valorous Seydou Hann than a lengthy description would. By then he had been nicknamed "the pious Hausa."

---

[7] Editor's note: Biton Coulibaly (d. 1755) was one of the Bambara kings of Segou.

[8] Editor's note: The Fulbe and Tukulor speak slightly different dialects of the same language, Fulfulde. To better understand this, and the many other complex ethnic and tribal distinctions found throughout this book, we highly recommend the appendix "A Note on Ethnicity" in Dr. Louis Brenner's book *West African Sufi: The Religious Heritage and Spiritual Search of Cerno Bokar Saalif Taal* (London: C. Hurst, 1985; second impression, 2005).

His household was run by his two wives, the first a daughter of Uthman dan Fodio[9] and the second the young *sharīfa* who was nevertheless not exempt from the storms of female jealousy. But the submission of Seydou Hann and his first wife to God's will attenuated the outbursts of these afflictions.

One day the master of the house obtained two heifers and presented them to his wives. He said to the *sharīfa*: "Choose the cow you like. The one you turn down will be the property of your sister Inna. You are a *sharīfa* and therefore deserve to have first choice."

The cow chosen by the *sharīfa* grew, calved, and gave forth scanty, thin milk, while Inna's cow gave birth to a beautiful heifer and was a marvelous milker. The second wife was consumed with jealousy and was untouched by the kind acts of Inna. The *sharīfa* complained endlessly and demanded that a new distribution take place. For three months, according to the story, Seydou Hann suffered the torments of hell in his own home.

One evening at the call to prayer he was leaving his vestibule when the *sharīfa* appeared at his doorway. "You won't go to the mosque," she told him, "until you have solved the problem of our cows. Do the distribution again and if you don't want to do me justice send me back to my family."

Seydou Hann, without losing his inalterable calm, answered, "In truth neither of your suggestions is possible to envisage. By redistributing, I would violate the law. Your own hands made the choice and they alone are responsible for it. In all justice you should have chosen the second cow. It was out of respect for the name of the Prophet that you had the advantage over Inna. I cannot now begin a redistribution which would leave nothing to chance. . . ."

He stopped for a moment before considering the second suggestion, and we can easily imagine the furtive smile that must have crossed his lips.

"If I sent you home, I would deny myself a cause of chagrin and worry. Now, in order to gain Paradise, I must suffer in my own home and I prefer to do so at the hand of a descendant of the Prophet.

---

[9] A *shaykh* of the Qadiri Sufi brotherhood who founded the Muslim Fulani Empire of Sokoto.

Would the Prophet therefore not be inclined to intercede for me (on the Day of Judgment)?"

Having said that, he went through the door and left for the prayer. But before leaving the doorstep of the house, he turned around and said, "Look, I advise you to come to an understanding with Inna. If she agrees to sell you her milking cow and calf, I'll pay for them for you."

Inna, who was in the shadows, had overheard everything. When her husband returned from the prayer, he found her waiting for him.

"I overheard your conversation with the *sharīfa*," she said. "In truth, I find you very impudent."

"Why do you say that? You know that I could not take part in an injustice."

"What part does justice have in a debate involving the seed of the Prophet?" she cried. "I was only looking for a way to please God and his Apostle. Since one of his descendants wants my cow, I'll throw everything into the bowl of the Prophet—the cow, its little calf, and the child who serves them. And were I not married, I would throw myself in as well!"

Seydou Hann's life revolved around his family and his school. At home, amongst all of his children, two of his daughters, Fatima and Aissata, were as remarkable for their wisdom as they were for their grace. Fatima had a burning desire for knowledge and passionately followed her father's classes; she attained a level of knowledge exceptional for women of that era. As for Aissata, the future mother of Tierno Bokar, she was the working linchpin of the household. All aspects of material life depended upon her. In addition to her practical qualities, she had inherited from her father a deep attraction to the mystical life.

The teachings of al-Hajj Seydou Hann achieved real success in the town. This was thanks only in part to the privileged position which he held in the eyes of the political leaders of Segou who looked upon him favorably. His students came both from traditional backgrounds as well as from the group of the most recent occupying forces.

Amongst the entourage of Amadou Sekou (the son of al-Hajj Umar left in charge by the latter as head of Segou), within his court, there lived a cousin of his called Salif. He was the son of Bokar Taal, one of the elder brothers of al-Hajj Umar.

Salif was a pious man. As a Tukolor prince, he followed the king and his army on their travels but spent most of his time instructing the offspring of the family of Amadou Sekou. His life, marked by piety, was therefore, whether he liked it or not, closely caught up with the political activity of the Tukolors.

Salif had studied the teachings of many masters and in particular was educated in the school of Tierno Seydou Hann. This was where he met the gentle Aissata whom he took as a second wife. It was from this union that Tierno Bokar Salif Taal was born in 1875.[10]

As the son of Aissata and Salif, the grandson of al-Hajj Seydou Hann, Tierno Bokar was born with the treasures of gentleness and a great aptitude for learning. Those called upon to be masters of men must necessarily subject their youthful qualities to some of the trials of life. Such masters are the products of a combination of their natural gifts and of the circumstances of their destiny. Tierno Bokar Salif Taal found these gifts within the family into which he was born. The agitated political life of his native province, characterizing the entire period of his education, gave his talents the opportunity to blossom.

During the final years of the Tukolor kingdom of Segou, Tierno Bokar Salif had grown up first on his mother's back[11] and then amongst the women of the family: Aissata, his mother, Inna his grandmother—the one who had regretted not being able to throw herself into the Prophet's bowl—and his aunt, the erudite Fatima.

Tierno became aware of life amidst a threatening atmosphere hanging over the city, which had been caused by the hostility of the Bambara and the Fulbe, who were not yet won over. In this climate of fear, the pious women taught him to fear only God.

Outside the home, the vicious punishment of those who had not yet submitted and the execution of rebels stirred up hatred. Yet, from the women who fed him and brought him up, Tierno Bokar learned to hate only his own faults and practiced "the greater *jihād*," the

---

[10] Editor's note: Louis Brenner, in his well-researched book on Bokar, *West African Sufi*, says that Bokar was "born in about 1883" and discusses the uncertainty regarding the precise date. The reader should note that in this present book, whenever an age is given for Tierno Bokar, it has been calculated from 1875.

[11] Editor's note: In many parts of the world, infants are first carried about by their mothers by tying them to their backs with a large piece of cloth, in much the same way as traditional American Indian mothers once carried their "papooses."

"greater holy war," that which the Prophet had said should be carried out against oneself.

The clash of weapons and the cries of warriors filled the city. War trumpets sounded the alarms, the departure of the cavalry, and the return of the king. In Salif's courtyard Inna grew elderly, Fatima was always at her writing, and Aissata was always lost in a dream. The three women gave voice only to the Name of God. In the street, the crowds spoke only of combat, of infallible battle plans, of enemies who were dying, escaping, or advancing. But around the young Tierno the only issue was Charity and Love, which conquer all hearts and which nothing can resist.

Tierno grew up and began his education. His intelligence and memory were opened up by the elderly Jire, who was of the Somono ethnic group and who was a *muqaddam*[12] of the Tijani order, himself a student of Seydou Hann. The lessons of transcendent morality which the child had always heard around him were now backed up by the Divine Word transmitted to him by his schoolmaster though the Koranic revelation. Beyond his teacher and beyond the Prophet, he grew accustomed to seeing none but God the Creator, and at the feet of God, a war-torn humanity, often pitted against each other in the name of this very God. In addition to the lessons he learned from his teacher were those he learned from the times.

In 1885 Amadou Sekou left for Nioro to block the road against the army of the French occupying forces, then under the command of Col. Archinard. In fact, he thought that Archinard's army, located not far from there at Kayes, would begin by attacking Nioro as a stepping-stone to laying siege to Segou. Before leaving, he left the administration of Segou to his son Madani, Tierno Bokar's cousin.

The noise of nearby battles, the probability of being occupied by the French, and the latent revolt of the local Bambara against their Tukolor occupiers stirred up an atmosphere of anxiety in the city.

Tierno and his family suffered less from the dangers at hand than they did from the horror they felt listening to news of battles and living amidst this hatred that disguised itself as piousness.

---

[12] *Muqaddam*: In Sufi brotherhoods, this is the title for the person who is charged with receiving neophytes and conferring upon them the basic initiation.

At the beginning of 1890, when Segou was just about to fall into the hands of the French, Tierno Bokar, then 15 years of age, had memorized most of the Koran, all of the Islamic rituals and laws, and much about the lives of saints. But his knowledge was not limited to this.

The role of the maternal family in the life of an African child is well known, especially that of the maternal uncle and grandfather. Now the maternal grandfather of Tierno was the elderly Seydou Hann, a great Sufi mystic, trained in the Qadiriyya school before entering the Tijani order. In the evening after a day of studying, Tierno would return home and become immersed in the uplifting, stimulating family atmosphere, where the lessons would continue with his grandfather. According to custom, a grandson can ask questions of his maternal grandfather at any hour of the day or night without fear of ever wearying him.

His aunt Fatima, the wise and enlightened "mother," could not refuse council to this young nephew who mirrored the curiosity she herself had experienced as a young girl. Her teaching and advice must have been absorbed within the context of the gentleness of Seydou's daughters. It was thus that the Taal child became familiar with the names of prestigious Sufis of the golden age: al-Ghazali, Muhyiuddin Ibn Arabi, Muhammad Ed-Dabbar and many others. Later, he would deepen and integrate their teachings. But already in his childhood, in his own courtyard during the endless African evenings, he learned the value of meditation, the richness of spiritual heritage, the vastness of knowledge.

Throughout his life the teachings that he imparted were influenced by the impressions of his adolescence. He was immersed in a "refuge of love and charity"[13] within the refuge of his own family, whose lives were tossed about at the mercy of the tormented times. Later on, his *zāwiya* was called "the refuge of love and charity," but alas, storms were awaiting him. At fourteen he learned, no doubt from the lips of his mother, from his dying grandmother, or from his aunt, this definition of religion:

---

[13] Translator's note: The word that we have translated as "refuge," used here and in the next sentence, is actually "cell," as in a monk's cell.

A woven disk, bearing on one side the word "love" and on the other the word "charity."[14]

One evening in March 1890 the elderly al-Hajj Seydou Hann died. He used the last of his strength to write a message to Amadou Sekou who at the time was in Nioro. He said to him: "Come take back what you have entrusted to me (the spiritual keys of the city) for the moment is approaching when God will take back that which He has entrusted to me (my soul)." After finishing the letter, he made this prediction to those around him:

"Soon we will no longer need a guardian for the spiritual keys of the city because the Tukolor are about to lose temporal responsibility for it. . . ."

Thirty-three days later, Archinard, at the head of the French army, entered Segou without encountering any resistance. The night before, in fact, Madani's forces had evacuated the city.

Tierno must have never forgotten that night when he saw his father for the last time. Salif Bokar Taal was swept up in the retreat because of his loyalty to the Amadou Sekou family. The husband of the gentle Aissata, a master of religion, the enemy of all hatred, left his home, his *zāwiya*, and his students to undergo the clamor of camps and the violence of war.

In the thick darkness punctuated here and there by a dim lantern, the Tukolor women and children watched the departure of the rest of the court from their doorways with heart-wrenching anguish.

Salif Bokar Taal, who was among the last to leave, was on horseback. Tierno walked alongside him until the city gate, accompanied by his father's younger brother, Amadou Taal who was not much older than Tierno himself. Before riding off for good, Salif stopped his mount and had Amadou Taal climb up behind him.

"And what is to become of me, Papa?" asked Tierno.

Taking Tierno's hand between his own, Salif enshrouded him with a warm, affectionate look and said to him, "I entrust you, my son, to God." These were the last words that Tierno heard from his father's lips.

---

[14] Editor's note: The "disk woven like a basket" referred to here is probably a flat, round, woven object used as a fan in some African countries. They often have figures woven into them and are hung on a wall as an object of decoration when not in use.

While returning to the women of the family with a heavy heart, was Tierno not already thinking about what he would teach us later on, that is, that material weapons can only destroy matter but not the principle of evil itself, which always rises from the ashes stronger than ever? Evil, he was to teach us, can only be destroyed by Goodness and Love. . .

When the last defenders of Segou had been swallowed up by the savanna, good old Jire, Tierno's teacher, attempted to shelter the family from the ravages of the conquerors. He made them leave Segou and housed them in Baraweli, in Somono country.

As soon as he was set up in Segou, Col. Archinard returned the command of the city to the Diarra, who represented the old Bambara royal family which had been defeated by al-Hajj Umar. Bodian, the new Bambara king, gave orders that all the Taal who were still in the area should gather in Segou. The refugees in Baraweli were therefore obliged to leave their refuge and place themselves at the mercy of the new authorities. Captivity was in general severe for the Tukolor. This land of black Africans seemed to have forgotten that theirs had traditionally been a place of tolerance and charity.

The elderly Jire, due to his Somono origins and the importance of his family, had a certain influence on the king Bodian, which he used to help the daughters of his late master. Thus Aissata, Fatima, Tierno Bokar, and his younger brother Aliu lived under fairly lax surveillance. They lived from the fruits of their own labor, in an isolated compound. All day the children braided together fences of rushes which were used to mark the boundaries of family homes. Aissata continually told her son that every man has to work, even, and above all, he who dedicates himself to serving God.

Young Tierno, the great-nephew of a conqueror, summoned by his birth to an enviable destiny of command, had known nothing of war except defeat and captivity, without ever experiencing the exhilaration of combat. For any other person placed in such a situation and tormented by the worries of this world, some hope would have remained: hope for a reversal of the situation, hope for revenge, the expectancy of better days. But the mind of this adolescent of Segou had been too much kept apart from the agitation of the century to need consolation or to seek a reason to act. From his earliest youth, he had grown accustomed to finding equilibrium and joy only from deep within himself, through a continual conversation with God.

Later on, he repeated this advice received from his mother:

Write the Divine Name *Allāh* on a wall, next to your bed so that when you awaken the Name will be the first image that your eyes fix upon. When you get up, pronounce it with fervor from the depths of your soul, so that it is the first word to come out of your mouth and to enter your ears. At night when you go to bed, fix your eyes on the Name so that it is the last image contemplated before being taken off into the temporary death of sleep. If you persist, the light contained in the four letters[15] will spread over you and a spark of the divine Essence will enflame your soul and illuminate it.

Out of a desire for vengeance on the part of the indigenous peoples against their former Tukolor masters, Bodian, the new Bambara king of Segou, went beyond the limits imposed by the new French military administration of Segou. In fact, Bodian had given one of al-Hajj Umar's own daughters to one of his servants.[16] This was too much to bear, and one of the sons of al-Hajj Umar, Aguibou Taal, who had become a personal friend of Archinard, intervened and obtained the liberation of all the Taal relatives.

Two years later, this same Aguibou Taal, accompanied by French troops, entered Bandiagara—where the French authorities had "appointed" him king—and established his government. With him came all the Taal and all the Tukolor refugees who wished to go to Bandiagara in order to distance themselves from the humiliations of the Bambara.

*

* *

What was this town of Bandiagara that took in the young man of 18 years? What was this town like at that time, a town which for 47 years

---

[15] The name *Allāh* in Arabic is composed of four letters: *alif, lam, lam,* and *hā.* These letters are the foundation of a substantial esoteric development within Sufi teachings.

[16] Translator's note: This can also be translated as "one of his slaves."

was to hear one of the purest voices of black Africa? Let us go back a bit further.

When in 1864 Tijani Aguibou Taal, the nephew of al-Hajj Umar and founder of the Bandiagara kingdom, set foot on this small plain, a sort of hollow in the middle of the Dogon cliffs, he found nothing there but a small hamlet. The site pleased him. It was situated in a depression surrounded by natural look-out posts, which would be easy to man and which were located at a good distance from one another. And so Bandiagara was founded and nicknamed "the great bowl." Tijani was undoubtedly an organizer and a skillful politician. Having decided to found a town, he caused it to rise up from the land and he settled it. All of the religious men of the region were required to build a house there and reside there three or four months a year.

Tijani encircled the city with a wall of dried mud. The few traces of it which remain today still bear witness to an area whose size does not compare with the Bandiagara of our time. Later, his cousin Mounirou made no change to the physical features of the town. He had inherited from his predecessors an easy and effective mandate which he attempted to improve upon even more.

One day in 1890 Amadou Sekou,[17] the son of al-Hajj Umar and former sovereign of Segou, arrived in Bandiagara followed by a procession made up of his sons, his horsemen, and his griots (songster storytellers). The reader will recall that Amadou Sekou had left Segou in the middle of the night for Nioro, with hopes of blocking the way of the French army and preventing them from advancing into the country. But when he witnessed the fall of Nioro in 1890, he left with his family to return to Bandiagara. When he arrived in that city, his younger brother Mounirou abdicated in his favor, in accordance with a law that had been established by al-Hajj Umar.

Bandiagara was then living in a glorious era characterized by valiant knights, sword fights, courtly love, and poetry contests. But the town suffered under the rule of Amadou Sekou from the fact that the sovereign lived in expectation of a fateful battle with the French, and also because he was powerless to dampen the hatred dividing his people. The co-existence of the former supporters of Mounirou

---

[17] Amadou Sekou was also called *Lamido Julbe*, "Commander of the Faithful," because he had inherited the religious function of al-Hajj Umar upon the latter's death.

(who had died shortly after his abdication) and the newcomers was, in effect, far from harmonious.

This situation lasted for about two years. In 1893, when Bandiagara was tearing itself apart, a third son of al-Hajj Umar, Aguibou Taal, approached the city backed by the infantry of Archinard. The town was taken, and as was mentioned above, Aguibou Taal was "appointed" king of Bandiagara by the French authorities.

Once again, Amadou Sekou and his family were forced into exile. They descended the Bandiagara cliffs and left for the south, looking for a new kingdom that they would never find. Amadou Sekou was accompanied by his eight sons and a few loyal companions. Salif Seydou Taal, the father of Tierno, was amongst them. Shortly after his departure, Aissata and her son Tierno arrived in Bandiagara with the convoy of the Aguibou Taal family, the new ruler. The father and son had only recently been separated. Salif was never heard from again.

*

*   *

The arrival of Aissata and her family caused a stir in the town. Aissata and her two sisters were preceded by a reputation of sanctity which they had not themselves sought but which was due to their unfailing gentleness, a faithfulness in carrying out their duties as wives and mothers, and in addition, their profound religious knowledge. Tradition says that their lives were so pure that they were invited, as was the custom, to leap over horses that were ill, a treatment from which a rapid cure was expected since purity carries with it all other virtues.[18]

Everywhere the sisters were received like princesses. All the clans in the town fought over them, as if to increase their prospect for divine favors. In Africa, when men want to show their sympathy and good will to a woman without a husband, they look for one for her. But Aissata refused to take sides and to choose a clan. She let it be known that she would remain faithful to her husband, the unfortunate Salif, as no news had come confirming his death. She ignored

---

[18] Editor's note: One of those virtues being the power to heal physical ailments. It is significant to note how the people of the region regarded purity as being a fundamental virtue.

the most flattering offers. "I cannot come to know any husband other than Salif," she said. "If he has abandoned me, it is against his own wishes; if he has fled, it is only out of loyalty to Amadou Sekou, the *Lamido Julbe*. And if he is alive, I have not been informed that he has repudiated me."

Since none of the factions could hope to become linked to this family, people distanced themselves from them little by little. Abandoned by the relatives and friends of her husband, Aissata turned towards the Hausa clan in whose midst her father had formerly lived. Hausa solidarity is justly famous in all the Soudan and this solidarity played a favorable role for the daughters of al-Hajj Seydou Hann. They were able to settle in the merchant quarter reserved for Hausas in the northeast of the city.

When the fighting finally stopped and peace returned to the country, Tierno Bokar was eighteen years old. He had endured all the trials of war with his eyes wide open. His extreme sensitivity caused him to feel these disturbing spectacles of life more intensely than they did anyone else, but he had been able to keep his freshness of soul intact.

Those who knew him at that time told us how joyous he was in the certainty that he had of being on the "right path." The women and elderly people who had brought him up knew how to expose him to everything while still shielding him from the poisoned atmosphere of the troubled times. Having already risen quite high on the ladder of the mystical life, he naturally possessed the values of a man who in many respects is no longer completely of this world.

*

* *

When he arrived in Bandiagara, Tierno Bokar had met a young man of his own age, Bokar Paté,[19] who was head of an association of young people. There were many such associations in Africa in the past, and he made Tierno Bokar a member. Bokar Paté was also an excellent tailor-embroiderer. In traditional Africa, tailoring was not a "profes-

[19] Bokar Paté's sister Kadija Paté would become my mother.

sion" in the modern sense of the word, but an art which even a noble was permitted to practice.

As the nephew of Aguibou Taal, king of Bandiagara, a military career was naturally open to Tierno Bokar. But his mother, the good Aissata, advised him to learn the art of embroidery. Under the supervision of Bokar Paté, Tierno became a great expert in this art. Often while embroidering, running his slender fingers over the clothes he was decorating, he recalled Aissata's advice:

Instead of taking men's lives, learn to cover their bodily nudity before being summoned to the honor of covering their spiritual or moral nudity by preaching to them about Love.

Tierno's general education was still incomplete; he was aware of this. Poverty had taken from him the courage to knock on the door of a master and the means by which to obtain the necessary books. Moreover, he was eighteen, the age of torment, the age of many dreams, of many pathways. He lived his dreams peacefully. They were all beautiful and mature. He perhaps did not realize how difficult the path that he had chosen would be and how little it would be understood by the world. But he understood to what peaceful happiness this path led. At an age of torments, he had found peace.

Although he had already mastered himself, it was still necessary for him to acquire the inclination to teach others, to transmit to them his knowledge and his serene certainty. He was to live the last forty-seven years of his life at Bandiagara, in his little compound, where the desire to teach would blossom and would become an urgent necessity. He would die without completely satisfying it because of the spitefulness and the ignorance of men.

It was a humble compound, a very modest settlement. At the end of a small street, it broadened into a courtyard that was used by everyone. A very low narrow door carved into a mud and straw wall gave out onto another smaller courtyard, onto which opened three or four small huts. It was a courtyard like 100,000 others in Africa: Two goats nursed their kids. A snarling yellow African mutt snapped at a fly that was bothering him. In a corner, a set of hoes. Laundry drying.

A little girl, a little black *tanagra*,[20] pounds millet and from time to time chases away two urchins with protruding bellies who come to lean on the mortar. An African courtyard, like so many that can be found under the sun, amidst the buzzing of wasps, the chirping of birds waiting in the distance for a grain of millet to be dropped. . .

The Hausa had received Aissata and housed her as the daughter of Seydou Hann, but being a younger cousin of the king of Bandiagara, she did not want to live on other people's charity. Though deprived of her former wealth, it was still up to her to feed three adolescents as well as her sister Fatima, who lived with her. At an age when other people are finally able to rest after looking back on what they have been through in life, the kind Aissata felt a heavy responsibility weighing on her shoulders. Her children were her worry; they were also the *raison d'être* for this woman without a husband, a strange anomaly in an African country. Above all, she had her eldest son in whom she saw her finest accomplishment. She loved all of them, but in her heart of hearts she admired Tierno, and undoubtedly the sacrifices that she had made must have seemed very mild to her. She lived modestly, preparing *dégué* (a sort of millet gruel) that the Hausa children would sell for her in the market.

Later, speaking of his mother, thinking about that woman who cooked millet gruel alone at all hours of the day, Tierno would say: "She nourished me with her milk and then with her sweat."

The family of Salif Taal, who were fugitives having to play the part of the "poor relatives," lived modestly in the shadow of the king without asking anything of anyone. The dignity of such a life could not but attract solid friendships. One of these friendships was to quickly change Tierno's life and would give him the opportunity to finish his education and share his teaching with others.

There was a young man in the association of young people into which Bokar Paté had introduced Tierno Bokar, who very soon became Tierno's friend. This was Tijani Amadou Ali Thiam,[21] the son of the chief of the large province of Louta. The three young men made

---

[20] Editor's note: *Tanagra* refers to a style of ancient Greek statuettes. These figurines portrayed women and children in great detail, engaged in the activities of everyday life.

[21] Tijani Amadou Ali Thiam would later marry my mother (see below). [Editor's note: That is, Amadou Hampaté Bâ's mother.]

up such an inseparable group of friends that all of Bandiagara called them "the three who are always together."

The chief of the province of Louta, Amadou Ali Eliman Thiam— the father of the young Tijani, very soon noticed the seriousness of Tierno Bokar and took an interest in him. Thiam wanted to help Tierno finish his education and so he entrusted the three young men to an excellent teacher in Bandiagara, Amadou Tafsir Bâ, a great mystic of the Tijani order.

Bâ was a very old man whose eyes had already for many years been shut off from the light of day, but he continued to teach and listen to readings from religious books, the text of which he often knew by heart. He possessed a library housing a great collection of works dealing with theology, scholasticism,[22] and the *Sunna* (the body of traditions referring to the Prophet Muhammad and his companions), Islamic law and everything concerning Islamic teaching, both exoteric and esoteric. He had acquired extraordinary learning that he had been able to embellish with Pullo[23] tradition.

From the first day, Amadou Tafsir Bâ was amazed at the spiritual depth of his new student and by his taste for introspection. He was even more surprised at his detachment from things of this world which, to Tierno, appeared to exist only in relation to the infinite love he felt for all creation.

Amadou Tafsir Bâ found in Tierno a student after his own heart and made him his favored reader. At his death, Amadou Tafsir Bâ left him a part of his library and entrusted to him the guardianship of his younger children.

After studying intensively with this teacher for eight years, Tierno Bokar was familiar with all the Islamic sciences. He knew God's revealed Word in its totality and in detail. He had meditated on the

---

[22] Editor's note: It is uncertain what this term is meant to indicate here. In a European setting, this would refer to works of such medieval writers as St. Thomas Aquinas whose thinking included both theology and ancient philosophy. Most probably, in this Muslim context, it refers to "theosophical" works of such esoteric writers as Ibn Arabi.

[23] Editor's note : The term "Pullo" is the singular form of "Fulbe," an ethnic group that is spread from parts of East to West Africa. Both terms refer to the people and culture of this area. The widest grouping of this ethnic identity is often referred to by the term "Fulani."

Koran. The esoteric knowledge of Amadou Tafsir, which completed that of Tierno's first teachers, had shed light on obscure parts in the sacred text. Tierno had reflected on and made his own the classical commentaries and more particularly those of the great Sufi thinkers. Nothing in al-Ghazali was hidden from him, and the *Meccan Revelations* of the great Andalusian spiritual master Ibn Arabi was his favorite book.

Amadou Tafsir Bâ was a Tijani mystic and he introduced Tierno to the secrets of the thought of the founder of the order, Shaykh Ahmad al-Tijani: *The Pearl of Perfection* (*Jawharat al-kamāl*), a particular prayer revealed to Shaykh Ahmad al-Tijani, and *The Desire of the Initiates*, a commentary on the writings of the great Master, had been learned and were continuously commented upon within Amadou Tafsir's hut. Finally, the magisterial religious work of al-Hajj Umar, *Al-Rimāh* (*The Lances*) was one of the most widely read books in the kingdom of Bandiagara.

Amadou Tafsir Bâ's main wisdom was to put his student on guard against the bondage that the texts imposed on students who did not assimilate them with joy. Tierno remembered this lesson and made it one of the pillars of his teaching. Had this principle not been approved and encouraged eight centuries earlier by al-Ghazali?

> Know that the key to the knowledge of God is the knowledge of the soul (*nafs*) as God Himself has said in Sura 41, verses 53 and 54 [of the Koran]. It has been reported that the Prophet said: "He who knows his soul[24] knows his Lord."
>
> If you tell me that you know yourself, I will answer that you know the matter that makes up your body, your hands, your head, and the rest. But you know nothing about your soul. If you are angry, you look for an adversary; if you are pursued by sexual desire, you seek to wed; if you are hungry, you seek to eat, and if you are thirsty you seek to drink. These satisfactions do not belong to you alone: they are yours, but they are also those of animals. Your duty is to discover what your real existence is. Who are you? Where do you come

---

[24] Or, "he who knows himself." *Nafs* means both the soul and the self; this word can be used to construct the reflexive form of verbs [e.g. "She hurt her*self* (naf*saha*)."].

from? Why were you created? In what do you find your happiness? In what do you find your unhappiness?

You have certain attributes which are also those of the angels. Your soul is what makes up the essential part of your being. The rest is foreign to you. You must know this, and also know that every creature has its own food and its own satisfaction. Farm animals are satisfied with eating, drinking, sleeping, and copulating. If you are one of them, try to satisfy your belly. Wild animals find their happiness in slaughter. Demons vie with one another in bad deeds. If you are one of them, take on their concerns. The angels find their happiness in the contemplation of Divine Beauty. Passions and anger are not the ways of their hearts. If you are of the same essence as the angels, try to know yourself and you will find the way that will lead you to contemplation. You will be liberated from the fetters of anger and passion. God has not given you these attributes for you to be a slave to them, but so that you will dominate them and make use of them on your journey. One will be your mount and the other a weapon. It is thus that you shall win happiness. . . .[25]

Tierno retained this lesson so well that he made it the first part of his religious course, from which we will quote extensively further below:

Neophyte, the Master created you. . . . God chose the most precious diamond, gave it to you and said: "Here, take care of this, but remember that I shall take it back from you. . . ."

As with Jire in Segou, Tierno found here, on each page of the Sufi texts, the fragrant essence of his mother's first teaching. Had al-Ghazali not said: "It is necessary to deprive the soul of some things that are permitted so that it does not aspire to things that are forbidden to it"? Inna, the good grandmother, had often presented this

---

[25] Editor's note: This passage is from Imam al-Ghazali's *The Alchemy of Happiness* (*Kitab-i kimiya-yi sa'adat*), chapter 1, on the knowledge of self.

concept to Tierno as a child. Very early on she had inculcated in him the idea of sacrifice as a self-discipline.

All the while perfecting his education, the young student became an accomplished embroiderer under his great friend Bokar Paté. He liked the work and above all it permitted him to contribute to the family resources.

When he had absorbed all the knowledge of his teacher and the latter had said to him: "I have nothing more to teach you," Tierno was twenty-six, the age at which a young man should take a wife according to Muslim propriety. Amadou Ali Eliman Thiam, who was becoming more and more attached to him, gave him his only daughter in marriage, Néné Amadou Thiam, whom we will find by his side throughout the rest of his life.

Two years later, Amadou Ali Eliman Thiam passed away and his son Tijani Amadou Ali succeeded him as head of the province of Louta. Tierno went to settle there so as not to be separated from him. It was at this time that my mother Kadija Paté, the sister of Bokar Paté, became the second wife of Tijani Amadou Ali when I was just a few years old. Tijani Amadou Ali officially adopted me and appointed me as his successor.

Tierno was in Louta when an insurrection of the Samo broke out, which put his friend's position in danger. The French Administration, having deemed the Thiams' repression of the indigenous Samo peoples to be too harsh, held Tijani responsible, condemned him, and deported him to Bougouni. My mother and I followed him there where we remained for seven years.

Separated from his friend, Tierno went back to Bandiagara with his young wife. Once again he took up his work alongside Aissata, along with her work and her concerns. The town welcomed him warmly and for several days the house was constantly full of people.

His old teacher Amadou Tafsir Bâ invited him to become a teacher in his own right and to take his place by teaching his fellow students. All of Tierno's relatives added their entreaties to those of Bâ. But Tierno refused. For four years he hesitated, not wanting to be anything other than his teacher's assistant. It was necessary for his teacher to die in order for Tierno to accept the task that awaited him.

THE TEACHER

The Bandiagara *Zāwiya*

At the age of thirty-three, complying with the wishes of his friends, Tierno Bokar agreed to direct the education of young children in Bandiagara. From that time on, his life would no longer belong to him, even though he had never considered it as his own. He dedicated everything he had and everything he was to the service of God and to those whom he taught.

An unacknowledged sadness had hung over the small compound in the Hausa neighborhood because the houses were without children. Suddenly all of this changed. The courtyards came to life. A rush of laughter and games swept away all traces of melancholy from the place. First of all, though, there was work to be done. Several small rooms had to be constructed as future dormitories for disciples coming from outside of the town. There were fifteen, twenty, and soon fifty disciples. During its heyday, the *zāwiya* counted almost two hundred students. The mare, chickens, goats, and dogs were a bit frightened. The women of the family were undoubtedly worried, but with children running in and out, joy penetrated the house. The joy departed only when the children did.

Very quickly the young master put together a schedule and adjusted the rhythm of his life to the one he had established for his students. A perfectly balanced life was rapidly achieved, and from then on he maintained an equilibrium within himself and with those around him. Not once in thirty-three years did Tierno ever modify the *zāwiya* schedule for any reason, except upon the death of his mother.

Tierno's constant repetition of activities and prayers was a source of peace. It coincided with the rhythms of his forebears. The African countryside, an ancient land, lives according to the rhythm of the seasons. The angle of the sun regulates the activities of the people, from hour to hour, from month to month. Everything is continuously renewed, and for centuries everything has been like this. Farmers have always thought in terms of the rhythm of this cycle, which is the same as that of their traditional religions.

The Sage of Bandiagara lived his life going from his home to the mosque, from the mosque to his friends but, wherever he was, he was always aware of the reality that those children had been entrusted to him. Later, he would feel the same about the adults who would become his disciples. On any given day of the week, in any season, at any hour, everyone knew where Tierno Bokar was and what he was doing.

A hard life? A desire for self-denial? No, certainly not. Asceticism is foreign to the deep-rooted thought of Africa, where the rule of life is to "live." Being sociable, the African asks of his spiritual guides, his elders, and other masters that they be models for him, and asceticism is not a way of conduct to be followed by a people so full of life in their everlasting youthfulness and even in their ancient ways of thinking. Simply stated, it was a life that seemed as clear and bright as crystal, as pure as prayer.

The master awoke at three in the morning. Kneeling, alone in his room, he prayed, surrounded by the thousand furtive sounds of the African night. He recited his *lāzim*[1] and bowed down three times. Then his mind turned to the supererogatory prayers[2] which he loved most of all. Finally, with head bowed and fingers running over his rosary, Tierno prayed and meditated until he felt that dawn was approaching. Then he went out, and going from hut to hut, though not without cheerfulness, he shook the matting that hung from the doors and cried out, "*As-salāt! As-salāt!*" ("Come to prayer! Come to prayer!") The student who slept in the master's vestibule was the first to wake up. He went out and called his fellow disciples to prayer. Mamadou Amadou Taal, the son of one of Tierno's brothers, led the children in prayer.

In the gathering glow of dawn, Tierno went to the town mosque. At this time, he fulfilled his function as co-muezzin.[3] The freshness

---

[1] *Lāzim:* The first set of prayers and recitations specific to the Tijani order. The *lāzim* must be recited twice a day: at dawn before the morning prayer, then in the late afternoon after the *'asr* prayer. See p. 201.

[2] Supplementary prayers beyond the five obligatory canonical prayers.

[3] Editor's note: The muezzin (or *mu'adhdhin*) is the one who calls Muslims to pray,

of the pre-morning carried his call, and his voice rang out above the terraces of Bandiagara. There are few Muslim cities that can boast of having a more sincere muezzin. He sang out his burning faith. He would have liked to awaken each of his fellow citizens personally and whisper his convictions into each ear. Once the call had gone out, he mingled in the courtyard of the mosque with those who had responded to it. He prayed amongst the crowd of believers. No-one ever saw him lead a prayer in public. He stood modestly behind the *imām*[4] or one of his substitutes.

The first prayer of the day was followed by the *wazīfa*, another Tijani prayer, recited in a group. Then, remaining alone in the mosque, Tierno again absorbed himself in meditation. Before returning to his students waiting for him in his *zāwiya*, Tierno performed ten more supererogatory *raka'āt*.[5] His silhouette was so familiar at this place of prayer in the town that he had been nicknamed "Papa Mosque."

As soon as he returned home, the children had their first meal of the day. They always waited for the master before beginning their breakfast. Later, wearing a simple *tantchikin*, a short sleeveless *boubou*, Tierno began to teach. A few older students gathered the younger ones into groups of five or six. According to their levels of education, the children were relegated to various corners of the courtyard under the awnings of the passageways.[6] Tierno took care of the eldest ones. After study of the Koran, which took place regularly every morning, they went on to the commentaries, approached from the point of view of law and of theology. Throughout the entire morning, the only subject was God and His attributes.

often chanting the traditional formulaic call to prayer (*adhān*) from the minaret of a mosque.

[4] *Imām* (and not *imān* as is often seen as a printing error). Literally, "he who stands in front." The person who leads the prayer is thus designated. In Shi'ite areas, the term is used for religious leaders or guides.

[5] A *raka'a* represents the basic unit of Muslim prayer: it is made up of all of the movements starting from the vertical position to the prostration. Each supererogatory prayer must include two *raka'āt*.

[6] Editor's note: This separating of those seeking learning into groups scattered about a central area, and with older learners often leading the younger, follows the age-old model seen in mosques all over the Muslim world, from simple mud-walled mosques of the countryside to grand marble mosques of large cities.

When the sun had reached its zenith and was beginning its downward course, the second meal was served. This was the time of the *zuhr*, the second prayer of the day. Mamadou, who was his nephew, led this prayer. Mamadou had not been his student, but had studied under his old friend Alfa Ali. However, Tierno entrusted the prayer and the supervision of the children in reciting the sacred Book to this young man, whom Tierno had not trained himself. We can see here yet another sign of the tactfulness of Aissata's son.

After the *zuhr* prayer, teaching began again until the *'asr* prayer (the mid-afternoon prayer) after which the students could attend to their own matters while Tierno recited his rosary. As the time for the *maghrib* (the sunset prayer) approached, the master left the house and returned to the mosque. He performed the *maghrib* prayer there and remained until the *'isha'*, the prayer at the beginning of nightfall. The night comes on early in Africa.

After this fifth and last canonical prayer, the master would yield to social customs, which he did joyfully, because this pious man, like most healthy and happy people, was a sociable person. He walked his old friend Tijani Amadou Ali Thiam home. The latter had returned to settle in Bandiagara after seven years of exile spent in Bougouni. Tierno never missed stopping by to see my mother Kadija Paté, who was the only one who dared to ask him the bluntest, most direct questions, ones that people never dared to bring up. For this reason, he had a great affection for her. Then he visited the homes of a few friends. He called at the Bodiel home and a few others. Then he returned home.

Every evening, after a light meal, Tierno presided over the evening gathering. These African evening gatherings have always offered the rarest of pleasures to those who know how to enjoy them. This is the time when the family gathers around a dim light. A guest passing by or on a visit is invited to join in the conversation, which turns to the most diverse topics. Until everyone is overcome with sleepiness, wonderful stories are told and marvelous legends are sketched out, created from scratch or based on ancient beliefs. Tierno often told the most beautiful story in the world, that of the creation and how man came to be. It was the time when the master spoke to his family and instructed them without any strictly pedagogical purposes. He spoke of God and conveyed His Word in a never-ceasing conversation, flowered with images, rich in examples taken from the Fulani tradition or other local traditions that he knew so well, infecting everyone with his quiet conviction. Late in the night, everyone returned home. The lights were blown out. In their rooms, sleep silenced everyone, the darkness brought night to the huts, the courtyard, to the entire *zāwiya*. In the morning, around 3 a.m. the master arose. . .

From Wednesday at the time of the *zuhr* until Friday evening, the students had a break which sent them back into the world. Tierno used this time for conversing with the sages of Bandiagara, for maintaining amiable relations, and for personal reflection. From the beginning of the time of this break, he isolated himself inside of his hut and for twenty-four hours consecrated himself to prayer and to meditation.

He always welcomed Thursday afternoon with joy. This was when his friend Alfa Ali, the Koran master, bent his long body through the low doorway. He was usually followed by the elderly men of the village. They settled in, and for hours discussed principles of Sufism. Saada Abdul Ciré, Tijani Amadou Ali Thiam, Moussa Noumoussa, and Koro Thiam were the most frequent at these meetings. All the participants prayed the *'asr* (the afternoon prayer) together in Tierno Bokar's compound. Friday morning, the meeting resumed in similar conditions, and continued until the hour of the *zuhr* (prayer at the beginning of the afternoon). During the morning the *'ulamā*[7] of the town examined the pious commentaries which Tierno and sometimes Alfa Ali submitted to them for judgment. Then they all went to the mosque to attend the Friday prayer together.[8]

In the heat of the afternoon the master made an extensive tour of the town and visited the families of his students. This was a long and tiring round of visits, but Tierno never failed to do it at any time of his life. On the way he prayed the *'asr* prayer, wherever he happened to be, alone or with friends. The *maghrib* and the *'isha'* prayer found him at the mosque.[9] When he finally returned home, he spent the evening

---

[7] Editor's note: *'ulamā* (sing. *'ālim*) refers to religious scholars in Islam. It should be noted that these are not "clergy" per se, since there are no Islamic clergy in the Western sense of the word. Here, it can be taken to refer to the men of the village who were learned in religious matters.

[8] This is the only prayer of the week which is obligatorily prayed in congregation.

[9] Editor's note: It may be useful for the Western reader to note how the author describes the progress of Tierno Bokar's day. He portrays very well how the traditional Muslim marked his day by the progression of the sun on its daily course, which then informs the faithful of the times for the various sessions of worship. Wherever adher-

in conversation with members of his family, seated on the ground in his usual posture with his legs stretched out in front of him, the right foot lying on the left.

Almost always dressed in white, he never was without his rosary, which he held in his hand or had rolled around his wrist. Sometimes when he was writing he would even hang it from his ears.

His every gesture was measured, linked to his will. He never allowed his limbs to hang loosely. He was fully conscious of and master of his body. His whole being radiated peace and inner joy. We felt him totally grounded within himself and in God. Everyone knew that when one was full of cares, one had only to sit next to him in order to rise again relieved and invigorated. As we said then, "We left our worries in his vestibule."

The strange thing was that his outer appearance went through changes that amazed us. On some days we thought we were seeing an old man of ninety, all wrinkled, his face ashen. His eyes, which were very large, then became red and sunken into their sockets.

At other times, his face was absolutely wrinkleless, his skin became smooth and luminous, the skin the color of black ebony, but of an ebony so shiny that one could almost see one's own image reflected in his forehead, especially at the time just before sunset. From the time of the *'asr*, his forehead became like a mirror. Maabal, a great Fulani mystical poet who was called "the most intoxicated of Tierno's students"[10] left us with this image of Tierno:

A constant smile that attracts you,
A forehead shining like a mirror,
But a mirror marked with a black mark from prostrations.[11]

---

ence to precisely measured minutes has not yet taken hold, Muslims will still refer to a particular time of day according to the times of prayer. For example: "I will meet you in the square before the *maghrib*." The passage of time flows with the rising and setting of the sun and moon, and the human fully enters this flow with the performance of acts of worship, his own natural cycle, timed to the natural cycles of the spheres. This may help us understand the flow of Tierno Bokar's day.

[10] Editor's note: It is common among Sufis to liken the state of being lost in God's Presence, cut off from all rational modes of thought, to "intoxication" or "inebriation."

[11] A small callus forms on the forehead of those who make many prayers with prostrations.

When the rainy season approached and until the end of the harvest season, the *zāwiya* schedule underwent several modifications so that the students could devote part of their day to work in the fields. Lessons were then given very early in the morning. When the lessons were deemed sufficient for that day, the youngest students, as was the custom, left for the master's fields. Tierno stayed with the *deftenkoobe*, that is, students of the higher-level class. As soon as it was midday, the classes ended and the master himself went to the fields to take the meal to the students.

With a staff in his hand and followed by several children and usually his dog, wearing the small conical hat of the Fulani, he made his way along the path and then had lunch with the young workers, going from one to the other and seizing the hoe himself. At harvest time, he took a major part in the collective celebrations. This man only very rarely knew sadness and the contemplation of nature gave him the finest of joys.

One year in which the harvest promised to be fruitful, Tierno admired the heavy millet heads along with everyone else. One of his students asked him:

"Tierno, do you not find that the French, who plant and care for flowers that do not bear fruit, act like big children and waste their time with useless and costly games?"

"Brother in God," he replied, "I do not share your view at all. He who cultivates flowers worships God, because these delicate parts of the plant, adorned with bright bursting colors, only open to greet God, for whom they are useful tools for the work of reproduction. Although the symbolism of flowers is not characteristic of our race, let us not speak against such symbolism. If you take a walk in the bush when the plants are flowering, look at the bees. You will see that each flower is a mystical pathway. Before making its honey, which God Himself has said is a remedy, the bee alights on each flower, the head of which is turned to the sun, asking for its contribution. As God has said at the end of verse 69 of Sura 16 (of the Koran): 'Herein is a sign for those who reflect.'"[12]

---

[12] Editor's note: In the original French version, the citation was given as verse 76. This may have been a misprint. The generally accepted number of the verse is the one given here, verse 69 of Sura 16.

He returned to the town, and without taking a moment to rest, went back immediately to the vestibule in his home where the older students were waiting. The lessons started again. The slightest movement, the most ordinary accident, a passing bird, a stem of millet that burst in the fire, anything was an opportunity for this lover of nature and her Creator to teach. He always repeated to his students: "Do your work, not in hopes of profit, but always do what you have to do as best you can."

It was not always easy to assure the material life of the *zāwiya*. Tierno had to provide the food, lodging, and the upkeep of two hundred people. However, he never asked the parents of his students for the smallest coin. It would have seemed to him scandalous that parents should be obliged to pay to have their children be given the indispensable elements of a spiritual and religious life. He had a deep horror of the "beggar marabout."[13] From his point of view, providing regular instruction did not give one the right to demand payment. The parents brought some offerings, but always less than what was needed. The harvests from the fields had ups and downs; they more or less provided everyone with their needs. Samba Hammadi Bâ, the eldest of the students, the one called the second son of Aissata, became a merchant. He did not keep the profits for his own use but maintained the *zāwiya* with them, convinced that he was only fulfilling a part of his duty.

To the Administration, the identity of Tierno Bokar was defined in this way: "Financial situation: possesses a mare and several goats. Resources: receives some alms and farms with his *talibé* (students)."

However, he did not intend to live from charity alone, even that of Samba Hammadi. During the free time allowed by the schedule, the students sewed together bands of woven cotton. The rolls of material were then sold in the market and the profits were used exclusively for improving everyone's existence. Material worries were totally foreign to the master. God provided for the growth of plants and for

---

[13] Editor's note: The term *marabout* is used primarily in Africa, particularly in areas where there has been French influence. It usually signifies a Muslim teacher, scholar, cleric, or holy person. In some places the designation can be passed as an epithet from father to son. Marabouts can have considerable influence in parts of Africa, and some are thought to have special powers. Although the term is not used elsewhere, there certainly are counterparts in other parts of the Muslim world.

all creation. One could always be assured of never being in need, he said.[14]

The women of the house participated intimately in the life of the *zāwiya*. They took over a part of the material responsibilities. One can easily imagine the joy with which the elderly Aissata presided over the food for the students whom her son nourished with his remarkable words. For twenty years she could be seen moving back and forth from the kitchen to the store-room taking care of this one and that one. In her free time she meditated, most often alone, sometimes in the company of her son.

All his life Tierno Bokar showed the most touching love for his mother. Twice a month, at daybreak on Friday, he was seen leaving the house with a bundle on his shoulder. On this day, the master did not go to the mosque for the morning prayer. What serious event could take him away from his devotional habit? Nothing other than filial respect. In fact, twice a month, Tierno went to the east of the cemetery, descended the banks of the Yamé River, and washed the clothes of the good Aissata. He thought that she had toiled enough for him.

Aissata's maternal concern for him did not diminish at all when a beard appeared on Tierno's chin, and no less when the beard turned white. She remained constantly seated at his side throughout all the circumstances of the master teacher's life. For twenty years, every class of students that passed through the compound of the son of Salif, and all the sages of the town who thronged there, all these witnessed the old woman taking in the words of the preacher with the same interest. Squatting down, she listened without saying a word; but if a distracted listener or disruptive student managed to direct the conversation towards a profane subject, Aissata knew, with one word, how to bring the group back to God. She liked to be involved in the children's life and reminded them of the traditional prayer in which her woman's heart included the believers of all places and of all times: "God, have pity on us, our ancestors, and all who have preceded us in the faith. . ." She attended all the meals but was only ever served by her son.

---

[14] This attitude was widespread in traditional Africa as well as in Muslim Africa at that time.

Tierno was not only the teacher of the children and adolescents who had been entrusted to him. The entire town sought his advice. He became the one whom Bandiagara consulted and followed on every occasion. He went visiting to some and received others. Everyone took in his words with respect, with gratitude.

He knew how to make a daily lesson out of the slightest gesture, the slightest remark, for himself as well as for those who had the good fortune of being present there.

One day, Soutoura, a woman of the neighborhood, came to find Tierno and said to him, "Tierno, I anger very easily. The slightest action severely affects me. I would like to receive a blessing from you, or a prayer to make me gentle, kind, patient."

Just as she had finished speaking, her son, a child of three who was waiting for her in the courtyard, came in, picked up a plank of wood and hit her violently between the two shoulders. She looked at the baby, smiled, and bringing him close to her, said, patting him affectionately, "Oh, the bad boy who mistreats his mother!"

"Why did you not lose your temper with your son, you who say you are so moody?" Tierno asked her.

"But Tierno," she answered, "my son is only a child; he doesn't know what he is doing; one does not get angry with a child of this age."

"My good Soutoura," Tierno told her, "go home. And when someone irritates you, think about this piece of wood and say to your-self: 'In spite of his age, this person is acting like my child who is three years old.' Be indulgent; you are capable of it, just as you have been with your son who has just given you a hard knock. Go, and you will never more be angry. You will live happily, cured of your difficulty. The blessings that will descend upon you will be superior to any that you could obtain from me. They will be the blessings of God and of the Prophet himself."

"He who puts up with and pardons an offense," he continued, "is like a large kapok tree[15] that the vultures soil when they rest on its branches. But the repugnant appearance of the tree only lasts a part of the year. At each rainy season, God sends a series of showers that

---

[15] Editor's note: The kapok tree (*ceiba pentandra*) is a massive tropical tree that produces large pods filled with seeds containing a silky floss that yields the kapok fiber.

wash it from its crown to its roots and clothes the tree again with a new foliage. Try to share the love that you have for your child with the creatures of God. For God sees his creatures like a father considers his children. You will then be placed on the top rung of the ladder, where, through love and charity, the soul sees and evaluates offenses only in order to better pardon them."

Tierno's words were so powerful for her that from that day on, Soutoura considered all those who offended her as children and reacted to them with only gentleness and patience. She corrected herself so perfectly that in the last part of her life the expression "patient like Soutoura" was used by people. Nothing could anger her anymore. When she died, she was close to being considered a saint.

Like a hunter, Tierno was always on the lookout for natural manifestations of Love. None escaped him, and he received regular nourishment from observing acts of kindness in the same way that others feed on the mediocrity or the dark side of life. He told his students about his conversation with Aya, his wife's niece, a little girl of five or six. Let's listen to him:

Little Aya likes to play with a strange collection of objects: a wax doll that she calls her daughter and a swaddled little piece of wood that she calls her son. She treats these objects with the greatest care. She looks after them like a mother caring for her offspring. She introduces her "daughter" or her "son" to every visitor and asks the latter to love them as she does.

One day, seeing her particularly absorbed in a corner of the room, I called her. She leaned towards me with her little hand open and her fingers spread apart as if to shut my mouth.

"What's going on?" I said to her.

"No noise. My children are sleeping."

"Those aren't your children, and they aren't sleeping."

"Maybe for you they aren't," she said, pouting. "But for me, even if they are made of wood, I love them like my children. I'm sorry I don't have breasts, like Mama, so that I could nurse them."

She thought for a second and then added, "But even without breasts, I have my tongue and my saliva. I'm going to use those until my breasts grow."

Then she grabbed her wax doll, put it to her lips and said, "Suck, I am your mother. I love you. Suck, and you will make me happy. Suck, suck . . . and don't cry!"

"My soul was deeply stirred," continued Tierno, "by this gesture of pure love. I then exclaimed: 'Love! Here is one of your manifestations offered to my sight to convince me of your power. Who but you can make wax or wood live just like true offspring?'"

Love. There was but this word on his lips. One of the greatest spiritual beings of Christianity called himself the spouse of "Lady Poverty."[16] Tierno had married "Lady Charity." If one were to remove the words "Love" and "Charity" from Tierno's teachings, then his sayings would become hollow.

How could one be surprised that the teachings of this man influenced those who followed him? Children and adults begged to be counted amongst his followers; yet, the humility of his heart was such that he always seemed unaware of this success.

One day a young man of Bandiagara came to find him. "Tierno," he said, "I've heard of you and your teachings. Only good is spoken of you. I wish to choose you for my master."

"Brother in God," he responded, "as flattered as I am, I must tell you first of all that I am a man sensitive to both material and moral possibilities. Also, I have some advice to give you that is worth months of productive study: A man never precisely matches his reputation. Admirers may falsify it by exaggerating his merits and detractors may try to underestimate him. To avoid such a situation, it would be good for you, and also perhaps good for me, for you to listen to me for days and days, to keep an eye on me for weeks and weeks, and to draw near me for months and months before deciding to choose me, not as your master, but as your teacher and your brother."[17]

There is no one who has been around Tierno who has not loved him and who does not still love him. His words still live in the hearts of all.

---

[16] Editor's note: The author is referring to St. Francis of Assisi. Also, note that in this section the author capitalizes certain virtues, such as Love and Charity, when he wishes to emphasize their exalted and fundamental status among the virtues.

[17] Tierno's sensitivity and humility were such that he never called his students anything but "my brother" or "my friend."

During his research into the events around the life of Tierno Bokar, Marcel Cardaire[18] met two of his widows in Mopti: Néné Amadou Ali Thiam, his first wife, and Aminata Ibrahim Taal, his cousin and second wife. Let's listen to Marcel Cardaire tell us about this encounter:

> The two women were bound together even more by the death of their husband. They lived close to one another, united by the sage's words that they had collected together. We saw these women sob till they could no longer breathe and then collapse on the matting in the tiny room that they were sharing as they recalled for us the last days of their husband. The tearless sobs of the elderly punctuated their account.[19] We soon noticed, however, that the words that they had received and piously preserved were words of hope and a source of peace. When their pain seemed the most intense, a younger woman entered the room. After the usual greetings, the new arrival, called Kowido, was informed of what we were seeking there. She rubbed the sand of the floor and recited with a firm voice the "Primordial Pact."[20] With her right hand, she drew in the dust the diagrams that the master had taught and that had illustrated his teachings. For a moment, the two old women followed the words of their husband on these lips which had brought them back to life. Then they closed their eyes. A smile floated across their two faces. Their grief had been laid to rest. The master had returned, and with him Peace and Hope. If the prayers of the old disciples of Bandiagara had not sufficed to convince us of our decision before this time, it was at this moment that the determination came to us to dedicate ourselves to our task of making this man live again so that our compatriots, both black and white, would be able to benefit from him.[21]

---

[18] See [the Author's] Preface.

[19] The reader will undoubtedly better understand their pain and chagrin when the conditions of Tierno Bokar's last days are known.

[20] This text can be consulted in the section titled "His Teachings."

[21] Cf. *Tierno Bokar, le Sage de Bandiagara* (Paris: Présence africaine, 1957), p. 40.

One day in 1927 Aissata Seydou Hann passed away, a septuage-narian worn out by the sorrows of her self-sacrificing younger years and by the care that she had devoted to the daily life of the *zāwiya*. However, she departed knowing full well the work of beauty created by the one whom she had brought into the world. Heaven spared her from sharing in the suffering that her son was to later endure. Tierno fulfilled his final duties to her, then closed himself up for a week in his grief. His friends became desperate. Kadija Paté, my mother, who was always able to say anything to Tierno, forced open his door and presented herself to him:

"Tierno," she said to him, "Allow me to remind you what you taught us. One day you said: 'When a man is born here below, I see his parents overwhelmed with joy and congratulate themselves and announce the event with great cries. When a man dies in the life of this world, I see his aggrieved parents bear on their faces and their clothing the sign of terrible desolation. Therefore, the best teaching about human insignificance is given to those who have a mind to reflect. Our human race desires life and flees death. Now what is it to be born? It is to enter into a field whence the only way out is the way of death, a one-way exit, which is the same for both the just and the unjust, for both believers and unbelievers. What is it to die? It is to be reborn to eternal life. The man who dies returns to the eternal source of everlasting existence. So it is then that we should rejoice.'

"Tierno, you told us this and now you are setting a bad example for us. The town is worried. Since the death of your mother, we have the impression that you are isolating yourself. It is even said that you are going to leave us and go east. Are you really going to abandon us?"

Tierno lowered his forehead. Then, lifting his head, he suddenly gave Kadija an enlightened look and thanked her for speaking to him. "Your frankness, Kadija, has released me from Satan's grip. But, you see, I have meditated so much on these questions that it seems that I myself have experienced the obscurity of the tomb and the eating away of the worms. I was apprehensive of all of this for my mother and also of the divine assessment of our works. But God will have mercy upon her, as she had mercy upon me when I was small. It was this deep reflection which made me remain in retreat and not the desire to leave you."

The next day, the *zāwiya* resumed its normal activity. Tierno asked all of his friends—adolescents, adults, the elderly, men, and women—to go to his place. When they were assembled, he said to them:

> My friends, it is said that I intend to leave Bandiagara and take refuge in the Holy Cities. This is not true at all. The holy places of Arabia are not the only places where one can worship God. One can worship Him here, in my compound, in my antechamber, in the office of the District Commandant,[22] in the Bandiagara market, and even in the cavity of a pig's tooth. Purity belongs to the man and not to the place. The purity or impurity of the man has nothing to do with the purity or impurity of the place. I shall stay in Bandiagara, and who can say that I too shall not lay down to rest under this same little tree that shelters the tomb of my mother, my aunt, and my two little godsons?

Tierno remained in Bandiagara and everyone's mind was set at rest. The voice of the Sage of Bandiagara was to make itself heard for another thirteen years. The first ten years of this period were calm. The *zāwiya* prospered, but around it, a storm was brewing. At the threshold of old age, Tierno Bokar was to again encounter insecurity. He was to know hatred, calumny, and treason without ever losing his serenity. Before going to lie under the little tree, beneath the pebbles that destiny had in fact laid out for him as his resting place, he still had to prove that he could welcome with the same gratitude, both the trials and the favors that came to him from Heaven, whilst giving thanks to God as if these trials were the same as blessings.

*

* *

---

[22] Translator's note: The French term "Commandant de Cercle" will be translated as "District Commandant." The title *Commandant de Cercle* refers to those officials who were the highest administrative authorities in a local district in French colonial Africa.

Some time after the death of his mother, Tierno received a letter that was to play a major role in the final direction of his spiritual life. This letter came from Alfa Hashimi Taal (brother of the king of Bandiagara) who had withdrawn to the Hijaz, in Arabia. Alfa Hashimi Taal reported on the variety of persecutions to which the fledgling Wahhabi regime was subjecting the members of brotherhoods. These "puritans of Islam" violently attacked all manifestations or vestiges of Sufism in Arabia.

Alfa Hashimi Taal, perhaps worried about the future of the Tijaniyya, discussed this problem with Tierno at length and transmitted to him some secrets known only to the master initiates of the order. In particular, he told him of a prediction that a spiritual master (*Qutb* or Pole) would soon appear from within the Tijaniyya whose mission would be to revitalize the order. Very precise details were given about the distinguishing signs that would allow this predestined man to be recognized. It was also indicated that his family origins would be unimportant, implying that he might appear within any social class.

Finally, Alfa Hashimi Taal specified to his correspondent the special prayers to say, the exercises of self-deprivation which would assist in recognizing the torch when it arrived, without risk of error. Amongst these was a fast of three years[23] interrupted only on the days when fasting is canonically forbidden. Tierno Bokar later told me that he had observed all of these recommendations to the letter.

This correspondence occurred sometime during the 1930s. Now, at this time a religious movement within the Tijani brotherhood was agitating the Muslim communities of the zones of the Soudan and the Sahel. A Tijani adept from the town of Nioro, Shaykh Hamallah—who was called Sharīf Hamallah because he was descended from the Prophet on his father's side—had been elevated to the function of *khalīfa* (Grand Master) of the order.[24] It was said that he had been given the mission of bringing the Tijaniyya back to its source by, amongst other things, returning to the original practice of the *wazīfa*, in which the prayer of *The Pearl of Perfection* (*Jawharat al-kamāl*) is

---

[23] This refers, of course, to an Islamic fast, which involves abstaining from all food and drink from the rising to the setting of the sun.

[24] *Khalīfa*: literally, "representative"; a title given to a supreme dignitary of the order who is supposed to represent the founder.

recited eleven times and not twelve times, a practice which had gradually been adopted.[25]

"Hamallism," (as this movement was called by the French Administration of the time) would spread from the banks of the Senegal River to Gobir, and from the gateways of the Sahara to the heart of the rainforest. Religious men exchanged letters and addressed questions to one other. The Taals, descendants or relatives of al-Hajj Umar, had learnt from the latter to recite *The Pearl of Perfection* twelve times. They therefore became fierce opponents of those who were called "the eleven-beads" because of the number of beads on their rosaries.

Being a Taal by birth and highly respected because of his spiritual influence, Tierno Bokar was invited to mix his voice into the chorus of curses. But it was inconceivable for a man like Tierno to come to a judgment without having heard the person who had been incriminated and without having weighed all of the facts. Therefore, he did not take a position and secretly awaited the opportunity to go to Nioro to judge for himself. This opportunity was to arise in 1937. We shall relate later on how Tierno met Sharīf Hamallah and how he recognized him as the one who had been announced by Alfa Hashimi Taal and how choosing to recognize him as such was to be the cause of all his ordeals.

Tierno Bokar's life entered its final phase in 1937. The master then embarked on what could be called the way of active mysticism, which was also for him the way of suffering.

At sixty-two, Tierno was experienced in all spiritual practices. He had followed the mystical paths revealed to him, never getting lost in their labyrinths. He had a solid inner assurance of his orthodox

---

[25] The prayer *The Pearl of Perfection* (*Jawharat al-kamāl*) was revealed by the Prophet Muhammad in a vision to Si Ahmad al-Tijani one day in 1781 at Bar-Semghoum in Algeria, with the injunction to recite it eleven times, and it is thus that it is practiced in the mother *zāwiya*. The recitation of twelve times was introduced by the elder students of the founder of the order (see p. 44) and taken up again later by certain branches of the Tijaniyya, including the Umarian branch.

The importance of the number eleven comes from its significance in Muslim numerological symbolism. Eleven is the number of pure spirituality and of esoterism because it symbolizes the unity of the creature bonded with the Unity of the Creator. It is the key to mystic communion. This number plays a great role both in Muslim symbolism as well as in African traditions. The number twelve, which comes from eleven, symbolizes action in the world and sacrifice.

faith, an infallible Ariadnean thread.[26] He was familiar with the most adventurous variations of the theme of God and His unity. He kept a cool head when the heads of others would begin to spin. An expert in the symbolic science of numbers, he manipulated them with a mastery only comparable to that of his fingers as they ran over his rosary. He possessed full knowledge of himself and strove to develop to ever higher [spiritual] levels.

He often sought out difficulties, to see if he possessed the patience and endurance that he had taught to others. One day he said: "I pray to God that at the moment of my death I have more enemies against whom I have done nothing, than friends." These are awesome words when one ponders upon the solitude of his final days. In his heart, therefore, he had wanted this trial. He considered that, until then, his life had not brought him a trial capable of revealing to him the degree of his own resistance, of his utmost capacity to leave everything to the will of God (*tawakkul*). From this point of view, it is true that many Sufis have asked God for martyrdom. . .

Nevertheless, he was aware of human limitations. Being aware of the responsibility that he had taken on by becoming a master to men, he did not invite his disciples to imitate his own attitude toward suffering, because he knew the various capacities of each one.

For years, Tierno Bokar had been saddened at constantly witnessing how the Spirit was watered down in the practice of the communal rites of the order. Above all, he complained that the spiritual precepts of the Tijaniyya were no longer respected.[27] Many adepts seemed to be more interested in money than in spiritual knowledge or moral perfection. Some naively imagined that they deserved something from God because of their giving money away, rather than by perfecting their conduct. To be a good student or a good disciple, they believed, it was enough to make donations to a *shaykh* and to receive

---

[26] Editor's note: Ariadne is a complex figure in Greek mythology, but who is now best known as the daughter of Minos. She fell in love with Theseus and gave him a ball of thread that she had been weaving so that he could find his way out of the dangerous winding passages of the Labyrinth. In this case, the author is probably suggesting, as have most Sufis since the early days of Islam, that a foundation of strong orthodox beliefs would be a protection for Sufis against errors in the often uncertain realm of esoteric practices and beliefs.

[27] The commandments are found in the third part of this book: His Teachings.

his "benediction." Needless to say, Tierno was much opposed to such practices.

Everywhere, religious fervor became lax, as if it had cooled down. Practices had fallen into a certain formalism. The disciples felt more strongly linked to one another as Tukolor rather than as brothers of the order. Loyalty to one's clan became confused with, and often prevailed over, the spirit of loyalty to the order. In short, the whole of the Tijani community needed a breath of authentic spiritual life.

It is known that the Tijaniyya, a brotherhood born in Algeria in the purest tradition of Sufism, had penetrated the black world through three routes: one that came directly from the north, descending from Algeria towards the Soudan and Timbuktu. The second came from the west along the Senegal River, and the third came from the east through the mediation of al-Hajj Umar, who had brought it from Mecca.

Al-Hajj Umar was already a Tijani before leaving for Mecca, but during the course of his pilgrimage he had been initiated and trained by Shaykh Muhammad al-Ghali, a direct student of Si Ahmad al-Tijani. Before returning to Africa, al-Hajj Umar had been elevated to the status of *khalīfa* of the order, with a special mission to propagate the Tijaniyya.

However, during the time in which our story is situated we are obliged to admit that the Umarian branch of the Tijani seemed to have lost most of the spiritual characteristics that it had drawn, directly or indirectly, from the *zāwiya*s of Fes, Témacin, or of Ain Mahdi in Algeria where the mother *zāwiya* is located.[28] At the time of the decay of the Tukolor Empire, the order seemed to have forgotten the tolerance and lofty thought that had been the hallmark of the teaching of Si Ahmad al-Tijani, the founder.

Suffering from this state of affairs, Tierno Bokar was additionally tormented by the emergence of Hamallism. For years, and from every side, he was asked about this. The Taals pressured him to take a position against this Tijani reformer who had dared to recommend

---

[28] Editor's note: We have kept the spelling used by Amadou Hampaté Bâ for various place names such as Témacin and Ain Mahdi. The spellings seem to be quite variable wherever French was used instead of local systems of writing. Thus, the forms "Tamacine" and "Ain Madhi" are found more commonly today for these places in Algeria that are associated with Tijani history.

that *The Pearl of Perfection* be recited eleven times, contrary to the practice transmitted by al-Hajj Umar. However, as we have seen, Tierno refused to accuse anyone without any proof. Throughout the long conversations he had with God, his conscientious soul asked to be enlightened about the truth of the affair.

Tierno's acute understanding of religious matters allowed him to sense intuitively the orthodoxy of a doctrine. When he was finally able to go to Nioro and listen directly to Sharīf Hamallah, Tierno found nothing objectionable in the former's propositions. On the contrary, Sharīf Hamallah's teachings inspired him because of the emphasis he placed on tolerance and submission to God. Tierno was also inspired by the Sharīf's tendency to place himself on a purely spiritual and not temporal plane, and by the references in his teachings to the highest levels of the human Intellect.[29] The pious exercises recommended by the new "Pole" of the Tijani were aimed solely at assisting initiates in reaching the highest levels of their being and in helping them remain at that level. In short, Tierno Bokar recognized the original teaching of the founder of the order, Shaykh Ahmad al-Tijani, in the doctrine preached by the Sharīf, which conformed both to the spirit and letter of Islam.

Once he had heard the Sharīf, Tierno was greatly relieved. He knew that he had found the truth which had been foretold to him in the letter from Alfa Hashimi Taal. Tierno was convinced that the voice of the Sharīf was going to irrigate and fertilize the Tijaniyya, which would henceforth be given new life, at once more intense and more pure.

It was during the year 1937 that Tierno Bokar met Sharīf Hamallah in Nioro. Before describing this encounter in detail, we must first explain what Hamallism was, how it appeared, and how it gave rise to the spurious problem of "eleven beads" and "twelve beads," a spurious problem that was nonetheless going to stir up a storm of hatred and violence. It was going to unleash the wrath of the Colonial Administration and, in the end, leave its tragic seal on the final days of Tierno Bokar's life.

---

[29] Editor's note: The author used the French term *Raison* ("Reason") here. We explain our substitution of the term "Intellect" for "Reason" in footnote 9 on pp. 171–172.

The Origin of the Practice of "Eleven Beads" and "Twelve Beads"

To understand the roots of Hamallism, we must first take a step into the past, to the life of the founder of this order, and sort out once and for all this question of the "eleven beads" and the "twelve beads," because this issue is at the origin of all the events that we shall relate in this book.

As we have already had the opportunity to point out, the prayer of *The Pearl of Perfection* was received by Si Ahmad al-Tijani in a vision he had of the Prophet, with the injunction to recite it eleven times, which is still the practice in the mother *zāwiya* in Algeria.

At a certain period in his life, Shaykh Ahmad al-Tijani had a dispute with the local authorities in Algeria who made his life impossible there. He had to leave Algeria and take refuge in Morocco. Above all, he wished to avoid any bloodshed amongst his many disciples that might be caused by such clashes. Protected by the sultan of Morocco, he was able to settle in Fes with all of his followers.

Every morning in the Fes *zāwiya*, after the dawn prayer, the brothers gathered with the Shaykh to recite the *wazīfa*, an ensemble of prayers that ended with eleven recitations of *The Pearl of Perfection*. It was the Shaykh's habit to give his benediction to everyone once the eleventh recitation had been completed.

One day he was delayed, and the students started the *wazīfa* without him. They had already finished the eleventh recitation of *The Pearl of Perfection* when the Shaykh was at last able to join them. Spontaneously, and so that the Shaykh could give them his benediction as was the custom, they repeated the prayer a twelfth time, after which the Shaykh blessed them.

Because the Shaykh had not made any observation, either positive or negative, as regards this innovation, the students of Fes preserved it and it is thus that the custom came about. It does not figure in any written teachings coming from the Shaykh himself, but it had been transmitted across Africa, in particular within the Umarian branch of the order.

When informed of this new practice, the mother *zāwiya* of Témacin did not oppose it, although for their part they remained faithful to the recitation of the eleven. The elderly initiated numerologists of the *tarīqa*,[30] explained: If the Shaykh said nothing, it is because, from an esoteric point of view, the number eleven equals the number twelve.[31]

Moreover, twelve being the number of sacrifice, of temporal action, even of war, it was appropriate to the state of exile in which the Shaykh found himself at that time. As for the number eleven, it is the number of pure spirituality, the number of esoterism and of mystical communion with God. It symbolizes the unity of the created being that is joined to the Unity of the Creator. It is also, amongst many other things, the [numerological] value of the divine Name *Huwa* (He), the name of pure transcendence which Sufis recite at the end of their mystical gatherings.[32]

This state of affairs continued for nearly a century without resulting in any problem.

In 1893, the mother *zāwiya*s of the Tijaniyya in Algeria heard the news of the capture of Bandiagara by the French. It seemed that the end of the Tukolor empire of Masina was nigh. The vitality of the Tijaniyya in black Africa seemed to be cut short. It was soon learnt that Amadou Sekou, Leader of the Faithful (*Lamido Julbe*) who had succeeded his father al-Hajj Umar in his spiritual function, had left the country, having been chased out by the French advance, and that there was no trace of him. Therefore, the Tijaniyya no longer had a *khalīfa*.

The *shaykh*s of the mother *zāwiya*s were concerned. A council of the Ain Mahdi and Témacin *zāwiya*s was convened. The *shaykh*s knew, through esoteric knowledge unique to their order, that a great master, a *Qutb* (Pole) was to manifest himself (this is what Alfa Hashimi Taal had foretold to Tierno Bokar), but they did not know where.

At the end of their meeting, they decided to send Shaykh Muhammad al-Akhdar[33] to the various territories of sub-Saharan

---

[30] *Tarīqa*: literally "way." This noun is the translation of order, congregation, or brotherhood (as applied to Sufism).

[31] Twelve is supposed to be an emanation of "eleven" for arithmosophical reasons which are too involved to go into here.

[32] See note 25, p. 40.

[33] Shaykh Muhammad al-Akhdar was a student of Shaykh Tahir, who himself was a

Africa, with a double mission: first, to find the person in whom all the signs predicting the *Qutb* would become clear, and then to bring all the Tijani communities that he would visit back to the formula of the "eleven beads." The Tijaniyya were no longer to take part in any form of temporal governance, nor in any outward actions. They should return to the number which symbolized pure contemplation and uniquely spiritual values. This change would be accomplished, of course, through outward forms as well as inwardly.

Shaykh Muhammad al-Akhdar set off to accomplish his double mission without knowing that his wanderings would last for years and that he would end up being taken to Nioro, where, after despairing at not finding the one for whom he was searching, he would finally find him.

He began by going to Egypt. From there, he reached the Anglo-Egyptian Soudan, then black Africa, visiting all the regions where the Tijaniyya had *zāwiyas*. But he did not detect the predicted signs of the *Qutb* anywhere.

He crossed Chad, Nigeria, and Niger, and finally arrived in French Soudan (Mali). He passed through Bandiagara, then following the Niger continued to Mopti and Segou before arriving in Bamako. Finally he learned that the town of Nioro had become the center of the activities of al-Hajj Umar after they had abandoned Dinguiraye. Another striking fact was that it was in Nioro that al-Hajj Umar had begun to lose control of his army and that the hitherto purely religious nature of his conquests had then slipped away from him. The Shaykh also learned about the history of Nioro, the true name of which, *Nūr*, means "Light" in Koranic Arabic. It seemed that a path of light had once stopped there.[34] Perhaps another might be born there. Moved by this presentiment, he decided to proceed there, hoping to find what he was looking for.

When he arrived in Nioro, Shaykh Muhammad al-Akhdar discovered a large Tijani community, including "elder students"[35] who

direct student of Si Ahmad al-Tijani and had been initiated by the latter.

[34] Editor's note: The story is told that a path of light, that is, an illuminated pathway like a light shining from above, had once led to Nioro and stopped there as an indication for people to understand the significance of the place.

[35] The members of a *tarīqa* continue to be called "students" even when they have

were extremely pious and learned, cultivated in Arabic and versed in mystical and religious sciences. The *tarīqa* had at its head Sharīf Muhammad al-Mukhtar who, having been initiated by the *zāwiya* of Fes, recited *The Pearl of Perfection* twelve times. When Shaykh Muhammad al-Akhdar arrived, Sharīf al-Mukhtar was away traveling.

The Tijani adepts of the town received Shaykh Muhammad al-Akhdar warmly, and hurried to his talks. The latter began to explain why it was necessary to return to the original recitation of *The Pearl of Perfection* eleven times. The Shaykh explained that the Tijani order was, by the grace of God, being discharged of temporal responsibilities, which were passing into the hands of the French, and so it was now incumbent upon the adepts to return to the numerical formula which corresponded to a vocation of pure spirituality and which conveys these virtues. Moreover, had not this way of reciting been revealed to Shaykh Ahmad al-Tijani by the Prophet of God himself? Had not the Shaykh explained this in his major work *Jawāhir al-Ma'ānī* (*Pearl of Meanings*), and had not the illustrious al-Hajj Umar himself commented on this passage in his own work *Al-Rimāh*?

Troubled by this, the Tijani of Nioro asked him for more explanation. "It is by reading the book of the Shaykh, the *Jawāhir al-Ma'ānī*, that you will understand," he told them.

Now an in-depth study of this book, though fundamental for the brotherhood, had been somewhat neglected until then. Apart from a few elder students, it was almost never read. The Sufi brothers asked Shaykh Muhammad al-Akhdar to give them some lessons in which this book would be read and commented upon. The Shaykh agreed.

At the end of their activities every day, the Tijani of Nioro, leading marabouts and simple adepts alike, came to listen to him. After a certain time, they were so convinced by the Shaykh's teachings that they asked him to "renew their *wird*." The *wird* is the name for the litanies (*lāzim* and *wazīfa*) which are recited at the time of initiation into the order just as the initiator (the *muqaddam*) received them from his own initiator, and likewise back to the founding Master.[36] Now it is

reached an advanced age and are themselves very learned. One then calls them "elder students."

[36] Each brotherhood (or *tarīqa*) thus possesses its own *wird*, which goes back to the

the custom in Muslim brotherhoods that upon meeting an initiate of high standing or one who is better placed in the "chain" of transmission, to ask him to renew one's *wird*, as a sort of confirmation.[37]

Shaykh Muhammad al-Akhdar agreed. Most of the marabouts of Nioro thus renewed their *wird* at his hand, but this time with a *wazīfa* comprising eleven recitations of *The Pearl of Perfection*. From then on, their rosaries were restrung such that a separator bead marked eleven rather than twelve beads.

When the ceremony was finished, the most senior of the students, who until then had remained on the sidelines, approached. He was called Tierno Sidi. Through deference towards his master Sharīf al-Mukhtar, who was still absent, Tierno Sidi did not want to receive the renewal of his *wird* before him. He asked Shaykh Muhammad al-Akhdar to first renew the *wird* of Sharīf al-Mukhtar.

"Would it not be preferable," suggested the Shaykh, "to wait until he returns?"

"Before he left," responded Tierno Sidi, "he authorized me to act for him as I would for myself in everything. Whatever you do, he said, I shall approve of it."

Shaykh Muhammad al-Akhdar reflected on this. Then he addressed the entire assembly of the brothers:

"If you all ask to have the *wird* of the Sharīf renewed," he told them, "I will do it. Reasonably, your master shouldn't be against something deriving directly from the teachings of Shaykh Ahmad al-Tijani

---

saintly personage who founded the order, and through this latter, to the Prophet. We shall see in the appendix on brotherhoods (p. 211) that these *awrād* (pl. of *wird*) are not very different from one another, being essentially made up of prayers in praise of the Prophet and of *dhikr*, or repetitions of certain names of God.

The recitation of the *dhikr* and of prayers specific to each *tarīqa* should normally be "received" during initiation into the *tarīqa*, in order to be fully efficacious and not to run any spiritual risk. Each "chain" that emanates from the great spiritual masters extends, unbroken, back to the Prophet himself. A special spiritual energy, or *baraka*, which originates in God Himself, is transmitted through the Prophet to all the "links" of this chain. This spiritual energy is an aid on the path of spiritual development, but, as Shaykh Tadili, a great Sufi master of Morocco, has said, "The initiation gives you the key to the gate of the garden, but it is up to you to make the effort to cultivate the garden."

[37] Editor's note: This renewing of one's *wird* is not practiced in all Sufi orders, but does seem to have been widespread within the Tijani order.

and through him from the Prophet of God. I greatly fear, however, that Sharīf al-Mukhtar might begin by accepting (the renewal of his *wird*), and then might reject it, which might stir up a lot of discontent." (A prediction that was to prove itself correct, as we shall see.)

The brothers insisted so strongly that the Shaykh ended up accepting. He began by drawing up *fatwā*s (a sort of official document establishing the affiliation of someone to the *tarīqa*) and the first one he completed was that for Sharīf al-Mukhtar.

From that day onwards his house was always full. It became a sort of *zāwiya* where people came to study and to pray.

It was at this point that Sharīf al-Mukhtar returned to Nioro. Once informed of the events, he accepted the renewal of his *wird* using the "eleven" formula. Gatherings always took place at Shaykh Muhammad al-Akhdar's house to receive his teaching, but from there the brothers went back to the home of the Sharīf to say their prayers and recite with him their *wird*.

Shaykh Muhammad al-Akhdar found this completely normal, because Sharīf al-Mukhtar was both the *shaykh* of the order and the leader of the community of Nioro. Shaykh Muhammad al-Akhdar had been entrusted with a mission: to reinstate the formula of the eleven recitations of *The Pearl of Perfection*. This mission had been accomplished. He had no other ambitions.

Yet, there was another mission which remained unaccomplished: the search and discovery of the predestined "Pole." Discouraged, Shaykh Muhammad al-Akhdar prepared to leave Nioro in order to continue his journey towards Saint-Louis-du-Senegal. But he did not want to leave Nioro without leaving a gift, a spiritual gift insofar as possible, to those who had so warmly received him and followed him. Shaykh Muhammad al-Akhdar suggested that each of the brothers should choose a particular formula from amongst the prayers, formulae, or *dhikr* that are unique to the Tijaniyya, which he as Shaykh would then ritually transmit to the disciple on behalf of his own chain of transmission, with all the *baraka* that was attached to it. This transmission was considered a gift of great mystical and spiritual value, the chain of Shaykh Muhammad al-Akhdar being particularly direct since he had been initiated by one of the great disciples of the Shaykh Ahmad al-Tijani himself.

The ceremony began. Everyone chose the formula of his choice, and received it from the Shaykh with an explanation of the particular methods of recitation that were attached to it.

Then came Sharīf al-Mukhtar's turn. He chose various formulae figuring on the list and the Shaykh granted them to him. Then he asked that the esoteric secret of each of them be explained to him. The Shaykh agreed to all of his requests. After this, the Sharīf named yet another formula. This time, instead of agreeing to give it to him, the Shaykh removed it from the list.

"I am sorry," he told him, "I cannot give this formula because it does not belong to me. It belongs to him who is predestined, whom I search for, and who alone will be qualified to recite it. However, in order that God might clarify this for me, I am going to make the *istikhāra*.[38] If in response I am told to give it to you, then I shall give it to you. But I cannot myself decide to transmit it to you. If I did it without special authorization and without you being the one that it is really destined for, this will do you more harm than good."

This last remark offended Sharīf al-Mukhtar enormously. The remark only added to the fact that his students, because of the great knowledge of Shaykh Muhammad al-Akhdar, had continued the custom of going to the latter's quarters to hear his teachings before going to Sharīf al-Mukhtar to accomplish the prayer.

Although hurt, the Sharīf withdrew without saying anything. In the evening, at his home, during the meal around which his usual griots (songsters)[39] and a few students were gathered, he declared:

---

[38] The *istikhāra* is a supplication taught by the Prophet which one addresses to God to ask Him to remove an uncertainty, or to clarify a choice or an obscure point. *Istikhāra* is generally preceded by a fast. According to the severity of this fast, one distinguishes between single *istikhāra* and double *istikhāra*. It is the second one which is in question here.

The response can come quickly or more slowly, directly or indirectly, in the form of a dream or in the form of an inspiration or a meaningful event. Sometimes it is a third party who receives the response in a dream in which he is told to transmit the message to the concerned person.

Advanced initiates and spiritual masters receive rapid and extremely precise responses. In general, they reserve this type of supplication for very serious situations and avoid using it for personal gain. This is because of their "courteousness" and modesty towards God.

[39] Griots constitute a particular caste, made up of troubadours, poets, and musicians,

"Today the new marabout told me that he possessed a name of God such that, if I pronounced it, it would do me more harm than good."

The griots, who were accustomed to flattering him, exclaimed, "Really, Sharīf, you have well deserved it, because we never would have imagined that you would give allegiance to another marabout in this land, much less to a man who turns up one day unannounced!"

Continuing along these lines in which they, like every respectable *griot*, were experts, they influenced the Sharīf so much that in the end, overcome by their eloquent indignation, he went to look for all the papers that Shaykh Muhammad al-Akhdar had given him, including the *fatwā* renewing his *wird*, and had them sent back to the Shaykh with the following message: "I give you back the eleven beads and return to my twelve beads." The prediction of the Shaykh was coming true.

And this is how the open conflict between the "twelve-beads" and the "eleven-beads" began, through a simple matter of wounded pride, which, in reality is foreign to all true religious sentiment.

The next morning Sharīf al-Mukhtar gathered all of his students and shared with them his decision to return to the "twelve beads" and to separate himself from the Shaykh. But none of his elder students, that is, the senior and more educated adepts, were prepared to join him in this. In the end, they joined Shaykh Muhammad al-Akhdar. When faced with this unexpected defection, Sharīf al-Mukhtar was deeply hurt. Embittered, he felt betrayed by everyone.

This is the point at which Sharīf Hamallah appears in our story.

Sharīf al-Mukhtar, like many dignitaries of Islamic brotherhoods, directed a Koranic school attended by young boys from the area and by several children of sharīfian families. One of the latter was the young Shaykh Hamallah ben Muhammad ben Sidna Umar. His father had been a merchant near Nyamani, on the Niger River. His mother was a Fulani woman of the Wassoulou country. When his parents

---

but also of genealogists who know how to sing the great feats of the ancestors of a family. They live off the donations that the nobles have traditionally been obliged to give them and they are often attached to a family. As the "living memory" of the community, their role in African society is extremely important. However, because they are "masters of language," it can happen that their influence on those who listen to them is not always positive, to the extent that the griots may stir up pride (in the negative sense).

came to settle in Nioro, they had entrusted the education and religious upbringing of the child to Sharīf al-Mukhtar.

Sharīf al-Mukhtar had predicted a great spiritual future for the young boy. One day, watching him carefully, he had said in front of other students: "The day will come when the sun of this one will be at its zenith, when whoever is not under his shade will be burnt by his sun!"

At the time of the first outburst between the "eleven-beads" and the "twelve-beads," the young Sharīf Hamallah was eighteen or nineteen years old. One evening he was going along a road which went past the compound of Shaykh Muhammad al-Akhdar who happened to be resting in the shade of his wall. It was the first time that the Shaykh had seen the young man. Something about him struck him. He questioned Sidi Abdallah, who was near him.

"Who is the father of this black boy?"[40]

"He's not a black," responded Sidi Abdallah, "he's a *sharīf*, a descendant of the Prophet. He's Sharīf Hamallah, the son of Sidna Umar."

For Africans, in fact, it is not color but birth which matters. As long as a man is a *sharīf*, even if he is as dark as ebony, he will be called a *sharīf*, therefore of Arab descent, and not black.

Shaykh Muhammad al-Akhdar kept silent for a moment and then said, "His foot is placed very high in relation to the earth."

All those present tried to outdo him: "It is not surprising. He has always caused wonder in people. He has even performed miracles, without seeking to do so and without taking pride in them."

As the days passed, Sharīf al-Mukhtar, noticing that his students did not come back to him, wondered what was going on with the Shaykh. He ordered young Sharīf Hamallah to attend their meeting and to report to him what was said there.

This is how Sharīf Hamallah went for the first time to Shaykh Muhammad al-Akhdar. He sat in the back of the room and carefully followed the lesson. When it was finished, he returned to Sharīf al-Mukhtar.

---

[40] This expression is common in African languages and has nothing pejorative about it.

"So, what did they say about me?" he immediately asked Sharīf Hamallah, convinced that he was the object of criticism and bad words.

"Nothing at all," answered the young man, "they did not even mention your name."

"But how did they spend their day?"

"Reading the *Jawāhir al-Ma'ānī* (*Pearl of Meanings*) and commenting on it."

For three days Sharīf al-Mukhtar sent the young man to take part in the meetings. Upon his return, he gave the same answer every time: "They didn't talk about you."

On the third day, Sharīf al-Mukhtar burst out furiously: "You too are amongst the traitors against me! They have won you over to their cause. Since this is the case, go and join them and don't come back ever again!"

Although he was unfairly banished, the young Sharīf Hamallah did not go to see Shaykh Muhammad al-Akhdar. Deeply upset and afflicted by a horrible headache, he went home. Since his birth, whenever he was upset, he would be besieged with such painful headaches that he would roll around on the floor and remain sick for entire weeks. Many cures had been attempted by every possible means, but nothing had worked.

His mother, Aissata, seeing him arrive in this state, rushed to a neighbor's to borrow a certain type of incense which she would often burn to assuage his suffering.

Her neighbor told her, "You would do better to take your son to the new marabout, Shaykh Muhammad al-Akhdar. Many people have already gone to him to ask for blessings."

In hopes that her son would finally find a cure, Aissata got her son up and took him to the Shaykh. The Shaykh immediately recognized the young man, whom he had been observing for three days without ever speaking to him. Turning to Aissata, he asked her how the headache had come about; but she wasn't able to give much of an answer. Addressing himself to the young *sharīf*, he asked him to accompany him to his room.

Once they were alone, the Shaykh asked him precise questions about the nature of his pain, the circumstances that had set it off, and what he felt. Sharīf Hamallah answered his questions in detail. When he had finished, the Shaykh remained pensive a few moments.

Then, leaning forward, he leveled out with his hand the fine sand on the ground in front of him and traced a word written in Arabic. It was a secret name of God that conceals the mysteries of the Tijani *Qutbuya*[41] which are preciously and secretly guarded by the master initiates of the order. It was a master word, one of those words which are only passed down mouth-to-mouth or that one writes in the sand so that no trace of it remains.

In writing it, the Shaykh had made an error by omitting to inscribe a certain letter of the word.

Then, lifting his head, he asked the young man, "Are you accustomed to seeing this word written or to hearing it pronounced, either in a state of wakefulness or during your sleep?"

"Yes, I'm used to seeing it," replied the Sharīf, "But in the word that you have written, there is a letter missing in relation to what I am used to seeing."

"What is this letter, and where is it missing?" asked the Shaykh.

Sharīf Hamallah leant over and traced in the sand the missing letter in the place where it belonged.

Immediately, the Shaykh gathered the sand up into his hand from where the sacred name had been written, placed it into a bag and gave this bag to the *sharīf*.

"Here," he told him. "This belongs to you. You are the *Qutb al-Zamān*, the Master of the Hour, the Pole of the Time, for whom I have searched everywhere. I ask you to renew my *wird*."

And, moved by an emotion that we can understand, the old master bowed before the young man, stretching the palms of his open hands in the form of a cup as is done in Islam to receive a blessing.

Sharīf Hamallah renewed his *wird* for him. Then, taking the bag containing the precious sand charged with forces of the mysterious Name, he gave it back to the Shaykh.

"I leave it with you," he told him, "I am still too young to assume outwardly the function that God has honored me with. Also, I ask you to keep this bag until the time comes for me to take charge of it."

---

[41] *Qutbuya*—a noun derived from *qutb* (pole). The term, which is untranslatable in French [and English as well], refers to everything having to do with the Pole.

Shaykh Muhammad al-Akhdar accepted and, although his heart was full of joy, for the time being he remained silent about his great discovery.

From that day on, however, the students began to notice unusual behavior on the part of Shaykh Muhammad al-Akhdar. As soon as Sharīf Hamallah arrived, the Shaykh moved aside to make a place for him on the same rug. Every time the young man took tea, if even a drop remained in his cup, the Shaykh seized it to drink it. In Africa as in all Muslim countries, these are the great gestures of honor and of respect.

Observing all this, the students said amongst themselves that the Shaykh undoubtedly felt a great consideration for the Sharīf, even if they did not know the precise reason why. Things continued like this for a time, the Shaykh having given up his plans to travel onward to Senegal.

One day, Shaykh Muhammad al-Akhdar was in a room with Tierno Sidi (the one who had asked that the *wird* of Sharīf al-Mukhtar be renewed in his absence), Hamedine Baro, and Kisman Doucouré, all of them "elder students" whom Shaykh Muhammad al-Akhdar had already named *muqaddam*s of the order, since he had the authority to do so.[42] He turned to Tierno Sidi.

"If I told you to swear allegiance to Sharīf Hamallah," he said to him, "would you accept it?"

"He's my son!" Tierno Sidi limited himself to replying, which could be understood in many ways.

The Shaykh added nothing. Then, turning towards Hamedine Baro: "And you, if I asked you to follow Sharīf Hamallah, to recognize him as your master, would you accept?"

"If you asked me to recognize a rooster as my master, I would recognize him," replied the latter.

Then, the Shaykh said to them, "I ask you to recognize Sharīf Hamallah as *Qutb*," and he told them about his long search, his discovery, the signs that he had recognized, and above all, the decisive sign of the secret Name destined for the *Qutb*, traced in sand and accurately corrected.

---

[42] In the *turuq* (pl. of *tarīqa*), a *shaykh* has the power to appoint *muqaddam*s.

It was on this occasion that he pronounced the word *Qutb* in public for the first time.[43]

The time came when Sharīf al-Mukhtar, more and more upset at not having been able to convince his former students to come back to him, decided to go on the offensive. He had the means of doing so, being at once the son-in-law and personal marabout of Bodian, the Bambara king of the country. His partisans, the Kaba clan of Nioro, as well as the members of the Bodian family that found themselves now allied with the Taal (the family of Hajj Umar), began a strong campaign against Shaykh Muhammad al-Akhdar.

One of the sons of al-Hajj Umar, who traveled back and forth between Kayes and Dakar to sell animals, roused the Taals by telling them that in Nioro a man dared speak against the "doctrine" of al-Hajj Umar and that he had instituted a practice contrary to that of their ancestor.

They did so well in stirring up trouble that they succeeded in bringing the French Colonial Administration into the affair, telling them that there would be fights and bloodshed if Shaykh Muhammad al-Akhdar were not expelled from Nioro. Always anxious to avoid an incident, the Administration asked no questions and decided to expel the Shaykh. It was made known to him that, not being a native of the town, he should leave it and go back to his own country.

The Shaykh prepared to travel and left in the direction of Senegal. When he was about to leave Nioro, some students came to greet him for the last time. He said to them, "I am very surprised that they have been able to banish me from my burial place. In fact, it was revealed to me that my tomb would be in Nioro. And now I am ordered never to return. This greatly surprises me. But God alone knows!"[44]

---

[43] Like all the events that took place at Nioro at the time, this scene was reported to me by an eyewitness, Kisman Doucouré, a marabout of Marka [ethnicity] from Nioro who had received his *wird* from the hands of Shaykh Muhammad al-Akhdar.

The details of what transpired between the Shaykh and Sharīf Hamallah during the private meeting were moreover confirmed to me by Moulay Ismail (see pp. 74-75), who heard them from the Sharīf himself.

[44] This information was given to me by a direct witness, Gata Bâ, a member of the royal family of Denianke. A prominent merchant who had played an important role in Senegal and in the French Soudan, Gata Bâ left for Abidjan after independence.

The affair created a great stir. Senegalese merchants in Nioro, Kayes, and Medina-Kayes who had valued the human and spiritual qualities of Shaykh Muhammad al-Akhdar, wrote to certain prominent marabouts in Saint-Louis-du-Senegal who were close to the central administrative authority in order that they might attest to the innocence of the Shaykh, the latter being, according to them, an agent of peace rather than a creator of troubles. They added that the Administration had certainly been misled into error.

When the Shaykh arrived in Saint-Louis, he made contact with these prominent marabouts who were, at that time, al-Hajj Malik Si, Abdoullaye Niasse, the Bou Kounta family, and the Shaykh Sidia family. They welcomed him with hospitality, but watched him carefully to find out with whom they were dealing, on the religious as well the human level. Over time, they found in him the very qualities that had been described to them by their Senegalese correspondents. Having reached this opinion, they intervened with the governor of Senegal to ask him to retract his decision to expel the Shaykh and to allow him to return to Nioro as he wished.

Their request was granted and it was thus that Shaykh Muhammad al-Akhdar, after about a year's absence, was able to return to Nioro. A little more than two years after his return, he took his last breath in the town where, as he had announced, his tomb awaited him. His passing away was to mark the beginning of the fiery and tragic religious career of Sharīf Hamallah.

The Destiny of Sharīf Hamallah

A large crowd accompanied the body of Shaykh Muhammad al-Akhdar on the day of his funeral. All of his students were there, amongst them Sharīf Hamallah. Upon returning from the burial, tradition would have it that the procession return to the home of the deceased. However, in an unplanned move the crowd spontaneously went to the home of Sharīf Hamallah and regrouped around him. This day in 1909 was the beginning of his public religious career.

From this day onwards, Sharīf Hamallah assumed his function as *khalīfa* of the order in a public and active manner, having been recognized by a great number of the brothers as possessing the necessary qualifications. He fulfilled his function as master, gave the *awrād*,[45] preached, commented on the holy books, guided the students, and spread his spiritual radiance and blessings on all—in short, he accomplished what was expected of him. His house became a veritable *zāwiya* and was never empty until the day he was arrested for the first time.

Believers, not only from Nioro but from neighboring towns and even from surrounding countries, crowded around him. It was a veritable sea of humanity. These crowds contributed to enflaming not only the Taal family and their allies, but also the Colonial Administration, who were always naturally concerned by large gatherings of men.

In 1920 the writer Paul Marty, an officer in the Colonial Administration, wrote:

> Sharīf Hamallah is still only a bubbling spring, but he is a spring which will become a great river. This can be predicted by the growing strength of the spring's current and by the virtue that is everywhere being attributed to its waters and to the convergence of neighboring streams.[46]

As Tierno Bokar was to explain to me one day, Sharīf Hamallah had assumed his spiritual leadership in 1909, the time when the world had entered into a cycle of Mars,[47] a cycle of troubles, conflicts, and wars.

"Every saint or prophet," he told me, "whose coming coincides with the beginning of a cycle of Mars will encounter more troubled times than peaceful days, but this will not diminish anything of his spiritual value. Our great master, Shaykh Ahmad al-Tijani, had recommended to his elder students: 'If you are slandered, do not slander. If you receive blows, do not return them. If someone refuses you a favor, offer to do one for him.'" Tierno added that Sharīf Hamallah himself respected this commandment to the end.

---

[45] Plural of *wird*.

[46] Paul Marty was in charge of Muslim Affairs: *Études sur l'Islam et les tribus du Soudan*, vol. IV, p. 218.

[47] This does not mean astrological or astronomical planetary cycles but numerological cycles linked to the symbolism of the planets.

The cycle of Mars that began in 1909 was to finish in 1945.[48] By that time, Sharīf Hamallah had been resting in the cemetery of Montluçon for barely two years, having died as a consequence of his deportation. How could the situation have deteriorated throughout these years to reach such an extreme point?

When Sharīf Hamallah arrived on the religious scene, the conflict between "twelve-beaders" and "eleven-beaders"—a purely human and not a religious conflict—already existed. He only inherited it. The fiery enthusiasm of which he was the object, and the success that he had, only served to fan the flames that were smoldering within all the supporters of the "twelve beads."

Things stayed that way, however, until a completely banal and purely human incident arose. This incident, in which the Sharīf had no part, has been called the "teapot incident." It lit the fuse and gave the conflict an open and irreversible character.

An interpreter named Mamadou Salim had had a silver teapot made by a craftsman and had given it for safekeeping to his wife, a descendant of al-Hajj Umar. This interpreter's master was Tierno Sidi, the one who had been initiated into the "eleven beads" by Shaykh Muhammad al-Akhdar in Nioro.[49] One day, wanting to honor his master with a gift, Mamadou Salim gave Tierno Sidi his teapot. Soon after that, the unfortunate Mamadou Salim was arrested by the French authorities and imprisoned. He died while in detention, leaving his family without resources.

His wife recalls that one day she saw her husband give the silver teapot to one of Tierno Sidi's messengers. She asked the latter to give the teapot back so that she would be able to sell it. Tierno Sidi answered that, unfortunately, the teapot had not been lent but given to him and he thus had given it to a third person, the Moorish leader of Tichitt. However, he added, if the Moorish chief still had the teapot in his possession, he would certainly not refuse to give it back to a descendant of al-Hajj Umar if she asked him for it.

---

[48] Let us note in passing that this present cycle of Mars has witnessed the two bloodiest wars of our era, the last one having ended at the same time as the cycle.

[49] Tierno Sidi had come to settle in Bamako so as not to get mixed up in the conflict confronting his former master, the Sharīf al-Mukhtar, and Sharīf Hamallah. He therefore had no relationship with Sharīf Hamallah.

The woman did not want to hear anything about it. She shouted out that her teapot had been stolen and took the matter to her brother Karamogo Taal, who at the time was the only known descendant of al-Hajj Umar in Bamako. He was a shopkeeper, illiterate in both French and Arabic. Very troubled, he summoned all the former *sofas*[50] of al-Hajj Umar, as well as the captives and griots who claimed obedience to him. When they were all together, he told them about the issue. His listeners, who for the most part had become domestics or cooks with the French who had settled in the town, decided to summon all the Tukolor present in Bamako.

Now it happened that amongst all the Tukolor of Bamako only two belonged to a noble and educated family: Bokar Diafara, and my adopted father, Tijani Amadou Ali Thiam, the faithful friend of Tierno Bokar.

After everyone had assembled and Karamogo Taal had put forward his sister's grievances concerning Tierno Sidi, my father Tijani Amadou Ali began to speak.

"Tierno Sidi is today the most remarkable personage of Futa," he said. "He is known for his knowledge as well as for his piety. In addition, he is a great *muqaddam*. His ties with the family of al-Hajj Umar are very strong. Therefore, it would be unfitting if we were to enter into a conflict with him over a teapot. I suggest that every Tukolor present in Bamako, be he a noble or a servant, make a contribution so that we can gather the sum of three hundred francs[51] which will be given to the sister of Karamogo Taal as compensation for her teapot."

When this proposal was put to the sister of Karamogo Taal, she exclaimed that it was an injustice, a maneuver typical of a Thiam,[52] and she demanded that her silver teapot be returned to her, the one that her husband had had melted down and shaped, and no other!

A short time later, the Tukolor held another meeting and sent two emissaries to Tierno Sidi to summon him and ask him to come explain the situation. Such a demand, within the context of African traditions

---

[50] *Sofa*: a name given to the warriors around a chief. Most often they belong to foreign ethnic groups.

[51] A very large sum for that time.

[52] The Tukolor are made up of two great families, the Taals and the Thiams, traditional rivals of one another.

based on the respect for hierarchy, was totally out of place. So Tierno Sidi responded to the emissaries[53] thus:

> Because of my age, my standing, and my rank in the *Tarīqa*,[54] I am the one who should call together a gathering of the Tukolor—it is not for them to summon me. However, if I am personally summoned by a grandson of al-Hajj Umar Taal (Karamogo Taal), I am ready to answer him out of respect for his grandfather.

Unfortunately, the emissaries had been badly chosen. One was known for his reputation of being a mischief maker, the other for his opposition to Tierno Sidi. They therefore were in complete agreement that upon their return to the Tukolor they would transmit an answer summarized in their own fashioning. They said:

> We have given the message to Tierno Sidi, but he made it known to us that he did not have to respond to a group of uncircumcised people! In other words, in plain language, to a group of insignificant kids!

Cries of indignation erupted everywhere. Feeling that they had been insulted, the Tukolor all rose up together against Tierno Sidi, except for my father, Tijani, and decided to organize a campaign of their own with a view towards ruining him. As most of them worked for members of the Colonial Administration, they were well placed for this kind of action. Each Tukolor was given the mission of setting his employer against Tierno Sidi by painting the blackest possible picture of him. After a certain time, this insidious campaign began to bear fruit. The commandant of the Bamako district began to hear from several sources about an "eleven-bead" marabout who was the very incarnation of dishonesty and of all possible faults.

When he had judged that the Tukolor minds were sufficiently prepared, Karamogo Taal, in the name of the Tukolor community

---

[53] The two emissaries were Bokar Yaya Dem and Karamogo Babali.

[54] Translator's note: *Tarīqa* is the Arabic word for "path" or "way" and is also used in Sufism to designate a Sufi order; thus in this case it refers to the local Tijani order.

of Bamako, legally charged Tierno Sidi with "appropriating a silver teapot belonging to a widow." The District Commandant, who was ill-disposed towards Tierno Sidi due to the efforts of the former's entourage, summoned him into his office. Without listening to any explanation, he sent the matter before the indigenous court. But Karamogo Taal and his friends had already gotten to the judge, promising him that he would be able to realize his dream of becoming *imām* of the Bamako mosque if he helped them win their trial.

The trial took place. Tierno Sidi lost and was ordered to return the teapot within a month, or he would be incarcerated. Fortunately for him, he was able to recover the teapot from the Moorish leader of Tichitt and returned it to the District Commandant within the allotted time.

For Tierno Sidi, at least, the matter thus seemed to be closed. But it was in fact to mark the beginning of a merciless war against all the "eleven-beaders" regardless of who they might be or where they came from.

Intoxicated by their easy success against a man of Tierno Sidi's standing and discovering the strength they had in unity, the Tukolor held a new assembly in which they decided to take the conflict to another level. Karamogo Taal harangued them, saying, "Tierno Sidi and his family are traitors to al-Hajj Umar because they have chosen the formula of eleven recitations. It is now up to us to bring them back to the formula of twelve; otherwise, there will be a total split between our clan and their followers. No Tukolor shopkeeper or merchant shall sell them anything anymore. They shall be boycotted by everyone!"

My father, Tijani Amadou Ali Thiam, from whom I have received all the details of this affair, was present at this meeting. Once again, he tried to make them see reason, but in vain. He asked them, "Would you dare, Karamogo Taal, and all who are present here, attack Tierno Sidi on religious matters? If Tierno Sidi is to be challenged with religious objections, it is for others to do it, and certainly not you who know nothing!"

In effect, of the five hundred people present, all were illiterate except Tijani Amadou Ali himself. Furious at these words, the Tukolor ejected my father from their assembly.

After their meeting, the Tukolor had letters written which they sent out everywhere: to all the countries, Senegal, Guinea, etc., wherever there were members of their clan, announcing their triumph over an enemy of al-Hajj Umar and asking them to boycott the "eleven-beaders" wherever they found them.

One of these letters arrived in Bandiagara. The chief of the canton, who was a Tukolor, assembled the committee of Bandiagara, presided over by Tierno Bokar. Alfa Ali, the Koran master and an old friend of Tierno Bokar, was also present. He had already been initiated into the "eleven beads" but had never spoken about it to anyone.

The letter was read, and then they asked Tierno Bokar his opinion. He declared,

"Personally, I will not take a position either for or against the 'eleven beads' without meeting the promoter of this practice and understanding on what grounds it is based. While waiting to learn more, I advise that we all remain with the tradition of 'twelve beads.'"

This occurred in 1917. The majority of Bandiagara thus preserved the practice of the "twelve beads" until 1937, the year of Tierno Bokar's trip to Nioro.

As can be seen, there was nothing political—as was believed by the French Administration—nor fundamentally religious in the origin of this conflict, because the implicated practice touched neither Islam nor the original teachings of Shaykh Ahmad al-Tijani. Until the campaign that was undertaken by the Tukolor after they had won the trial against Tierno Sidi, "twelve-beaders" and "eleven-beaders" had co-existed peacefully. In the mosques, after the canonical Islamic prayers, each person peacefully recited his Tijani *wird*, fingering the beads of his rosary, be they eleven or twelve. In fact, no-one paid much attention to it.

But from then on, the lions were unleashed and the formidable administrative machinery was put into action. For the French authorities, the "eleven-beaders" had become the target. In the eyes of many, "Hamallism," which was the most representative movement of the "eleven-beaders," became suspect and was seen as the cause of problems. Pressed hard by important and influential Tukolor marabouts, the Administration became embroiled in a quarrel which in fact did not concern them at all.

On his side, Sharīf Hamallah was unaware of the stratagems of intrigue and lived in a world estranged from the outward rules of diplomacy. With regard to the French Administration, he never strayed from an attitude of perfect dignity, but also one of total independence, which could be interpreted as disdain, even hostility. He sought no honor, was not concerned with winning medals, did not pay visits to the authorities of the time, and paid homage to no-one. In short, he stayed away from all worldly matters. This was a dangerous attitude at a time when the Colonial Administration had a strong tendency to think that whoever was not with them was against them. It did not take much more for the authorities, who were worried about the growing popular success of the Sharīf and were urged on by the Tukolor, to consider him to be a dangerous rebel who was devising secret, dark plots and was just awaiting a propitious moment to start a revolt.

In 1920 Paul Marty could still write: "Vis-à-vis us (the French Administration), his attitude is courteous but reserved. He only comes to the District office upon a formal summons. It seems that with a bit of astuteness, he could be easily controlled."[55]

Unfortunately the Administration did not listen to Paul Marty, who was better informed than they were because of his post of being in charge of Muslim affairs. In addition, he was well connected with marabouts of all followings. The Administration preferred to listen to those who trotted out the bogeyman of disorder and revolt, predicting that terrible troubles would come from the Hamallists. Such are the ways of history.

From that time on the situation became continually worse. The Sharīf was held responsible for even the most minor incidents, and these were used as pretexts to persecute his students. This was the beginning of arrests and mass deportations.

A minor brawl took place in Nioro in 1923 which motivated the summoning of Sharīf Hamallah to Bamako, some six hundred kilometers from his residence. The Governor, whose entourage had set him against Sharīf Hamallah, rudely received the Sharīf:

"It is said that you claim to speak directly with God. So ask him, if you are able, to smash my head with the roof of my palace," he guffawed.

Through an interpreter, the Sharīf offered the following response: "Interpreter, tell the Governor to open his mouth wider (literally, in Bambara: 'to make best wishes'). I have no interest in asking God to

---

[55] *Études sur l'Islam et les tribus du Soudan*, vol. IV, p. 218.

grant him life or death. I only know that when God puts a man at the head of even five people, it means that God has some consideration for that man, all the more so when he places the man as the leader of a country as large as the Soudan. Now when God has consideration for a man, he grants his wishes. It would have been more valuable for the Governor to ask God for a long life so as to better profit from the function that he has. Living is certainly better than dying because, here at least, he is assured of having an excellent position, whereas he does not know if the same will be in store for him in a future life."

We can easily understand that for an all-powerful Governor used to hearing only: "Yes, sir, as you command, Governor," that he could not accept such words. At a fever-pitch of anger and indignation, he immediately ordered the deportation of the Sharīf. He was not even permitted to return to Nioro to see his family. He was handcuffed, and immediately taken to Saint-Louis-du-Senegal where he was put under house arrest.

In 1924, some incidents took place in Kiffa (in present-day Mauritania). Even though the Sharīf was then residing in Saint-Louis, he was held personally responsible for them. The incidents were used as a pretext for removing him from Saint-Louis, where his influence had begun to spread to the population and had provoked several conversions, and he was transferred to Muderdra in Mauritania.

In 1930, while Sharīf Hamallah was still in Muderdra, fights broke out in Kaedi (Senegal) between members of the Marka ethnic group. It was known who the instigator of these incidents was, but he was a Hamallist. Again, the blame was put on Sharīf Hamallah, who was deported from Muderdra to Adjopé in Ivory Coast, a particularly humid area. Undoubtedly, it was known that the best way to kill a Moor, used to living under a tent in the open air, was to make him live in a humid house. . .

From then on, access to Ivory Coast was forbidden to all Moors so that none of them could make contact with the Sharīf. That is why until 1936, when the Sharīf returned to the Soudan, the Moors were constantly expelled from the Ivory Coast.

Throughout this period, life became impossible for the Hamallists. They were accused of any trouble that the Administration encountered. If someone refused to pay his taxes, he was accused of Hamallism. To take revenge on an enemy, it was enough to denounce him as a "dangerous Hamallist" and he was dragged off without any explanation. The followers of Sharīf Hamallah, particularly all of his main *muqaddam*s, were deported and dispersed into the four corners of West Africa and French Equatorial Africa. But by a strange twist of fate, these measures were to work against the desired intention. In fact, everywhere where there were Hamallists in exile, they settled down and founded *zāwiya*s that were soon very successful. From every link that was separated from its chain, a new chain arose. In this way, the activities of Sharīf Hamallah's enemies—who were inciting an administration that knew little about spiritual problems—seemed destined to continual failure.

In 1936, thanks to the formation of the Popular Front,[56] all political prisoners were freed by the decision of the French government. Sharīf Hamallah could finally leave the Ivory Coast and return to Nioro.

But his enemies were still present and they had not been disarmed. The prominent Tukolor marabouts, seeing the new Administration lose interest in the Sharīf, feared that the advantages that they enjoyed would be passed on to the Sharīf, whose popular following was growing all the time. Thus they decided to attack him again and so searched for a pretext. They did not delay in finding one.

Upon his return, Sharīf Hamallah had declared to his students who were celebrating his arrival, "This will not last. I still consider myself to be a traveler." Because of the permanent insecurity he found himself in, he had shortened the length of his canonical prayers, making them two *raka'āt*[57] instead of four, which is permitted by Islamic law in cases of traveling, danger, or war. He had not advised anyone to imitate him, but this did not prevent some of his students, especially those belonging to the Marka ethnic group and who were always traveling for their trade, from following his example.

---

[56] Editor's note: The "Front Populaire" was a broad coalition of left-wing parties that won the French National Assembly election of 1936 and stayed in power until 1938. While in power, they changed many previous government policies.

[57] Editor's note: A *rak'a* (pl. *raka'āt*) in Islam is a "unit" of ritual worship. It includes required and optional recitations from the Koran along with certain physical gestures and movements. Several *raka'āt* are combined to make up the various canonical prayers at the heart of Muslim daily practice. When a prayer is shortened, as in the circumstances described above, some *raka'āt* are omitted from the prayer.

As soon as they learned about this, the antagonists of Sharīf Hamallah agreed to warn the French authorities that Sharīf Hamallah was preparing a "holy war" because he was praying two *raka'āt* instead of four.[58] They simply neglected to explain that this practice—which is, indeed, valid in times of war—is also valid for simple journeys and states of insecurity.

The Sharīf was summoned. Again, the meeting was memorable. The Sharīf asked the commandant how many *raka'āt* the French had prescribed so that he might know if he had gone against their orders. Fortunately, the Sharīf was sent home without troublesome consequences.

The attention of the new Colonial Administration of the Popular Front was no less focused on Sharīf Hamallah, whose dossier acquired a political coloring. At the time, the ominous words "holy war" were not easily dismissed. From that day onwards, surveillance of the Hamallists was redoubled and they were considered "anti-French." Oppression against them multiplied, which began to irritate some.

This state of latent persecution continued without the French Administration deciding to take any clear action against the Sharīf. Disappointed, his enemies looked for a new way to create difficulties for him from which he would not be able to escape. They found a means of accomplishing this by organizing a cruel provocation which was to result in the fatal incidents of Assaba. This was in 1940.

A marabout family of Nioro (the Kaba Diakité) that was opposed to Sharīf Hamallah was looking for a way to provoke an incident. Now it happened that the Kaba Diakité had traditionally been hosts (i.e. landlords) of a Moorish tribe who were enemies of Sharīf Hamallah's clan. This ancestral opposition was intensified by the fact that the tribes allied to the Sharīf had, along with him, embraced the Tijaniyya order, whereas the other tribes belonged to the Qadiriyya order. As always, religion served as a pretext for a conflict that was of purely human origin, which in this case was a tribal rivalry.

The Kaba Diakité asked their tenants to provoke their ancestral adversaries, which did not displease them. They did not hold back. One day when their tribe was traveling about, they encountered a

---

[58] See note 5, p. 26. Of the five daily Islamic prayers, three are made up of four *raka'āt*. These can be reduced to just two prayer cycles in situations of travel, danger, or war.

caravan which was carrying the eldest son of Sharīf Hamallah. They immediately threw themselves upon the caravan, seized the young man and began to insult him: "You and your family are false *sharīfs*. But we are going to clear up this matter. Fire from God should not be able to burn a *sharīf*, isn't that right? Well, we're going to try it." And they kept the young man upright, barefoot on some burning sand that had just been used to prepare a *mechoui*.[59]

Before being seized by his enemies, the son of Sharīf Hamallah had forbidden his companions to intervene to defend him. In fact there were fewer of them than their assailants and he feared that the confrontation would end up in a massacre. Therefore, his companions did not move, champing at the bit. After the torture, they rescued the young man. The soles of his feet had been badly burnt and they took him to Nioro where he had to be hospitalized. An investigation was begun.

Perhaps fearing turmoil or new provocations, Sharīf Hamallah forbade all of his followers, even members of his family, to visit his son in the hospital, advising them instead to wait until the Administration had done its work and until justice had been rendered and the guilty ones were brought to light. Therefore, the *zāwiya* stayed completely out of this affair.

This silence worried the Administration, who wondered whether something was being planned. In order to test the waters, the commandant summoned Sharīf Hamallah. He asked him what he thought of this matter and what he thought would be best to do about it. To this unexpected question, the Sharīf answered in his usual way, again very direct and lacking in diplomacy: "Where, then, does justice come from? Certainly not from me. Moreover, I personally am not the victim. The victim is an adult and well known. The question should be addressed to him. Since it is your duty to provide justice, and since you have seen the victim as well as the torturers who were arrested, I don't understand why you are asking me what I think should be done."

Those responsible for the incident had in fact been arrested, and then put under house arrest in Nioro in a camp where they lived ordi-

---

[59] Translator's note: *Mechoui* means roasted meat. In some areas of Africa, meat is cooked in a clay pot buried in the sand or earth. To "have a *mechoui*" can also refer to having a large family or communal celebration at which one or several whole animals are roasted on a spit.

nary lives and where they were brought everything that they needed. Two months later, they were simply released.

Happy at having gotten off so easily, they then composed a poem with a provocative title: "Around the Grill," a poem which they spread all over Mauritania by singers who were accompanied by drums. Now, the Moorish tribe to which the wife of the Sharīf belonged, the mother of the young man who had been tortured, was a warrior tribe. In Mauritania there are three types of tribes: marabout tribes, warrior tribes, and merchant tribes. These tough warriors, whose pride had been stung, had waited in vain for a reaction from Sharīf Hamallah. Exasperated, they came to find him to ask him what should be done. "Leave it to God to render justice," was his response.

For the moment, they accepted deferring any action, and things might have remained as they had been if their adversaries, seeing that no reaction was forthcoming, had not outdone themselves by now composing a new song, this one even more insulting than the first. It was addressed to all non-Tijani Moors and entitled "Come to the Rescue, Nothing Will Happen"—that is, you won't have to risk anything. This new song was also spread all over the country.

This time it was too much for the young man's uncles, who were particularly targeted through this poem. "Although Sharīf Hamallah may let himself be dragged through the mud," they said, "we shall show our enemies that we have always been victorious over them." Having said that, they gathered a troop of warriors and left on a campaign against the tribe that had attacked their nephew. The provocation was bearing its fruits.

They found the ones they were looking for at a place called Assaba, a place of sterile sand dunes. Alas, overcome with fury, they massacred their enemies on the spot. Hardly any of them escaped.

Feeling that they had now avenged their nephew, they immediately calmed down. When seven civil guards accompanied by a doctor came to arrest them, they showed no resistance, although they could easily have killed all of them. This shows that their action was a purely private one and had nothing to do with the "anti-French revolt" of which they were to be accused.

The reaction of the Administration was severe. Let us remember that this was 1940, the time when France was torn between Vichyists and Gaullists. To be accused of hostility towards France amounted to being accused of plotting with the enemy, the Gaullists in this case.

The Administration was sensitive to events in Europe and had been pushed to the brink by the enemies of the Sharīf who were portraying him as a dangerous rebel. They could not imagine that the reserve of this man came primarily from his detachment from purely worldly events. In striving to apply the teachings of Shaykh Ahmad al-Tijani to everything, he did not even want to react to the torture of his son. "If you receive blows, don't return them." Because they did not understand him, the Administration suspected the worst of him.

Once again, he was considered personally responsible for the events of Assaba. Not finding any proof of his participation in these events, and for good reason, it was not possible to bring the Sharīf into court. However, an administrative procedure was applied to his case which gave the Governor the right to deport him if he wanted to, according to his personal decision.

Very early one morning a group of guards came to get him. Dressed in a light cotton *boubou*, he walked in front of them. Even then, he did not react. Although only one word would have been necessary to raise thousands of men to defend him, he did not even go back into his house to get clothing, out of fear of waking his family; the cries of the women would have provoked a riot. So he followed the guards, never to return. The few witnesses to this scene report that the only words he uttered were those that are pronounced during the pilgrimage and at the moment of death: "*Rabbi labbayka! Rabbi labbayka!*" "Lord, here I am! Lord, here I am!"[60]

He was taken first to Gorée in Senegal, then to Cassaigne in Algeria, then to Vals-les-Bains in Ardèche (in France) before being transferred to Evaux. There he contracted a lung disease and was transported to the hospital of Montluçon where he died in January 1943.[61] He reposes in Montluçon, in the Eastern cemetery where his tomb has attracted more and more African pilgrims.

---

[60] Editor's note: The *talbiya* (i.e. the formula *labbayka*) literally means "at thy service." It is repeated by all pilgrims to Mecca to state that they are performing this rite to fulfill their religious obligations and to renounce any egotistical reasons that they might have besides the pure service of God. Here, it is Sharīf Hamallah's way of acknowledging that this turn in his destiny is of God's design and that he accepts his fate. He puts himself utterly into the hands of God and states that even in this ordeal he intends to serve God's will.

[61] Dr. Charles Pidoux, who later became our friend, was at this time sequestered in

This was the outward destiny of Sharīf Hamallah, the man "whose feet rested very high above this earth."

It was necessary for us to trace out his life in order to throw light on the events of which Tierno Bokar would be the victim, events which were set into motion the very day after his meeting with Sharīf Hamallah.

The Meeting of Tierno Bokar with Sharīf Hamallah

In 1937, about a year after the Sharīf returned from Ivory Coast, Tierno Bokar had the opportunity to go to Nioro, which he had wanted to do for a long time.

That year, Tierno had been summoned to Bamako to preside over the division of the estate of his eldest half-brother, Amadou Salif Taal. His faithful friend Tijani Amadou Ali Thiam accompanied him.

At the age of sixty-two, Tierno Bokar was traveling to a very large city for the first time. The farthest his preceding trips had taken him were to Segou and to Mopti. In Bamako he saw for the first time some modern technologies such as electricity, railways, and airplanes. Seeing these things helped him satisfy a bit of curiosity, but he also acquired a few images that he would fortunately be able to use in his later teachings.

The estate was settled amicably. Tierno then called me to his side and declared, "Amadou, I must now gain a clearer understanding of the situation of the Tijaniyya. In Dinguiraye, Nioro, Kayes, Segou, and Bamako everyone is constantly asking questions about the orthodoxy of the 'eleven beads' within the Tijani order. I have always answered that I could not pass judgment on this matter without personally seeing Sharīf Hamallah, who has become one of the most popular masters of the Tijaniyya Way. I therefore intend to take advantage of this journey to go to Nioro too."

Evaux for political reasons. He got to know Sharīf Hamallah there and provided us with a precious eyewitness account of the end of the Master's life. It was thanks to the Doctor that we were able to find the tomb of the Sharīf in Montluçon.

Because of my personal experience as an official in the French Administration, I considered it my duty to alert Tierno to the consequences that might come about for him.

"Rightly or wrongly," I told him, "the Sharīf of Nioro has a bad reputation with the Administration. He has been portrayed as 'anti-French' by eminent religious leaders whose words the authorities would not doubt because they consider these religious leaders to be allies. By now, the divorce (of the authorities from the Sharīf) is complete. The problem has been complicated by the intransigence of the Tukolor on one side and the zeal of the Marka and the Moors on the other. Disputes that have absolutely nothing to do with religion have been superimposed on the matter. The 'eleven-beaders' are now opposed not only by the 'twelve-beaders,' who are even fellow Tijanis, but also by members of the Qadiri brotherhood. It would be best for you to stay out of this, or else ask to see the Sharīf on an official basis, with the agreement of the authorities."

"I am not averse to requesting anything whatsoever, you know that," he answered. "But if it were known that I am going to Nioro, who knows what measures all the parties involved in this matter would take. I prefer to take everyone by surprise."

"You risk making many enemies, Tierno, and attracting difficulties from every direction."

"Have you ever known a man of God who has lived and died without difficulties? Find me an opportunity to go to Nioro incognito."

I did as he wished and was able to organize his trip as he had requested. Leaving his friend Tijani Amadou Ali in Bamako, Tierno boarded a broken-down truck. For twenty-four hours he bumped along a track that stretched over 450 kilometers of sand furrows, stones and thorns. The truck arrived in Nioro around eleven in the morning, an hour before the *zuhr* (midday) prayer.

On that very day, soon after the dawn prayer, Sharīf Hamallah had called his trusted right-hand man, Amadou Ould Brahim, who was the most educated of his students, and had said to him, "Amadou, today I'm going to receive a stranger. He will be the one who follows me in al-Hajj Umar's succession. Please make sure that he does not feel homesick [that is, make him feel at home]."

So, when Tierno arrived at the *zāwiya* at around eleven in the morning, Amadou Ould Brahim and other students rushed to receive him. When he had stated his name (Tierno Bokar Salif Taal), Amadou Ould Brahim, recognizing a member of the family of al-Hajj Umar, was overcome with surprise: "Shaykhna [our Master] predicted your arrival today," he exclaimed.

Amadou Ould Brahim immediately sent someone to tell Sharīf Hamallah that the stranger he had predicted would come had in fact arrived. Sharīf Hamallah was not accustomed to leaving his home before the *zuhr* prayer, and so Tierno was settled into a small room in the compound. He washed, changed his clothes and organized his baggage and then went to wait in the *zāwiya* amongst the students.

Just before the *zuhr* prayer, the Sharīf appeared. Everyone could see that he wore exactly the same clothing as Tierno: the same *boubou*, the same *tourtil* (a light *boubou* worn as underclothes), the same cap. It was said that each was the reflection of the other. While Tierno remained silent, as he told me later, Sharīf Hamallah rushed up to him, held out his hand and smiled, "Well, we are dressed in the same way."

At that moment the call to prayer was sounded. Everyone lined up in rows behind the Sharīf's prayer mat, as he usually led the prayer.[62] A disciple of sharīfian origin, Moulay Ismail, was placed in the first row, right behind the Sharīf. Moulay Ismail gave his place to Tierno and then stepped back into the second row, and each one of those who were behind him also went back one row.

The Sharīf stepped into his place. Before beginning the prayer, he turned around and saw Tierno behind him; pulling him by his *boubou*, he drew him to his right side in order that he join him on his own prayer mat. Moulay Ismail and all those who had gone back a row again moved forward a row and took their usual places.

---

[62] When Muslims pray together, one man must always be positioned in front of the others to "lead" the prayer. This is the *imām*. The believers arrange themselves behind him, shoulder-to-shoulder in very straight horizontal rows and follow his movements.

Anyone can be the *imām*. An *imām* who is appointed by a community permanently exercises this function in the mosque. In general, the choice falls upon a man who is renowned for his piety.

This was not merely a gesture of courtesy on the part of the Sharīf. He intended, through this act of great spiritual respect, to encourage a similar attitude towards Tierno in his students. In fact, some of them had learned through hard experience to regard any stranger—and particularly a Taal—as an agent sent by the Tukolor to spy on their *shaykh*. Tierno's surname made him particularly suspicious in their eyes. By having the stranger pray by his side, the Sharīf "covered him," in a sense, with his own mantle.

After the ritual prayer, Sharīf Hamallah, as was his practice, remained for thirty minutes praying in a low voice. Then he gave his blessing to everyone and turned to Tierno Bokar and said, "I would have liked to have you stay with me, but your Tukolor relatives in the town might be offended and feel awkward if they want to visit you. You will therefore stay in the compound, but in the home of Bouyed Ould Sheikh Siby."

He turned towards Moulay Ismail, the one who had given his place to Tierno, and said, "Moulay Ismail, you shall be at the service of Tierno Bokar during his entire stay with us. Forget your status as a *sharīf*, and serve him."

Then, as was his habit, Sharīf Hamallah returned to his quarters and only came out for the *'asr* (middle of the afternoon) prayer.

Once Tierno was settled in the home of Bouyed Ould Sheikh Siby, Moulay Ismail came and placed himself at his service. He looked after all of his domestic needs, making his tea and keeping him company. Apparently, Tierno and the Sharīf saw each other only at the times of prayer.

Tierno had been there for three days when one night Moulay Ismail was struck with dysentery and was obliged to leave his room several times to go to the lavatory which, as in many African compounds, was outdoors, surrounded by a small wall. Thus it was that at 3 o'clock in the morning Moulay Ismail saw Tierno Bokar leave his room and go towards the house of Sharīf Hamallah. His curiosity was aroused, and he wanted to see where Tierno would go. At the same moment, at the side of the Sharīf's house, he saw a ray of light coming from the lamp that the Sharīf usually carried with him once evening had fallen. The ray of light approached Tierno. It was the Sharīf. They met half-way and began to speak in low voices, while walking slowly. Moulay Ismail did not hear what they said to each other, but he remained there and watched them in stunned surprise. He saw them make their way towards the Sharīf's door with slow steps, speaking all the while, then turn around again and walk away and then come back to the door, continually going back and forth. This went on until the call for the morning prayer, after which each one returned home.

This is how Moulay Ismail discovered that Tierno Bokar and Sharīf Hamallah saw each other every night, starting at three o'clock in the morning when all of the *zāwiya* was fast asleep. That is to say that during his stay, Tierno slept very little. Moreover, he never used the bed that the Sharīf had had prepared for him. When sleep overtook him, he stretched out on the skin that his host had offered as a prayer mat.[63]

Tierno stayed at the Nioro *zāwiya* for fifteen days. Later, he told me that he had had fifteen meetings with the Sharīf, which means that they saw one another every night from the beginning of his stay. He told me that during their nighttime meetings, he was able to ask the Sharīf all the questions he had wanted to in order to determine his position. Let us not forget that since receiving the letter of Alfa Hashimi Taal, Tierno had been informed of certain mystical means that would permit him to recognize the new Pole of the Tijaniyya. The fact remains that Tierno, who was not naive, was entirely convinced of the spiritual validity of Sharīf Hamallah in regard to the Tijaniyya as well as to Islam in general. He also asked the Sharīf to renew his *wird* for him using the formula of "eleven beads," which the Sharīf agreed to do.

A large gathering with all of the students was organized for this purpose a few days before Tierno's departure. He knelt facing the Sharīf, his hands crossed on his knees, his chest bent over, his chin on his chest.

Sharīf Hamallah, who was younger than Tierno, asked him, "Tierno Bokar, of us two, who is the elder?"

"I was born before you but you are older than me."[64]

---

[63] All of these details were related to me by Moulay Ismail. See note 43 on p. 56.

[64] This means the following: "In the Tijaniyya, I began before you but you have come farther than me." This is a way of rendering homage and recognizing the superiority of someone. The value of one's spiritual superiority is considered, in Africa, as if it were one's age. One would say, for example, of a young man who is particularly wise: "This young man is older than his father."

"We wish that the descendants of al-Hajj Umar might all have been like you. But whatever God does is well done. As long as there are descendants of al-Hajj Umar on this earth, there will always be at least one who will inherit his ancestor's love for the Prophet and his descendants."

After a moment of silence, the Sharīf got to the heart of the matter. "Bokar Salif, have you ever made a spiritual retreat? Have you ever performed *istikhāra*[65] in order to release yourself from indecision?"

Tierno, who had until then remained in the same position, straightened up. He said:

What a coincidence! I knew that this would be the first question you would ask me. In fact, I made such a retreat, and this is why: For some time, darkness reigned at the depths of my heart. I received letters from my *Foutanké*[66] relatives and even from Sharīf al-Mukhtar saying that I should not follow the path of Sharīf Hamallah and that neither they nor the Administration wished to see crowds gather around him. I read these letters in my *zāwiya* to some of my friends. But the unknown weight that pressed on my chest became heavier. My compatriots rejoiced, yet I could not understand the reason for their joy. The Tijani doctrine that I consulted did not enlighten me on the matter. The Tukolor *'ulamā'* whom I questioned cursed you and your followers. It was then that I decided to make the *istikhāra* so that God would make known to me who you are in reality.

Seven days after I had finished the *istikhāra*, God sent me a dream. I saw eleven men walking at daybreak and amongst them I recognized Sharīf al-Mukhtar. They were all covered with prickly heat sores[67] and suffered from severe itching. They were staggering through the sand tearing their clothing and scratching themselves until they bled. I joined them, and

[65] See note 38 on p. 50.

[66] *Foutanké*: a native of Fouta, in Senegal, which is where the Tukolor are from.

[67] An eruption of small pimples that appear on the body during great heat and which itch intensely.

as soon as I did, I caught their disease. We came to a rise and we observed from there a vast pool which stretched as far as the eye could see. The water of this pool was white, like milk. "We're going to wash ourselves and drink" said one of those amongst us.

We hurried on. A winged man appeared out of the water. He spread out his arms and said to us, "It is forbidden to come into this pool."

"There is a *sharīf* amongst us. Let us drink."

"I know all of you better than you know yourselves," he replied, "but you shall not go into the pool until its owner arrives."

A tornado-like wind arose and lifted a sparkling cloud from the horizon. A chant came from this cloud. We recognized the formula from the *dhikr.* "*Lā ilāha illa 'Llāh.*"[68]

Gripped with fear, we saw this strange cloud coming over us. It rushed into the sky with the speed of a galloping horse. When it reached the zenith, it broke up. It was composed of a multitude of winged men and the movement of their wings was producing pulses which were striking us. The men entered the pool and vanished. As one, the twelve of us started ahead to follow them. The guard stopped us with a gesture. Another gust of wind brought us a second cloud of winged men who repeated the same actions as the first. And then a third. Each time, the clouds were more brilliant and the voices that chanted the sacred formula became more harmonious. Behind the third cloud, there appeared a man on a horse. The rider was masked, and he held a rosary in his hand. At the horse's head, al-Hajj Umar held the bridle.

At this point, the Sharīf interrupted Tierno and asked, "How did you recognize al-Hajj Umar?"

Tierno replied:

---

[68] This is the chanted recitation of the first part of the profession of Islamic faith: *Lā ilāha illa 'Llāh,* which means: "There is no god but God" or "No god if not God." This *dhikr* [i.e. invocation] is an essential part of the *wird* of all Islamic brotherhoods in general.

His name was written in letters of fire on his chest. The horse reared in the wind. Al-Hajj Umar clung to the bridle. A gust of wind made the horse's mane stand upright and caused the face-covering of the horseman's turban to slip away. I attest before God that I now realize that the face which appeared to me then was yours.

The horseman said to the guard, "What do these people want?"

"They want to drink," he replied.

The horseman got down from his horse and advanced towards the pool. A gust of incredible ferocity then arose, compared to which the preceding gusts seemed only light breezes. We twelve men were scattered within the cloud of dust. The man who had your face took the milky water into his cupped hands and sprinkled me with it. My thirst and itching stopped. I heard a voice louder than the wind shout into my ears, "You shall drink and you shall wash yourself; but later, not today. . ."

I awoke shaken by this dream. Since then, I have stopped reading in public and copying for distribution the letters that condemn you, and which had cast turmoil into my soul. This dream took place four years ago. It is so present in my memory that sometimes I wonder whether it was a dream or not.

However, my torments did not cease then and there. The importance of the decision that I had just taken seemed as clear as day to me. I had broken ties with my relatives. I suffered so much that three days after the response to my *istikhāra*, I performed another, this time a single one.[69] I had the good fortune to see al-Hajj Umar himself in a dream and he reassured me. The desire to meet you had continued to grow in me for four years. The death of my elder brother gave

---

[69] Editor's note: According to Amadou Hampaté Bâ, this second personal supplication by Tierno Bokar for God's guidance in making a decision was different from the first in the length of the fast. The author explained in footnote 38 (p. 50) above that the fast of the "single *istikhāra*" is shorter than that of the "double *istikhāra*." Such a categorization and these particular practices appear to be either regional or perhaps specific to Tijani adepts. Although the origin of *istikhāra* is certainly traceable back to the Prophet, in many parts of the Muslim world it is less formalized and rigorous, and even discouraged by some *'ulamā'*.

me the opportunity to go to Bamako and today I have come
to you.

"Aren't you afraid of the anger of your relatives?" the Sharīf
asked Tierno. "Their hearts will be full of anger. They will treat you
as someone who has humiliated their family and they'll fight against
you. Look at my hand," he added. "It is as if it contained a red hot
piece of coal and the hand of anyone I meet is filled with explosive
powder. All I have to do is give you the *tajdīd* [70] for it to explode.
Aren't you afraid?"

"It will make no difference to me," answered Tierno.

The Sharīf asked him the same question three times, and three
times Tierno replied: "It will make no difference to me."

The Sharīf was silent for a moment, and then raised his head and
turned towards the Moorish students who filled the room, and said,
"I take Shaykh Ahmad al-Tijani and all of you present as witnesses.
Today I shall give Tierno Bokar the key that will permit him to open
all the secrets contained in the abode of Shaykh al-Tijani."[71]

Then, taking Tierno Bokar's hands into his, he proceeded with the
tajdīd: "I renew your *wird*. I renew your rank of *muqaddam*, this time
in the rite of the 'eleven.' Once more, I declare that the 'twelve' is
not an error. For any *muqaddam* whom you have already designated
and who consents to follow you in the rite of 'eleven,' if he asks for
tajdīd, give it to him. I will confirm him in the rank of *muqaddam*. On
the other hand, you shall not name any new *muqaddam*."

Then all the students came forward, and each one in turn took the
hand of Tierno Bokar and asked for his benediction.

Moulay Ismail later told me that Sharīf Hamallah, talking one
day about Tierno to his followers, had said, "Of all the men whom I
have been destined to meet, Tierno Bokar is the one who has most
deeply penetrated the secrets of the Tijaniyya that are contained in

---

[70] *Tajdīd*: renewal of the *wird* [Editor's note: that is, the litany particular to a Sufi
order].

[71] Editor's note: By this, the Sharīf presumably meant all of the most esoteric "secrets"
accessible to those who achieve the highest levels of spiritual realization within the
Tijani Sufi order.

the *Jawāhir al-Ma'ānī* (*Pearl of Meanings*)[72] and in *Al-Rimāh* (*The Lances*), the book of al-Hajj Umar."

A few days before Tierno's departure, after the *'asr* prayer when the heat of the sun was beginning to fade, Sharīf Hamallah asked all of his students to accompany him on the walk which he used to take outside of Nioro to get some air. He walked into some peanut fields which bordered the town and suggested that the students collect the nuts that remained buried in the earth after the harvest.

After they had entered the field, each one went his own way to collect the nuts. The Sharīf placed what he collected in his palm. When his hand was full he stretched it out to Tierno and said, "Take this! Here's a good supply."

The students saw this, and as soon as they had gathered a handful of peanuts, they came to give them to the Sharīf, who in turn gave them to Tierno saying, "Add these to the others."

As soon as Tierno's *boubou* flap was filled with several kilos of peanuts, the Sharīf gave the signal to return to the compound. The elder students were familiar with the usual reserve of their master, and they knew that his gestures were never empty of meaning. According to them, the Sharīf had shown extreme consideration towards Tierno on that day. Tierno always kept and treasured those peanuts, never wanting to give them away.

On the evening before Tierno's departure, the Sharīf had provisions for the journey taken to him.

"I'm going towards the area where sugar is found," said Tierno. "Keep your provisions."

"I would like you to take a little of everything that I eat," the Sharīf replied.

The servants brought baskets of dates, cuts of dried meat, and a goatskin full of cow's butter. They brought three kilos of tea, five chunks of sugar, and also apples from the city, which the Sharīf liked.

---

[72] Editor's note: The Arabic word *jawāhir* (the plural form) that is used here is usually translated as "gems" or "jewels," but "pearls" seems to be a less common meaning, and was given as the author's translation (though in the singular form) for the Arabic. It is significant that some other meanings associated with the word are "essence," "substance," or "quintessence."

At dawn the next morning, taking leave of the Sharīf (whom he would never see again), Tierno Bokar Salif climbed into a truck that was to take him to his first stop-over, Koniakari, in the Karta of Diombogho. As rapidly as his vehicle might have traveled, the news that preceded it traveled even faster:

"A Taal has betrayed the cause of the 'twelve'!"

The Beginning of the Persecutions

Tierno had hardly received his *tajdīd* when the news became known all over the town. The chief of the Taal in Nioro immediately telegraphed all the cities and regions where there were Taal to inform them that Tierno Bokar had just betrayed the cause of al-Hajj Umar and that it was necessary to cut all family ties and relations with him. At every stop along the road between Nioro and Bandiagara the descendants of al-Hajj Umar waited for their cousin. Tierno's trial had begun.

In Koniakari, where a branch of the family lived, no-one received Tierno. To one who is accustomed to African hospitality and the sacred obligation that it imposes on those who must give it, there could not have been a more serious insult.

However, it had been possible that things might have turned out dramatically worse, because the Taal of Koniakari had decided to provoke Tierno as soon as he arrived in the town. They informed the chief of the district, Dembasadio Diallo, of their plan. Fortunately, he had been initiated into the Tijaniyya by Tierno, and was very attached to him. His official function did not permit him to show this attachment openly, but he knew how to break up the plot.

"Your disputes concerning 'eleven beads' and 'twelve beads' do not concern me," he said to the Taal. I am the chief of the district and represent the French authority in this region and I shall lock up anyone who tries to disturb the public order in any way."

Cooled down by this warning, the Taal of Koniakari were silenced, and Tierno was able to pass through the town without trouble and to continue his journey.

In Kayes, the Tukulor paraded down to their chief, Bassirou Mountaga Taal, and urged him to act against Tierno's presence. Bassirou was more sensitive to family traditions than to current rivalries, even those decked out with "religious" epithets, and refused to listen to them.

"If it is necessary for me to oppose my cousin Tierno Bokar," he said, "I shall confront him personally, and I alone shall make this decision."

Somewhat relieved, Tierno took the train to Bamako from Kayes and arrived in the capital of the Soudan in the last days of June, 1937.

As soon as he got out of the station, he summoned me. Needless to say, I was waiting for him impatiently. I went to the house where he was staying. After the usual salutations, I questioned him without delay.

"Tierno, did you see the Sharīf?"

"I did," he said.

For several long minutes, he fixed me with an intense look which gave evidence of his deep thinking. Then, breaking the silence, he added, "I saw the man. I found him and I found myself in him. I recognized him. All that I had, I laid at his feet.[73] I asked him to give me what he had, and he gave it to me.

"I will not oblige any student, relative, or friend to follow me in this path. But as for me, even if my skin were to be separated from my flesh, my flesh from my nerves, my nerves from my bones and my bones from my marrow, and if my marrow were then to let go of Sharīf Hamallah, I would let go of my marrow!"

Seeing how firm his decision was, I asked him, "Since the time that Sharīf Hamallah gave you the *tajdīd*, have you yourself given it to anyone?"

"No."

"Tierno," I said, "I had the honor of being amongst the first four little students of your Koranic school. Of us four, I am the only sur-

---

[73] What is understood here are the chains of transmission that he had received before. [Editor's note: That is, the Sufi initiatic chain that stretched back to the Shaykh Ahmad al-Tijani himself. The Sharīf "renewed" Tierno Bokar's esoteric connection to the great spiritual mysteries. One might view the initiatic chain as the many branches that are attached to the trunk of a tree. The Sharīf permitted and assisted in Tierno Bokar's letting go of one branch of the Tijani "tree" and taking hold of another one.]

vivor. Today, I would like to be the first of your followers. I would like to be your *tiolel*."[74]

He looked at me for a long time.

"I ask you to think hard about this," he told me. "The Sharīf told me that his hand contained a burning ember and that the hand of those to whom he gave the *tajdīd* contained gunpowder. He warned me of the danger. I told him that it made no difference to me. But you, have you thought this over well?"

"Since it makes no difference to you, it is also the same for me," I answered him. "My desire is to be behind you in everything. Even in Paradise, I would like you to enter before me and I only follow behind. I shall be with you everywhere and unconditionally. I ask you to now renew my *wird*, too."

I held out my open hands to him, in the position of one who is receiving. He proceeded with the *tajdīd*, then he recited the chain of transmission: "Abou Bokar Salif (that is, himself), Amadou Hamma Ullah (Sharīf Hamallah), Shaykh Muhammad al-Akhdar, Shaykh Tahar, Shaykh Ahmad al-Tijani, and Sayyidna Muhammad, the Prophet of God." That is the chain that I received from him. Then he blessed me.

I could not help, however, being worried about him and I shared this worry with him.

"Tierno, do you realize that you yourself have just thrown the burning ember into the gunpowder? Your family will not forgive you. Terrible difficulties will be created for you, and your reputation will be tarnished."

He responded:

I thought you were more mature. Have I wasted my time preparing you? "My" honor, "my" family, "my" chicken, "my" horse, my. . . , my. . . , always "my." You see, Amadou, foam only forms on the surface of the waters when the waves are high, pounding strongly against each other and finally crashing onto the shore.

---

[74] The *tiolel* is [what one calls] the first small fish that is caught following an earlier fishing trip from which one returned empty-handed.

This is how it is with so many expressions such as "Give me," "You did not give me," "You shouldn't have that," "He had," "I would like to be," etc. These move about in our hearts like wild waves, or frightened sheep. They will rise up to darken our vision and block up our hearing, great dark clouds, loaded with lightning and thunder. These clouds, bearers of calamity, will make the sky and the horizon seem dim to us. And we will no longer be able to detect the serene aspect of the firmament, sprinkled with stars, nor fields of fine grass on the sides of hills which tumble down towards the regions where God is worshiped for Himself.

"If this is so, then all is well," I said.

I asked him for permission to go to Dakar because, to my knowledge, the source of all the difficulties having to do with the "eleven beads" was in that city in the person of certain major Tukulor marabouts who had the ear of the colonial government. The idea had come to me at that very moment to hold in that city a public lecture on Islam and on the Tijaniyya, which would be done in such a way as to clear up this matter once and for all. I decided to present a detailed study of the rites of the Tijaniyya and their meaning because the disciples, more often than not, content themselves with a superficial attachment or are insufficiently enlightened. I hoped, naively perhaps, that this would contribute to dissipating misunderstandings. In any case, I did not speak to Tierno of this idea that had come to me.

"I am going to perform the *istikhāra* concerning your trip," he told me. "I would like you to wait until I have received some insight into this before you make a decision on anything."

Three days later he told me that he had received an auspicious response and that I could leave. I was ready. I took the train that very evening.

He accompanied me to the station. I can still see him, dressed all in white as was his custom, wearing a simple *tourtil* beneath, his head bare. He held a long bamboo pole. In the station he gave me his last blessing and we separated. I saw his face and bright forehead disappear. I was leaving full of enthusiasm, my head full of ideas and nourishing the hope of being able to fix things. I did not know that I would never see him again.

During my stay in Dakar, I was able to carry out my first public lecture on Islam and the Tijaniyya under the sponsorship of a newly formed association called the "Muslim Brotherhood." The lecture was a great success. Alas, this success only further exasperated the prominent Taal marabouts who were already relentlessly pursuing the ruin of Tierno.

For his part, Tierno had taken the road back to Bandiagara. Tijani Amadou Ali Thiam, his faithful friend, was again with him. The first big city they stopped in was Segou, the old town on the bank of the river where Tierno had spent the years of his youth.

Mountaga Taal lived in this city. He was the grandson of al-Hajj Umar and the son of *Lamido Julbe* Amadou Sekou, who had left the area before the French conquest. The Taal were forewarned of Tierno's arrival and they knew that conforming to custom the first thing that he would do would be to come and greet Mountaga as head of the Taal clan in Segou. Therefore, they organized a large reception in Mountaga's home to welcome Tierno in their own way. The griots themselves were there as well. Of all those present, there was not one learned person, not one man qualified to engage in a discussion of religious matters.

As expected, Tierno Bokar, accompanied by Tijani Amadou Ali, appeared at the Mountaga home as soon as he arrived in town. As soon as he entered the room, there was silence. He pronounced the usual greetings, to which they responded reluctantly. Mountaga, as head of the Taal, questioned him straightaway.

"It has become known to us that you have asked for the *tajdīd* from Sharīf Hamallah and that you have recognized him as the Grand Master of the Tijani order. Is this true?"

"Yes."

"Is Sharīf Hamallah greater than al-Hajj Umar or is he only as great as al-Hajj Umar was?"

"From what point of view?"

"From the point of view of knowledge, sanctity, and from all points of view."

"Your question is not well formulated," said Tierno, "because in no way can a dead saint be compared to a living one during the lifetime of the one still living.[75] It is said that a living saint always takes precedence over a dead saint, but the living saint owes respect and consideration to the dead saint and should imitate him in fulfilling what is appropriate for his time."

There was an indescribable uproar. From every side, the cries of the courtiers rang out: "Renegade! . . . You have abandoned your family. . . . You have demeaned al-Hajj Umar. . . . You are against al-Hajj Umar! . . ."

Although he was not learned, Mountaga was a very pious man, and also reasonable and moderate. He silenced the assembly. Then turning towards Tijani Amadou Ali Thiam, he said to him, "From my point of view, if anyone here has the right to speak, it is you. You are here and you say nothing. What do you think of Tierno Bokar's action?"

"I think," responded my father, "that if Tierno Bokar had brought back from his journey a box full of gold, those who at this moment are simply following others in condemning him, and who have no knowledge of the questions at hand, would divide his gold up amongst themselves without asking him about its origins and without worrying about its purity.[76] Now when it is a question of religion, Tierno Bokar is the judge and not the accused. You are indignant because Tierno Bokar recites his rosary with eleven beads instead of twelve, but most of you yourselves do not pray either with eleven or with twelve beads, nor are you worried that these days your children go to night clubs more often than to the mosque. For you, that is acceptable!"

Upon these words, he was silent.

For those present, all of whom were of the Taal, this was not common sense but was the simple reaction of a Thiam. Weren't the Thiam the traditional family rivals of the Taal? Weren't they known to never use flattering language? In any event, these words greatly displeased Mountaga, who took offense.

---

[75] By this it is meant that when times change, conditions also change, as do external attributes and accomplishments. Only principles and fundamental values remain immutable.

[76] From the Islamic point of view, material goods are pure or licit if they have been honestly acquired, not only by the current holder of them, but also by those who have transmitted them to him. Thus it is necessary to know the origin of goods in order to know if they are licit.

"Since I know your positions now, Tijani Amadou Ali," he said, "yours and that of Tierno Bokar, let us go our separate ways. Never again will there be anything in common between you and us!"

Tierno and his friend withdrew. The next day, they left the city and went in the direction of Mopti, the last main stopover before Bandiagara.

In Mopti the news of Tierno Bokar's rallying to Sharīf Hamallah had already become known amongst the French authorities. Informed by the leading Taal marabouts, the colonial government in Dakar had sent precise instructions to the commandant of Mopti: He was to ensure that Tierno Bokar's return would not disrupt the public order. At the least threat of trouble, Tierno Bokar was to be deported and placed under house arrest far from the territories at the bend of the Niger River.

The "chief interpreter" of the commandant of Mopti at the time was Umar Sy. He was very attached to Tierno, who was his marabout. As with every chief interpreter, he was privy to the secrets of the gods and the commandants. He had caught wind of the matter long before Tierno's arrival. In his desire to protect Tierno against the frame-up being organized against him, he undertook a clever maneuver.

As soon as Umar Sy learned that Tierno had left Segou, he went incognito to Bandiagara that very night in a friend's car. He asked for a meeting with Tijani Aguibou Taal, who was the son of the former king of Bandiagara, and who was then head of the canton of Bandiagara and head of the Taal clan in the city.

"Tijani Aguibou," he said to him, "your cousin Tierno Bokar is going to arrive in Mopti tomorrow, probably in the evening. From what I have learned, he is in danger of being deported because of the *tajdīd* that he received from Sharīf Hamallah, and they are counting on using you against your cousin. So I have come to ask you not to let yourself be manipulated. I will be with you in this matter. If you accept my help, I can, for example, inform the commandant that you have decided to come fetch your cousin, that you have great influence on him because of your position in the family, and that you give your word to the commandant that there will be no trouble. I will add that this is a family matter in which the Administration should not intervene, and that you take it upon yourself to resolve the matter yourself. We will say that those from Dakar, Nioro, Kayes, and Segou do not really know Tierno Bokar, never having lived with him, whereas you do know him and have always been close to him and have even entrusted one of your sons to him as a student. If you come, make sure to bring a few notables with you. But be careful! When you are in the presence of Tierno Bokar, only say that you have come to collect him and nothing else. Neither you nor those who accompany you should speak of religion in front of Tierno, so as not to provoke a reaction on his part or any imprudent words."

Tijani Aguibou Taal, who loved Tierno very much, agreed. Umar Sy returned to Mopti that very night, the two towns being only seventy kilometers apart. He went to the office of the commandant the next morning, just as he did every day. That evening, Tierno Bokar arrived in Mopti, where he spent the night, since he didn't have to meet the commandant until the following morning.

At the beginning of this second eventful night, Umar Sy came to find Tierno to warn him of the plot that had been organized against him. "They want to make you out to be an agitator who is ready to light the fuse here," he told him. "Don't get involved in this game. Listen to my advice on how to stop them from sparking a fight that would be associated with your name, even without you. Your cousin Tijani Aguibou Taal is coming to meet you. You know his uprightness. I ask you to follow him in the name of family tradition. Once it becomes a question of family tradition, no issue of religion should come up."

"Indeed," answered Tierno, "once we find ourselves in just such a situation, I will consider myself a servant of Tijani Aguibou Taal. He can do with me what he wants. This really has nothing to do with religion."

Umar Sy breathed a sigh of relief. Now that he was assured that Tierno Bokar would not refuse to follow Tijani Aguibou Taal, Umar informed Tierno that he would have to present himself to the commandant the next morning. After these two busy nights, he finally returned home to get some rest.

The next morning he went to the District office very early in order to be sure that he could speak to the commandant before Tierno's arrival. The commandant had just settled into his office when Umar brought up the subject: "Commandant, I believe that the fears of the colonial government in Dakar are not well founded and that the information that has been given about Tierno Bokar is not accurate. In fact, we are not going to have any kind of trouble at all."

At that time, chief interpreters generally enjoyed the complete trust of the district commandants, who greatly valued their advice. The commandant of Mopti, whose name was Levavasseur, felt more at ease after this assertion. As with every self-respecting commandant, his only concern was to avoid his district being disturbed by even the slightest complication.

For his part, Tijani Aguibou Taal—accompanied by Tierno's old friend Alfa Ali, his first cousins Sada Wane and Mamadou Ibrahim Ali, and a few notables—had arrived in Mopti early in the morning. They went directly to the house where Tierno was staying.

"I heard," he told him, "that you had returned. I have come to take you back to Bandiagara. I want us to leave the town immediately after you visit the commandant of the district. I don't want you to stay here even an hour afterward."

After Tierno had agreed to this, they all left together for the commandant's Residence. As soon as they arrived, Tierno was brought into the office of the commandant, who asked him the following question in French: "Tierno Bokar, are you prepared to return to that practice of which you are one of the great leaders (that is, of the 'twelve beads'), and that's the end of it, yes or no?"

The chief interpreter Umar Sy turned towards Tierno as if he were about to translate the commandant's words for him, but realizing all the nasty consequences that a sincere reply from Tierno could bring about, he took it upon himself to invent a harmless question, the essential result of which would be that Tierno would visibly be able to answer "yes" by nodding his head. So he "translated" for him the following sentence: "Tijani Aguibou Taal, the chief of Bandiagara, accompanied by notables, has come to take you back with him to Bandiagara. Are you ready to follow him?"

With a great nod of his head, Tierno answered "yes," which the commandant could see with his own eyes. Then the interpreter turned back to the commandant and said, "Tierno Bokar is going to follow his brother, who is both his chief and his elder. He cannot go against orders given to him by his brother. The latter has asked him to reintegrate himself into the family, which he is going to do."

In the mind of Commandant Levavasseur, this meant that Tierno was breaking with the "eleven-beaders" and reintegrating himself into his family and taking up the "twelve beads" again. For him, everything was settled.

However, there remained a complication for Umar Sy to address. In the same office there was an African clerk who spoke French and who had heard and understood everything. The ever-astute Umar Sy turned to him and said, "This is purely a family question," he told him. "And as Africans we cannot aid in the deterioration of a family, otherwise we will be accomplices in it. I'd like you to exchange a few words with Tijani, then tell the commandant, 'Tijani Aguibou Taal has confirmed to me himself that Tierno Bokar agrees with him.'"

The clerk, conniving with the interpreter as all clerks do, spoke briefly with Tijani and then said to the commandant, "Commandant, Tijani Aguibou Taal has come to collect his brother[77] and his brother agrees to follow him in everything. That way, there are no problems!"

Umar Sy had found an eyewitness.

This was how Commandant Levavasseur, unbeknownst to Tierno, was misled by the cunning of his chief interpreter. The interpreter's only intention was to avoid the deportation of his Master, and he wasn't able to foresee that this mistake would come to light much later, with very oppressive consequences for Tierno Bokar.

In his district registry journal the commandant wrote, "Today, Tierno Bokar Salif Taal and the members of his family presented themselves to me. The marabout Tierno Bokar is taking up the 'twelve beads' again and abandoning the practice of the 'eleven beads.' His relatives have come to collect him. Everything is settled, the matter is closed."

He also sent a telegram to this effect to the Governor General of Dakar to inform him that the matter had finished.[78]

The prominent Tukulor marabouts of Dakar learned about the event through friends in the colonial government. Knowing Tierno's strength of character, they doubted the reality of this denial. Wanting to know where they stood, they called upon their partisans in Bandiagara to verify if Tierno had indeed gone back to the practice of the "twelve beads." Of course, it was observed that Tierno continued to

---

[77] In Africa, cousins [were at the time of the original publication] called "brothers."

[78] I obtained all of these details from Umar Sy himself who died in Mopti a few years ago.

calmly recite his rosary with "eleven beads" in the mosque, with the blessing of the head of the region, his cousin Tijani Aguibou Taal.

Unable to attack Tierno on this front, the marabouts took their offensive to another level. They thought that they could estrange Tierno Bokar from Sharīf Hamallah by sending insulting letters to the latter and signing them "Tierno Bokar." When these letters arrived at the Nioro *zāwiya*, certain students who were as a rule suspicious of anything having to do with the Taal, took the bait and tried to set the Sharīf against Tierno. However, the master exposed the trap.

"No," he told them, "the man I saw would never go back on his word. Moreover, these letters are not in his handwriting, which I know. If he had needed to write to me, he would have done it with his own hand. Therefore, do not let yourselves be misled by people who are hoping for this very result."

Faced with this new setback, the marabouts decided amongst themselves to go and find Tijani Aguibou Taal, the chief of Bandi-agara.

"Tierno Bokar has misled you," they said to him. "He hasn't stopped practicing the use of the 'eleven beads.' We must act against him in the way that all of our ancestors have laid down for us."

Tijani Aguibou's answer was straightforward. "The Taal who are pushing me to deal severely with Tierno Bokar," he said, "already had him in their hands before he returned to Bandiagara. Why did they not act themselves and get rid of him in their home territories? In any case, as long as I am alive, no-one here will touch Tierno Bokar. He is better placed than any of us to know what is valid or not in matters of religion."

And there the matter rested. Tierno had gone back to his previous routines, his lessons in the *zāwiya* and his prayers in the mosque. When he recited his *wazīfah*, he fingered the eleven beads of his rosary and everyone closed their eyes. Without knowing it, he was living his last days of happiness and peace, far from the pettiness of men.

THE ORDEAL

Peace did not last even a year. On May 21, 1938, Tijani Aguibou Taal died and the succession of the chieftaincy of Bandiagara was open. From then on, this accommodating and well-placed cousin would no longer protect Tierno, who was to suffer the repercussions of the incidents that would accompany and follow the nomination of the new chief.

After various maneuvers that were aimed at getting rid of other candidates to the succession, a postmaster, Moktar Aguibou Taal, was assigned to be Chief of the district of Bandiagara by the French Administration. This was due to direct action by the prominent Taal marabouts of Dakar, to whom Moktar Taal thus became indebted.

Until then, Moktar Aguibou Taal had had excellent relations with Tierno Bokar. One could even say that he was devoted to him. But an old Diawando,[1] who had a personal account to settle with Moktar, was to set things off.

This old Diawando, called Aguibou Ousmane, had first of all supported another candidate for the chieftainship. He was made the victim of a ruse by the Taal marabouts of Dakar, who had caused him to imagine that he might be deported, and so he had finally been forced to publicly rally around Moktar Aguibou. The indiscretion of an administrative clerk allowed him to find out about the trick that had been played on him, although too late. He swore to take revenge and to find a way to make Moktar Aguibou the most unpopular of any chief ever to have existed or who would ever exist in Bandiagara.

He began by becoming an intimate of Moktar Aguibou, sticking close to him, displaying total devotion to him, and making himself indispensable. In short, he did this so well that Moktar ended up considering him his best advisor. Everything was in place to edge the new chief of the county into severe difficulties.

---

[1] The *Diawambe* (plural of *Diawando*) are a non-Pullo ethnic group, but who speak Fulfulde, living mostly among the Fulbe. They are reputed for their intelligence and their trickery.

The old Diawando saw that it might be possible to make Moktar very unpopular in Bandiagara if he could set him against Tierno Bokar. Tierno was very much loved in this town where renouncing another person was viewed harshly, no matter the reason. He hoped that a sudden change of heart on the part of Moktar in favor of the enemies of Tierno would earn Moktar the contempt of the population, without thinking of the consequences that could result from this for the aged teacher.

Therefore, one day, when he found himself alone with Moktar Aguibou Taal, he said to him:

Moktar, there is one thing that threatens your authority. I'm sorry to have to talk to you about it, but since I promised to help you and you promised to listen to me, my duty is to alert you to this. It's about your cousin Tierno Bokar. He has established something in Bandiagara, something that was not done under any of your predecessors, the former chiefs of the city. And because he has dared to do it under your command, it is because he has no consideration for you. Everyone says you are weak and are not worth anything, but this is because they confuse your courteousness with weakness. It is my duty to tell you that, when one is chief, one has to put courtesy aside. Believe me, if you do not crack down on Tierno Bokar by forbidding him to practice the "eleven beads" you will be the last of the Taal.

This was the quickest way that the plotting Diawando could devise to place Moktar in a difficult situation.[2]

Alas, Moktar Aguibou did not have the wisdom of his predecessor, Tijani Aguibou Taal. Rather than inform himself by going and confiding in Tierno or even discussing it with him, he let himself be drawn into the old Diawando's game and listened only to his own indignation. Could he have thought that by acting against the "eleven beads," the bane of the Colonial Administration and of the Taal mar-

---

[2] Later on, once his revenge had been achieved, Aguibou Ousmane himself told a number of notables in Bandiagara how he had been able to maneuver Moktar and boasted about it even on the market square. This is how I was able to get to the bottom of the affair, through diverse sources.

abouts to whom the former were beholden, that he would enter into their good graces? In any case, the first Friday following this meeting, when the main communal prayer, attended by Tierno Bokar and his students, was just finishing, Moktar Aguibou stood up and began to speak:

"*As-salaamu alaykum!*" Peace be with you!

"*Alayka as-salaam!*" Peace be with you! responded the crowd of the faithful.

"I am Moktar Aguibou Taal, chief of Bandiagara by the grace of God and chief of the family of al-Hajj Umar. That which was not permitted under any of my predecessors will not be permitted under Moktar Aguibou. I am speaking of the practice of the 'eleven beads.' For those who do not wish to respect the way laid out by al-Hajj Umar, I will pluck out their feathers just as one does with a sacrificial chicken, beginning with their leader. To be more direct, I am addressing myself to you, Tierno Bokar Salif, since it is you who want to establish something which has never existed here before."

These last words fell on total silence. Those present were dumbstruck. Each one waited for what would happen next.

Tierno Bokar was sitting in the first row of the faithful. As soon as he heard Moktar pronounce his name, he got up, picked up his slippers and left by the southern door of the mosque without saying a word and without looking back. Following his example, his students also rose and followed him out without saying anything. For the last time in his life, Tierno crossed the doorway of this place of prayer where he had spent so many hours of his existence.

Later on, he did not say why he had kept silent. However, one could suppose that since he had never agreed to take part in any polemics, that then, more than at any other time, he had not wanted to throw fuel on the fire and thereby risk an incident which in the end would cause his students to be the victims. So he went silently towards his home, accompanied by his students. They told me that once at home, he sadly exclaimed, "What then do they have against the number eleven? Don't they see that the mosque itself sits on eleven pillars?"

After Tierno had left, Moktar, even more furious because of this silence which he undoubtedly had not expected, continued his abusive language, saying, "Good! They have left this mosque. Well, they will never enter it again. From now on I forbid them access to it! I forbid them to gather to pray together anywhere! I forbid any two of them to walk together!"

This was almost an excommunication. Because Moktar Aguibou was considered as a representative of the powerful Taal clan and was also protected by the French authorities, there was no question of the people going against his orders. For Tierno and his friends, this was the beginning of an inflexible quarantine that was going to lead the gentle man of God to live his final days in almost total solitude.

Leaving the mosque, headman Moktar Aguibou Taal hurried to the commandant of the region of Bandiagara, Commandant Ortoli, to tell him that they were witnessing a fresh outbreak of the "eleven beads" and that Tierno Bokar, although he had agreed to reintegrate the "twelve beads" into his practice, had returned to the practice of the "eleven."

Now it so happened that Commandant Ortoli had been the assistant of the district commandant of Mopti when Tierno had been received by the latter. Ortoli had himself seen the minutes in the commandant's official logbook reporting that Tierno had renounced the "eleven beads" to return to the fold of the "twelve." Convinced that Tierno was a complete hypocrite, he summoned him into his office.

As soon as he saw him he attacked him, saying, "Well, Tierno Bokar! It seems that after returning to the 'twelve beads' you have abandoned them again to go back to the 'eleven beads'?"

"I don't understand," responded Tierno, who, naturally, was ignorant of all the convoluted strategies that had been employed by the interpreter Umar Sy in Mopti. "Since I adopted the 'eleven beads' in Nioro in 1937," he added, "I have never abandoned them and have not ceased practicing them to this day."

These words enraged Commandant Ortoli. He reminded Tierno of the conversation in Mopti when he had appeared to have recanted. Very surprised, Tierno replied that under no circumstance would he ever have disavowed the Sharīf of Nioro. Of course, he could not convince Ortoli of this. In the eyes of the French Administration, Tierno was from then on seen as a man of bad faith. Umar Sy's little trick, inspired by good will, had turned into a drama.

Ortoli wrote to the commandant of the District of Mopti to warn him that Bandiagara was going through a revival of Hamallism. His report was transmitted to the government of the Soudan. In return, instructions came back to deal severely with Tierno Bokar and his disciples. This was the beginning of the open persecution.

To start with, all Tukulor women who had married a student of Tierno Bokar were ordered by their parents to leave their husbands and go back to their families. Now at that time, no-one, man or woman, could go against an order received from their parents, whatever the circumstances might be. Of course, the appeals brought by the husbands to the Administration led nowhere. An epidemic of divorces raged throughout the town. The custody of the children, when there were any, was given to the mother.[3]

The *zāwiya* was closed. The day-students had to go back to their families in the town. The students who lived in the *zāwiya* were scattered to the four corners of the country. Some young people were automatically registered in the office of military recruitment, drafted, and sent into the army. In just one family, that of Ali Bodiel in Bandiagara, four brothers of the same father and mother were called into active military service on the same day, contrary to military regulations.

Tierno was spied on day and night. A record was made of who entered or left his compound, and his visitors were interrogated or deported. From that time on, Tierno never again left his compound. He left it again only on the day of his death. The pressure exerted on his visitors was such that soon only a handful of faithful friends would dare to come to see him.

Material life became more difficult day by day. No one would sell him anything. One can well imagine the distress of this family of about twenty people who were unable to go out or to get provisions, and, in any case, who had no revenue to assure their subsistence. While the members of Tierno Bokar's own clan, brotherhood, and religion abandoned him without remorse, his friends the Dogons of the escarpment, some of whom were newly converted, assured his sustenance

---

[3] Editor's note: This would be a highly unusual situation in Muslim cultures. Peremptorily removing the rights of the father's family in regard to the children would be unheard of in even a single case, much less in the numerous cases in this situation.

and that of his family. At night they came, secretly slipped up to the compound, and threw goatskins full of millet and condiments over the wall, which permitted them to survive.

Despite these terrible conditions, Tierno, who lived with only his family and four or five students, remained the same. He continued to teach those around him and always remained just as serene as ever. However, once we take into consideration the extreme sensitivity that was one of the features of his character, we would be entitled to imagine that behind this serenity which was the fruit of his communion with God, suffering was not absent.

Did he remember in those days these words that he had said to us in 1933?

> In truth, the tongue of he who adores God is like a blazing firebrand. For those who idolize material values, this causes constant trouble. For fear that it might burn them, they drench it with the muddy water of calumny, thinking that by doing so they might save the thatched hut that shelters the idol of falsehood and covetousness. Brother in God, you who comes to the doorstep of our *zāwiya*, have you decided to sing the hymn of Truth, at all costs? Remember these verses:
>
> "Woe unto every vile slanderer,
> Who amasses and counts his riches!
> He thinks that his riches will make him immortal.
> Nay! He will be cast into al-Hutamah" (one of the names of hell).
>   —Koran, 104:1-4

For my part, I did not know what was happening. When I got back from my journey to Dakar, I was assigned to Bamako where, since July 1937, I was more or less under house arrest and unable to leave the city. When I returned from my leave of absence, I could not hope to ask for another leave for another three or five years. I received no news from Bandiagara, 800 kilometers away from Bamako. It was only after the death of Tierno that I was able to go to Bandiagara, thanks to the understanding and help of my District Commandant, André Morel, a good man.[4]

While carrying out his research on the life of Tierno Bokar, Marcel Cardaire had met the widows of Tierno in Mopti, as mentioned earlier, and he had asked them about the last days of the Master. Let us listen to his report, as it was presented in the first edition of this book.[5]

> The small number of his faithful followers, fewer each week, was suffering from the situation that they had been put in and they did not conceal this fact. These people rejoiced in the thought that their master was overcoming all of the petty tricks that were being aimed at him. They were elated by the thought that the viciousness of men had led Tierno to take refuge all the more intimately in the arms of his Creator.
>
> His communion with God practically never ceased. He seemed perpetually serene and remained from dawn to the end of the day within the house that he loved and amongst all the others. Huddled over, his eyes closed, he would escape. All life that remained in him was concentrated in his thin hands which fingered the rosary all day long. Sometimes he went into the now-deserted *zāwiya* and those around him were surprised at his apparent indifference to the sights that tormented them. The little rooms were empty, the courtyards abandoned. The rolls of cotton which had formerly brightened up the school as if they were party decorations no longer dried on rocks and lines, looking like so many white snakes. The large fires were extinguished, the earthen jars overturned, the doors gaping like mouths in an anguished face. The wind shook the useless matting.

---

[4] During this trip to Bandiagara, I had a meeting with Commandant Ortoli and was able to explain the true substance of this matter. He was an honest man. He realized that a mistake had been made and put things back into order in the town. Up to the time of his departure from Bandiagara, the practitioners of the "eleven beads" had no further cause for worry.

[5] *Tierno Bokar, le Sage de Bandiagara*, p. 65. I point out, however, that in some places I have had to correct certain small errors of the account or to make certain additions.

The Master was, in effect, being beaten to death. A small swallow fallen from a nest had once brought this man to tears; he felt the crying of a child as if it were a stab-wound; his words had preached tolerance and love, but today sectarianism and hate were beating him down. He met these old enemies once more in the twilight of his life, when his voice was weakened. Hadn't even speaking been forbidden to him?

Betrayals multiplied around him. His own nephew, Alfa Ali's former student whom he had appointed to monitor his Koranic school, the man whom he had perhaps groomed the most, went over to the side of Moktar. His closest friends came only on nights when there was no moon, and later they did not come at all. Calumny and hatred had created an emptiness around the compound. For those ignorant believers or for those too attached to the misunderstood teachings of the Umarian brotherhood, Tierno was seen as one who had lapsed into heresy and who had proudly withdrawn into his error. For those who were indifferent, he was someone to be avoided because he was in disgrace with the local chiefdom and the Colonial Administration. Finally, in the eyes of the Taal, he had betrayed his family, a fault that could not be pardoned. Visiting him became an act of courage, even of recklessness.

Without intending the slightest harm, rumors from the town were reported to him as well as the remarks of his enemies. Each time he would respond, "They are more worthy of pity and prayers than of condemnation and reproach, because they are ignorant. They don't know, and unfortunately, they don't know that they don't know."

Tierno sought more and more refuge in prayer and meditation. However, during his pious exercises, his body sometimes betrayed him.

The next rainy season would certainly destroy one or the other of his little rooms because the roofing materials needed to be replaced. Tierno knew very well that he wouldn't live to see the next rainy season, but it was necessary not to show his weakness. He used the last of his strength to give his last lesson through a final example. Pride had nothing to do with his behavior. Pride was as far from Tierno as it could be. He forgave hatred and betrayal. All who listened to him had the impression that, for him, man only existed to be forgiven and God existed so that He could grant him grace. . . . And Tierno's forgiveness of men was sincere, as was his thanks to God for the new trials that fell upon him.

No one knew what he was experiencing in the secret of his heart because he did not want to share it with anyone. His wives wept; his servants were simple people who admired him but who often did not understand him. . . .

He used up the last of his strength. He was irremediably broken. His health declined from day to day. He no longer ate, he hardly slept, and he grew visibly thinner. In their simplicity, those around him endeavored in vain to sustain him by feeding him.

The coolness of December and January did not improve his state in any way. Physical suffering was soon added to his mental suffering. He became covered with boils. A serious infection started on his right temple, then on the left. With a razor he cut the one that seemed the most inflamed. His head began to swell. A doctor was called, but it was too late. Septicemia had set in. He was overcome by horrible headaches which never again left him or let up until the end. He lay down never to arise again.

Lying alone in his small room, Tierno lived through days and nights of fever. Between two prayers, the sounds of which overcome time, he was either freezing under his blanket or streaming with sweat on his matting. Gone forever was the laughter of students, the chanting of the Koran, and the murmurs of conversations lasting well into the night that would lull one to sleep. The coolness of the morning and the call of the muezzin coming from the mosque which had been forbidden to him would pull him from his drowsiness. A cock would crow. Turtledoves, then a coucal[6] would greet the sunrise. In the courtyard, Nene or Fatumsuka, the servant, would be pounding millet. Those passing by the door would

[6] Editor's note: The Senegal coucal (*Centropus senegalensis*) is a bird in the cuckoo family known for its loud cries in the early morning hours.

speak in a low voice. The dog—son or grandson of the dog who had previously escorted the master—would appear on the doorstep. The unhealthy odor of the fever would stop him and he would go away with his tail down. The morning would pass. The midday heat brought silence again, then life would start up again. Pestles banging in the mortar would add to the throbbing of blood in his ears. Cock, cat and dog fights. The sounds of life in the courtyard. Life continued while he was fading away in painful solitude. The call of the muezzin would mark the end of the day. It was the saddest time of all. There, at the foot of the royal palace, the call to prayer would sound for all, except for him and his family. Then night would fall.

Every evening the headaches became more intense. His face was swollen, his features were deformed, but his eyes, shining with fever, retained their customary gentleness. No complaint about his pain ever escaped his lips. Nene, his first wife, confided to us, "He went to death as if to a celebration."

Someone suggested calling a local healer since European medicine had proven ineffective. Tierno was against this, and said, "Don't do anything. It is not these remedies that I need. The doctor himself could not do anything for me. I asked him to come, not in order for him to cure me, but only so that it could not be said that you did not do everything you could for me."

"From time to time," continued Nene, "the pain became more intense. It would distort his poor features. And Tierno would ask God aloud for strength to endure his hardship."

One evening, February 8 or 9, 1940, Nene came to listen at the doorway. Tierno was speaking: "My God, take my life. Kill me, take from me this existence and receive me in death. I know that You will give back life to me as soon as You take it from me."

The easterly wind, cool and dry, shook the matting that hung over the door. A gust of wind brought a few echoes from the town to the dying man. Tierno came out of his conversation with God for a moment, saying, "Poor Bandiagara. . . . If Bandiagara only knew! If the people of Bandiagara had only known . . . they would have taken much money out of their pockets to prolong my life. But they do not know. . . . My God, forgive me and forgive them because they do not know."

We can testify with complete certainty that the pious Nene had never heard of the lamentations of Sayyidna Issa (Jesus) on Jerusalem.[7]

Nene pushed aside the matting and entered the room. She collapsed at the feet of her husband and burst into tears.

"No, do not cry," he told her.

But Nene could not stop her sobbing. Nor could she stifle her sobs as she related the following to us:

"Today, it is his body that is gone, but he carried our soul away with him. His departure plunged us into darkness. There is no light left in the house. Material light illuminates only dwelling-places. He, however, was the light of our souls."

This woman had borrowed from the vocabulary of her husband. Fifteen years after the death of Tierno, his very words filled the little room in Mopti and we choked up.

It was that same evening when he lamented Bandiagara that Nene heard her husband address her for the last time, saying, "I am leaving you. . . . I entrust you to God as my father entrusted me to Him."

To his second wife he had said, "Aminata, I forgive you. Know that even if my body leaves you all, my soul is near you. When you are in doubt, spread out your hands and if from the place where I shall be, souls can answer, you will hear me."[8]

During the following night, Tierno's pain never let up. He spent the night in prayer. In the morning he was exhausted but still lucid. He felt his end was near. Overcoming his suffering and his exhaustion, he sat up and asked to make his ablutions. His servant Fatumsuka brought water.

---

[7] Editor's note: The author is referring to passages in the gospels of Matthew (23:37) and Luke (13:34).

[8] Editor's note: It is likely that Tierno is referring here to the posture that Muslim supplicants often assume in private prayer: they place their arms in front of them, bend their elbows, and slightly cup their hands in front of their faces, giving the impression of being a humble supplicant seeking blessings from above.

This woman told us herself of the happiness she had seen on the face of her master when he realized he could still carry out these sacred rites which his grandfather had taught him so many years ago in Segou. Exhausted by the effort this required, Tierno collapsed on his matting and during the course of the morning, entered into his death throes. It was the 19th of February, 1940.

The women had left his room. The wives had gone back to their quarters. Fatumsuka stayed on the doorstep of the small room on the other side of the courtyard that faced the dying person. A few still faithful friends remained near Tierno: Samba Bâ, the student and servant Thiamba, and also the father of Yousef. When Tierno lost consciousness, they thought the end had come. But he had only fainted. The dying man opened his eyes, but his gaze seemed far away. Yousef's father, a pious man, leaned over the matting.

"Tierno," he said, "say the *Shahāda*."[9]

The master had often spoken of these final moments of man and he had always said that if the tongue was paralyzed, if the mouth refused to open to pronounce the supreme words attesting to the existence and the unity of God, the believer could always testify silently, by touching his chest with his index finger, a symbol of unity.

"Tierno, say the *Shahāda*!"

Then the three men saw Tierno's right wrist and his outstretched index finger rise slowly to the level of his heart; his gaze became veiled, and as slowly as sand runs out between one's fingers, life escaped this old worn out, pained and wretched body. The three men knew it was death. Something alerted Fatumsuka, who understood before they made the slightest gesture that Tierno lived no more. She exited and went through the deserted *zāwiya* announcing the death. The chickens and the young goats scattered before this woman in tears. Sobs were heard from the master's wives. Fatumsuka went from courtyard to courtyard as if the disciples might

---

[9] "There is no god but God," the last testimony of a believer, the last words that should leave his mouth before death.

come out *en masse* to share in her pain, but she only saw gaping doors, cold houses, empty rooms. She returned to Nene and Aminata.

One of the three witnesses of the death left to inform first Alfa Ali, and then the chief of Bandiagara, Moktar Aguibou Taal. As is the custom in Africa, the death put an end to the quarrel. Tierno, laid low by the spitefulness of men, had appeared before God at that very moment. The grandeur of that moment was felt even by those who had been bent on destroying him.[10]

Then the women's voices rose in a spontaneous chorus in honor of the deceased: "Taal! Taal! Taal![11] You were waiting for this day to come, you were prepared for this journey. You had already sent the necessary provisions ahead before you. You will find an honorable reception awaiting you. You worked in preparation for this voyage. You will not be disappointed because a wonderful reception awaits you. You gathered orphans unto you, fed the hungry, calmed the distressed, and responded to every appeal that was addressed to you. And each time you responded, you did so only with the intention to please God and His Prophet, and not for your own glorification."

In Islam, one hastens to return to the earth that which, despite everything, has never ceased to belong to the earth. Tierno's body, wrapped in a shroud, was placed on a bier. In accordance with tradition, the wives were asked to come and grant forgiveness to him for any offenses that he might have committed against them during his life. But they answered, "It is we who ask him for pardon. It is we who made him suffer. He was always a faithful husband, a benevolent elder brother, and a wise teacher. This is all we have to say: 'Taal! Taal! Go in peace!'"

It was now the end of the morning. The body was taken to the cemetery. The entire town followed behind its chief, the cousin of

[10] Editor's note: This ends the section taken from the first edition, as noted by the author on p. 98.

[11] In Africa, the repetition of a man's clan name as a salutation is a way of honoring him and, through him, of honoring all of his line, from which it is expected that he will never be separated.

the deceased, who led the remains to their final resting place. Oh, the inconsistency of man!

The only ones absent were those of Tierno's students who were still in Bandiagara, because Moktar had forbidden them to be present. Conforming one last time to the teachings and to the example of their master, they did not protest. They withdrew into Tierno's courtyard. Fervently, they began to chant the *Shahāda: Lā ilāha illa 'Llāh,* "There is no god but God," the great words of Islam to which Tierno had molded both his life and his heart.

It was thus that Tierno Bokar was buried in the ground at the feet of his mother, under the little tree, as he had one day predicted. Bandiagara went into mourning for three days on the order of the local authorities. Minds became uncertain. What was the truth? The friends of the deceased received several visits, which continued to multiply. People came to ask Tierno's friends for his forgiveness. And Tierno began to live once more. . . .

Like Sharīf Hamallah, Tierno Bokar was the victim of the ignorance and obscurantism of men who confused clan loyalty with religious commitment and who had forgotten that tolerance is a fundamental principle in Islam (*No compulsion in religion. . .*[12]) as well as in the Tijani order (which forbids one to remain three days without speaking to another because of anger, under punishment of being excluded from the *Tarīqa*).

But let us not heap condemnations upon them. It has been seen throughout this account how a sort of fatal destiny linked all the events together and then destroyed all the roadmaps. Over the years, ill-informed men became caught up in the game and may even have thought sincerely that they were defending a just cause. "They did not know that they did not know. . ."

In any case, intolerance, closely related to ignorance and to a lack of spiritual maturity, is not limited to any one race or to a particular community. It is a common human disease. All eras and places have known it. Even today, more or less woven into certain murky realms of our being, intolerance always threatens to bare its claws as soon as we encounter in our neighbor something different that we cannot understand. That is why we need spiritual masters who are at the same

[12] Koran, 2:256.

time doctors of the heart. This was what Tierno Bokar was. His call for union and for understanding was addressed beyond his entourage to all people.

"I wish with all my heart the coming of a time of reconciliation amongst all religions of the earth, a time when these religions will unite and support one another to form a spiritual and moral canopy, an era when all religions will be at peace in God by resting upon three supports: Love, Charity, Brotherhood."

Part 2

His Words

The word has been sacred for millennia in this country, where only sages had the right to speak and where oral tradition was endowed with the same rigor as the most sacred writings. Because black Africa was without a practical system of writing, it has nurtured veneration for the spoken word, of the "life-giving word."

Aissata had said to her son: "Learn to cover the physical nakedness of men before covering their moral nakedness with your teachings." Traditional weavers are initiated into the symbolism of their craft, in which each element has a specific meaning and of which the whole symbolizes the "primordial creation." They all know that as they give birth with their fingers to a length of cloth, which progresses like time itself, they are doing nothing other than reenacting the mystery of the creative Word.[1]

The importance of the word, and concern for its value, for whether it is good or bad—a new "language of Aesop"—assumed an essential importance for Tierno Bokar.[2]

> Speech is a fruit whose skin is called "chatter," the pulp "eloquence," and the kernel "common sense." From the moment a being is endowed with speech, whatever the degree of his development, he is in the class of the most privileged, because speech is the most marvelous gift that God has given to His creation.

> Speech is a divine attribute, as eternal as God Himself. It is through the power of the Word that everything was created. By bestowing upon man speech, God delegated to him a part of His creative power. It is through the power of the word that man, too, creates. He not only creates to secure the indispensable necessities of his material existence, but also to secure the viaticum [i.e., a purifying sacrament—Ed.] that

[1] See our *Aspects de la civilisation africaine* (Paris: Présence Africaine, 1972) and "Africanisme" in *Enciclopedia del Novecento* (Rome: Instuto dell'Enciclopedia Italiana, 1976).

[2] Editor's note: The ancient moralist and storyteller Aesop was once asked to identify the best of things and the worst of things. To both he replied, "Language," because of all the good and all the bad that it can bring about.

opens for him the doors of beatitude.[3] A thing becomes that which the Word tells it to be. God says: "Be!" and the created being responds: "I am."

In the first part of this book we reported some of Tierno's words. It would have been awkward indeed to focus on his life and to try to outline it without citing something of what he said in relation to those events that were milestones in his life. The master's words are the essential element of his story. How better to elucidate the "message" that he has left us than to allow the one who unfolded it to speak?

We can never say often enough that the essential characteristic of Tierno's words was that they were spoken in one of the most humble places in the world, the master seated on an infertile soil that was by turns scorched by the sun and eroded by the rain. Tierno usually spoke in Fulfulde (Fulani). Although he was a good Arabist, which permitted him to study texts in depth, he always taught in the local languages. Besides Arabic, he knew four African languages, as well as the traditional knowledge of the main ethnic groups of the savanna.

He had an aversion to those who expressed themselves in anything other than ordinary language. One of the characteristics of "sorcerers"[4] was to use impenetrable language, and Tierno often used this same appellation to ridicule those who through intellectual snobbery made a show of expressing themselves only in Arabic, even when addressing people who did not know this language, in the belief that they were dazzling them.

His message was meant to be understood. Had the Prophet not said: "Speak to people according to the level of their understanding"?

I personally collected the accounts and reflections that follow from the mouth of Tierno Bokar. I was always close to him from my earliest childhood. I was born, as they say in Africa, "in his hands." How many times when I was little did he carry me on his back in my parents' courtyard! And what wonderful stories he told me that I could not yet understand! My mother had often said that as a rather sullen baby, my face only lit up when he came to take me in his arms.

---

[3] An allusion to the spiritual virtue of reciting sacred texts and divine Names.

[4] Editor's note: That is, a person who claims or is believed to have magic powers.

Amadou Hampaté Bâ

The present courtyard of Tierno Bokar's house

A Hausa disciple standing in front of the door to one of the rooms in the courtyard of the Tierno Bokar home

A Hausa disciple of Tierno Bokar walking through the neighborhood in Bandiagara where Tierno Bokar lived

The interior of the mosque at Bandiagara

The Aguibou Taal Palace in Bandiagara, opposite the mosque, is now a museum

Scenes of Malian life: the weekly market in Djenné

Scenes of Malian life: a back street of Timbuktu

Scenes of Malian life: the Great Mosque of Mopti

Scenes of Malian life: a Dogon village

The elderly Alfa Ali

Disciples gathered around Aissata's tomb

An elderly Hausa disciple stands behind Aissata's tomb;
in the foreground, Tierno Bokar's tomb

When I was seven years old, I was entirely entrusted to him so that he could take charge of my religious education as well as the formation of my character and my social comportment. I only left him on the day when, like all sons of chiefs, I was "requisitioned" by the authorities to be sent far from Bandiagara to the French school which was then officially known as the "School for Hostages." But I came back to be near him during my holidays.

This continued until, as a young man, I became a civil servant and was posted to Upper Volta. No longer able to teach me directly, Tierno transmitted to me, by correspondence, answers to questions that I asked him. He dictated his letters to a friend, Mamadou Sissoko, who knew how to write in French.

It was particularly in 1933 that I received his teaching more intensively and in more depth than ever before. Until then he had, in effect, always taken into account my age and my level of comprehension. That year Upper Volta had been eliminated as an administrative territory. Having been put on extended leave awaiting a new assignment, I took advantage of the time to immediately rejoin Tierno and had the good fortune of being able to spend the better part of this providential year of leave with him in Bandiagara.

It was mainly during this stay in 1933 that I made notes of the teachings and of the anecdotes that are to follow. Moreover, Tierno entrusted me with the mission of making known the schematic teaching that he had invented under the name of *Mā 'd-Dīn* and which appears at the end of this book. It goes without saying that I could only present the exoteric, outward aspect of this teaching, only that which could be written down and presented in the form of diagrams. Esoteric knowledge cannot be presented according to a logical plan. In Islam, as in many other religious traditions, esoteric knowledge is taught by word of mouth and is more akin to a lived experience than an intellectual type of teaching.

We are very aware that any attempt at classifying and labeling this message in its entirety can only be incomplete, even artificial, and would have made the master smile. A book cannot reproduce the full force of these words as they were heard in Bandiagara, where they resonated with such life and love. However, it is incumbent upon us, we who have inherited an oral tradition, to try to transmit what we can of it before time and forgetfulness erase it from the memory of men.

A particular difficulty exists in going from Fulani to French because of differences in structure that characterize these two languages. Fulani, like Arabic, is a synthetic language in which each word can carry many different (although related) meanings according to its position in the sentence and to the level of meaning at which a person can comprehend it. By contrast, in French, which is not a synthetic but an analytical language *par excellence*, each word possesses a unique and precise meaning; hence the difficulty in transporting an idea from one language to another without affecting the conciseness of the expression, or the style, or the pungency of images. The reader is asked to pardon these inevitable shortcomings.[5]

For Tierno Bokar, the power of the divine creative Word, as with all uttered words, was linked to vibrations.

"In the universe," he taught us, "and at every level, everything is vibration. Only the differences in the speed of these vibrations prevents us from perceiving the realities we call invisible." And he gave us the example of the propeller of an airplane that becomes invisible after attaining a certain speed of rotation.

But when the creative Word is written, its mystery can be approached through the traditional science of letters and numbers. The perspectives opened through explanations in this domain allow us to sense, or sometimes to glimpse what seems to be an immense edifice of astounding consistency, where primordial principles underlie the whole of the living world and are found even in the very heart of apparently mundane realities.

Immersed in mysticism—and by this we do not mean a life cut off from the world, but a life in which the inner relationship with God accompanies and enlightens every moment lived in this world— Tierno Bokar was the very incarnation of love and of goodness. Firstly, his love for God was absolute and without reservation; then came his

---

[5] Editor's note: The author is certainly not using the terms "synthetic" and "analytical," as applied to language, in the same way as modern linguists do. We can probably get an accurate sense of what he intends by looking at the definitions for these terms given in the *Dictionary of the Académie française* (8th edition), according to which synthetic language is language that "expresses complex relationships with a single word." From the same source, analytical language "expresses an idea by breaking it down" (or: "parsing it").

love for all living creatures, from human beings to the most humble creatures of nature, whether animal or vegetable.

Tierno Bokar loved all men, without consideration of race, religion, or social status. The distinction that seemed to him the most senseless was when men band together under different religious insignias and declare themselves the enemies of others. Do not all men, and most particularly those who are animated by sincere faith, carry within themselves a "particle of the Spirit of God"? Tolerance was thus to become the permanent concern of his students, as it had been the basis of the teaching of Shaykh Ahmad al-Tijani as well as one of the main fundamentals of Islam.

Tierno Bokar focused his attention on the society in which he lived during his earthly journey, a society whose equilibrium was so often compromised. But for him, Love and Charity provided the key to all hearts and the solution to all problems.

A monumental program! He who dedicates himself to following it must return often to a refreshing, vivifying source in order to find the strength to progress further along the spiritual path. For Tierno Bokar, there was only one source capable of constantly reinvigorating those who become weak. It was the mystical Spring[6] around which one meets religious men of all religions and of all times.

"Tierno," I asked him one day, "what are the respective roles of the *Sharī'a* (the revealed Law) and Mysticism?"[7] He answered:

> The *Sharī'a* and Mysticism (initiatic teaching) are two different aspects of Religion but which complement one another and are not able to exist one without the other.
>
> The essential objective of the *Sharī'a* is, by its very severity, to preserve man from the decadence of irreligion. It is comparable to a carpenter's plane that smoothes a wooden

---

[6] Translator's note: In French, *une source* can mean "spring" as a source of water as well as the origin of something.

[7] Editor's note: Since the specific form of mysticism practiced by Tierno Bokar and his students was Sufism, we can safely assume that this is what is being indicated by the French term "la Mystique" used here. The Arabic word *Tarīqa*, meaning "the Path" (i.e. the mystical path), is frequently paired with *Sharī'a* to show the interdependence of the Sufi mystical path and the practices of the general body of believers within Islam.

plank. The *Sharī'a* compels the believer to improve his or her conduct and prevents a person from falling into the depths of a disorderly life where no spiritual growth can come to flower.

Without a strong *Sharī'a*, moral defects will soon express themselves and encourage moral corruption. The fundamental pillars[8] of the *Sharī'a* are like canals through which the imperfections that soak into hearts are allowed to drain away.

If we liken the *Sharī'a* to a network of canals, mysticism will be likened to irrigation. The role of this irrigation is to open the human spirit to the Knowledge of God (*ma'rifa*), which is like a kind of subtle water, in the absence of which the spirit becomes like dry, burning earth.

Mysticism comes from two sources: First, from a Revelation made by God to an elect of His choosing; that is, to a Prophet who teaches and propagates this Revelation. Second, from the [lived] experience of the believer or, for one who is destined for the divine Light, from a direct intuition which is the fruit of his long meditative and religious practice.

In its first aspect, Mysticism comes directly from the Source, contained and preserved in the sacred Books. In each form of *The Religion*,[9] these Books are like vessels in which one collects rainwater. Just as with physical water, these vessels must be preserved from all pollution, in the interest of the very life of the community.

In its second aspect, Mysticism is comparable to water that human ingenuity is able to divert through the use of dams and canals. Any theologian can draw portions of a spiritual teaching from the Holy Books—those carefully guarded vessels. But he can also dig another canal, one that is adapted to the contours of the land; that is, one that corresponds to the

---

[8] The fundamental pillars of the *Sharī'a* are, firstly, the canonical obligations of Islam (faith in the Unity of God, prayer, alms-giving, fasting, pilgrimage), then the various moral and material prohibitions that a believer should respect, and finally all of the recommendations taken from the example of the Prophet and his Companions.

[9] The eternal Religion: the various known historical religions are but manifestations in time and space of the eternal Religion.

mentality and to the level of development of the people of his own time.

In order to make us understand the limitations of an attitude of simple, blind, and narrow imitation (*taqlīd*), he provided us with the following parable:

The Well

The well that receives its waters only from outside itself receives at the same time a thousand things that have been caught up by the current. Such a well is exposed to all this litter and to something even more dangerous: to find itself dry as soon as its water has been drawn out. On the other hand, the well whose "eye"[10] is situated within itself has no need of rain to fill it. Its water, filtered through the cracks of the earth, remains abundant, pure, and fresh, even during times of greatest heat. It is the same with those whose faith in God depends on outward relations and with those who take their faith from their own meditation and intimate conviction. The first are subject to variation and their faith is not exempt from doubt. The second group remains steadfast. They are in the full Light, the full moon of their faith, which never knows darkness.

Tierno called the well which only receives its water from the exterior "the well of *taqlīd*." It belongs to those who only blindly follow outward examples: "Someone said this," "Someone did that," instead of finding in themselves a certitude born of their own experience, or even from personal reflection when confronted with an unexpected circumstance.

Tierno reminded us in this respect of the following *hadīth*:[11]

---

[10] In Fulani, as in Arabic, "eye" and "spring" (*source* in French) are expressed by the same word.

[11] *Hadīth*: An account relating the words of the Prophet or an anecdote about his life.

One day the Prophet wanted to send one of his companions to Yemen. He called Mu'adh ibn Jabal to teach Islam there. He asked him, "How will you apply the law? How will you dispense justice?"

"I shall dispense justice according to the Koran," answered Mu'adh.

"And if you are confronted by a case that has not been anticipated by the Koran?" asked the Prophet.

"I will apply the *Sunna*,"[12] Prophet of God."

"And if the *Sunna* has not made provision for the case?"

"I will refer to *Ijmā*.'"[13]

"And if *Ijmā'* had never handled such a case?" asked the Prophet.

Mu'adh was somewhat taken aback, because in Islam, the Koran, the *Sunna*, and Consensus are the sole three sources of law and of jurisprudence. But since he was a man who prayed and meditated, he had found in himself the way of divine inspiration (*ilhām*).

After a moment of reflection he answered, "Then I will perform *ijtihād*" (effort at personal reflection).

The Prophet looked at him and then said, "Go and perform *ijtihād* whenever it is necessary. As long as Islam includes men of your like, it will not become like a slender tree with few branches." (That is, which provides neither shade nor protection.)

Reliance on *taqlīd* is normally a feature of those marabouts and believers who are purely exoteric in their outlook. It is not a question here of rejecting conscious and voluntary imitation of the prophets and saints, which is, on the contrary, very beneficial to the spiritual life, but to denounce blind, narrow-minded imitation, in the name of which all those who do not conform to the established norm are condemned.

[12] *Sunna*, "Custom": All of the sayings and deeds of the Prophet that should be imitated. *Sunna* is a source of jurisprudence.

[13] *Ijmā'*, "Consensus": All of the opinions or customs of the Companions of the Prophet, also a source of jurisprudence.

One day, wishing confirmation upon this point, Tierno Bokar went to Segou to visit Niaro Karamogo, the greatest marabout of his time, one of the "most learned students" of al-Hajj Umar. He intended to ask him for his thoughts on *taqlīd*.

When Tierno arrived in front of the compound of Niaro Karamogo, at least three hundred students were assembled to listen to him. Tierno went through the first door, with his question in mind. Just as he came up to the second door, he saw at the far end of the courtyard the marabout with his head tilted forward as he began to pound on the cushions on which he was leaning, saying forcefully, "*Taqlīd*! *Taqlīd*! Say, all of you, without any doubt or dispute, that he who applies only *taqlīd* in his Muslim devotions will go to hell! The only question is to know whether he will be able to get out of it or not."

Tierno told us this anecdote with a smile, specifying that this, of course, was only an image by which one might adequately portray the seriousness of *taqlīd*.

It is certain that *taqlīd* is a tendency that is found everywhere, not only in Islam. It has prevailed, as it undoubtedly still does, in many environments that are not necessarily religious. Both the ancient and contemporary history of mankind shows us countless examples. This is a weakness inherent in man, and this is why Tierno Bokar insisted so often to us on the dangers of *taqlīd*. He always encouraged us to become fully informed before taking a position, to never stop at the surface of things, and to remember the gift given to us by God: Intelligence, Higher Reasoning, which is a subject that he expounded upon in his lesson *Mā 'd-Dīn*.[14]

The Three Lights

The eye (*'ayn*) that lies in the depths of each person needs light in order to see the world in its true reality and, above all, to perceive divine Reality. But not all paths are accessible to everyone.

One day, while he was teaching about the concept of Light (*Nūr* in Arabic), I asked him, "Tierno, how many mystical lights are there?" He replied:

[14] See p. 181.

Oh my friend, I am not the one who has seen all the lights. I shall nevertheless talk to you about three symbolic lights:

The first is that which we get from matter by rubbing it, thus causing combustion. This light can only heat or light up a limited space. It corresponds symbolically to the faith of the mass of individuals who have only advanced a little along the mystical ladder. At this stage, adepts cannot go beyond imitation (*taqlīd*) and the letter. The darkness of superstition surrounds them, the cold of incomprehension makes them tremble. They remain huddled up in a small corner of (their) tradition and they make as little noise there as possible. This is the light that gives life to believers when they find themselves at the degree of faith called *sulb* (solid).[15]

The second light is that of the sun. It is superior to the first in that it is more widespread and more powerful. It lights up all that exists on earth and warms it. This light symbolizes the middle degree of faith on the mystical path. Like the sun, it dissipates the shadows as soon as it comes into contact with them. It is a life-giving source for all creatures. It symbolizes the lights that hold adepts at the mystical degree of faith called *sā'il* (liquid). Just as the physical sun gives light and warmth to all beings, who from this perspective are all brothers, the adepts who have reached the middle degree of light see and treat everything that lives under the sun and receives its light as brothers. Because of its indispensable preparatory role, they do not scorn the first light, but they are no longer like insects that dance around a flame and sometimes get burned. The first light, just as that which it symbolizes, can be extinguished or relit depending on the circumstances; it can be transported from one place to another; in other words, it can change in form and strength. However, the second light remains fixed and unmovable in its perennial existence, like the sun. It will always come from the same source and will never falter throughout the ages.

The third light is that of the center of all existence; it is the light of God. Who would dare to describe it? Its darkness

---

[15] See pp. 119-120.

is more brilliant than all lights combined.[16] It is the light of Truth. Those who have the good fortune of reaching it lose their identity, and become like a drop of water when it falls into the Niger River, or rather into a sea infinitely more vast in breadth and depth. In attaining this degree, Jesus became the Spirit of God, Moses became His Interlocutor, Abraham became His Friend, and finally, Muhammad became the Seal of His Emissaries.[17]

The Three Degrees of Faith

Having thought about what he had just said, I asked him, "Tierno, how many types of faith are there?" He replied:

O my brother, I don't know exactly. Faith is neither countable like the population of a farmyard, nor measurable like the distance from Bandiagara to Mopti. It cannot be weighed like the millet of Bankassi or the fruits of the Dourou market. For me, faith is the amount of trust that we have in God and the degree of our conviction; it is also fidelity to our Creator. Faith becomes warmer or cooler, it varies according to people and places.

I am willing to outline faith in this way to make it easier to understand: The first is *sulb* faith which I shall call solid faith; the second, *sā'il* faith, which I shall call liquid faith; and finally *ghāzi* faith, the most subtle, which is like a gaseous vapor.

1. The first degree of faith is suitable for the common man, for the masses, for marabouts attached to the letter. This faith is upheld and channeled by the prescriptions imposed by a Law which itself is taken from revealed texts, be they

---

[16] Editor's note: This is intentionally paradoxical and enigmatic. The author has said that there are no words that can adequately describe the light of God. In referring to the "darkness" of the light of God, he is making the point that its full glory confounds our understanding and language, yet it is still immeasurably greater than all other lights combined.

[17] All of these qualities applied to the prophets are taken from the Koran.

Judaic, Christian, or Muslim. At this stage, faith has a precise form; it is inflexible, hard like a rock, whence the name I attribute to it. Faith at the degree of *sulb* is heavy and immobile like a mountain. If necessary, it prescribes armed warfare to assure its place and make it respected.

2. *Sā'il* (liquid) faith is the faith of men who have worked and successfully confronted the trials of *sulb*, the rigid law that permits no compromise. These men have triumphed over their faults and have embarked on the way that leads to the truth. The elements of *sā'il* faith flow from knowledge and are related to the truths from which they come, without one ever having to think about their origin or their existence from time immemorial. These truths gather and come together to form a living body that is in perpetual movement, constantly moving forward like the flow of drops of water, emerging from mountain hollows, coursing through varied terrains, accumulating at obstacles, then swelling from streams into rivers to finally rush into the ocean of Divine Truth. This faith, like its liquid symbol, washes away the faults of the soul, wears away at boulders of intolerance, and spreads everywhere, always taking the form of its receptacle. It penetrates human beings according to the contingencies of their moral make-up. *Sā'il* faith disciplines the adept. It makes him a man of God, capable of hearing and appreciating the voice of all who speak of the Creator. It is vivifying. It can solidify and take on the nature of hail when it has to deal with souls who have remained at the first degree. And it can sublimate and rise up in a vapor, like *ghāzi* faith, into the heavens of Truth. It establishes the regime of the city of peace, where man and beast live side by side, where the three kingdoms live as brothers.[18] Those who possess this faith rise up against war.

3. *Ghāzi* faith is the third and last term. It is the privilege of an elite within the elite. Its constitutive elements are so pure that, released from all material weight that would hold them down on the earth, they rise like smoke into the heaven

---

[18] Editor's note: The "three kingdoms" are the animal, vegetable, and mineral domains of existence.

of pure souls, permeating them. Those who attain this faith worship God in truth and in a light beyond color. The Divine Truth flowers in the fields of Love and of Charity.

For Tierno, loving and serving God amounts to no more than a very small part of returning to Him what is His due, because compared to the infinite nature of the gift that has been given to us, all that we can offer necessarily remains miniscule.

The Miserly Merchant

"Is it reasonable," he would ask us, "to refuse a small portion to Him Who has given you everything?" [Then he would tell this story:]

A merchant who, through greed, tightens the cord of his purse and refuses to give a penny to someone who had financed him when he was starting out, can be considered as an example of moral ugliness. But how much greater is the ugliness of a man who refuses to worship God, from Whom he has received the very spirit of life, which is both the source and the result of Love? To God belongs all that is in the heavens and earth—can one refuse to give a part to Him who has created and given everything? Certainly not, and yet this is what is done by those who are lost and distracted in the labyrinths of earthly life.

Thinking Beings

Many people came to Tierno with the hope of obtaining material benefits or miraculous powers, thanks to his blessings or his prayers. "Give me the secret of such and such a Name of God or of such and such a prayer," they asked him. He replied:

O adept, you who come to the threshold of our *zāwiya*, do not think that we have miraculous means of curing souls. We refer our brothers to holy verses. Reflect upon the following:
"May the illusory life of this world not lead us astray and may temptation not turn us away from God" (Koran 31:33).[19]

---

[19] Editor's note: A more literal translation of this portion of the verse would be: "Let

Be in God's hands like a child in the hands of his mother. Seek for nothing other than the desire to please Him. You who come to us, and whom we consider not as a pupil, but as a thoughtful brother, before entering the *zāwiya* where one seeks Love and knowledge, meditate well on this verse and allow it to illuminate you:

"One of His wonders is to have created you and spread you over the earth as thinking beings" (Koran 30:20).[20]

Ask Him to do with you what pleases Him.

Tierno rebelled against the idea that any being could be excluded from God's love. He scorned the distinctions made by those "attached to the letter" and chose to ignore those who make this love the privilege of only orthodox believers.

For my own part, I could not understand how only Muslims could be the beneficiaries of the mercy of God. I reflected on the smallness of their number in relation to the whole of humanity, both in time and in space, and I said to myself: "How could God, in front of a mound of seeds, take only one handful of these seeds and reject all the others, saying: 'Only these are my favorites'?"

I had often heard around me, especially from certain marabouts, that non-Muslims were *kuffār* (infidels) and that they would go to hell. This angered me, as if I myself had been one of those unhappy infidels. So one day I took advantage of a class to ask him about this subject that was troubling me:

Does God Love Infidels?

"Tierno, you always speak of God's love which embraces everything. But does God also love infidels?" He answered:

not the life of the world beguile you, nor let the deceiver beguile you, in regard to God." The source of translations of the Koran used by the author is not known.

[20] Editor's note: Translated more literally, this verse reads, "Among His Signs is this, that He created you from dust; and then, behold, ye are men scattered (far and wide)!" The author's translation is emphasizing the aspect of intelligence implicit in the Arabic word *bashar*, "human being."

God is Love and Power. The creation of beings comes from His love and not from some constraint. To detest that which is the result of the Divine Will acting through love, is to take a position against the Divine Will and dispute His wisdom. To imagine the exclusion of a being from primordial Love is proof of fundamental ignorance. Life and perfection are contained in Divine Love, which manifests Itself in a radiating Force, in the creative Word that brings the living Void to life.[21] From this living Void, He makes forms appear that He divides into kingdoms.

May our love not be centered upon ourselves! May this love not incite us to love only those who are like us or to espouse ideas that are similar to our own! To only love that which resembles us is to love oneself; this is not how to love.

Being a man, the infidel cannot be excluded from the Divine love. Why should he be excluded from ours? He occupies the rank which God has assigned to him. The act of a man debasing himself can bring about a punishment for him, but without thereby provoking an exclusion from the Source from which he came.

It is necessary to reflect upon the legend of Korah and Moses.[22] Korah was the most perverse of beings. He had received his share of the finest riches that a man can enjoy on earth. From these, he had made a paradise for himself, access to which, he said, was forbidden to Moses and to his God. Moses asked God to chasten Korah.

God replied, "I have entrusted the earth to you. Act as you see fit."

The Prophet Moses then addressed Korah, "O infidel! Mend your ways and return to your Lord, otherwise you shall receive a punishment that will be cited as an example."

---

[21] Tierno compared this living Void, pure potentiality, to the mathematical notion of zero, the starting point containing the seed of all numbers that emerge from it. He does not mean here "nothingness," but rather "non-manifested."

[22] Editor's note: This story of Korah (called Qarun in the Koran) is constructed of elements from the Koran, which mentions him very briefly, the Old Testament, and other legends whose source we do not know.

"Call upon me all the misfortunes you want, I fear nothing," replied Korah.

So Moses ordered that the earth swallow up Korah and all of his possessions. Korah, ensnared by his feet and unable to loosen the hold, understood that he was lost. He repented and asked Moses to forgive him.

"You believed yourself to be stronger than God," Moses replied to him. "You have rejected the Eternal, and me, His Messenger. Now you are defeated and your riches are no more. The earth will swallow you up slowly; you shall be subjected to this punishment until the end of time."

It was thus that Moses excluded the infidel from God's love. He caused him to perish after having pronounced his judgment, and he expected the approval of the Almighty. But the ways of God are impenetrable and the Lord reproached him severely, saying, "O Moses! Korah called upon you seventy times in repentance and you remained deaf to his plea. If he had called upon Me but one time, I would have saved him."

Moses was confused. God added, "Do you know why you did not have compassion for Korah? It is because to you he is neither your son, nor a being that you have created."[23]

This intentional juxtaposition of "son" with "created being" clearly shows us that God, Who has not engendered and Who was not engendered,[24] has for those He created the same love that a father has for his children. He was generous to the children of Adam, without differentiating amongst their states.

In this regard, Tierno told us about a major event in the life of Shaykh Ahmad al-Tijani when he was living in Morocco, where he benefited from the protection of the Sultan. During a public talk, a troublemaker who wanted to embarrass him asked him a trick question. He asked, "Does God love infidels?"

---

[23] Editor's note: Whereas, for God, even one as wicked as Korah is still considered as a "son" and one of His created beings.

[24] An allusion to a phrase in the Koran 112:3.

Basing his response on commentaries of the Koran, the Shaykh dared to answer, "Yes, God loves infidels." This was an unexpected answer at that time. There was a great outcry. Indignant, the audience left the room. Only eleven faithful disciples remained around the Shaykh, those very ones who later would see the birth of the Tijani order.

Marcel Cardaire, himself a fervent Catholic, had been touched by the attitude of openness and love that radiated from the teachings of Tierno Bokar. Let us allow him to speak:

> The first lesson that the "brothers in God" learnt was a lesson of religious tolerance.
>
> In the small rooms of Tierno's disciples, the teaching that was described to us took on new dimensions according to the rhythm of the seasons. It became true nourishment. In this country of simple technologies, we heard simple sentences fall from simple lips. The words penetrated better than if they had been pronounced in one of those temples or mosques that give homage more to the prowess or refinement of man than to the majesty of the Creator. And moreover, these words that we have collected in no way resemble what one hears in other places of worship. These were words in their pure state, words spoken not to exalt man, neither speaker nor listener, but rather truly animating words, spoken with such sincere feeling for the other as to cause God to live in the heart of the unbeliever, to vivify his faith, and to give a meaning to the lives of everyone.
>
> In these small rooms we heard maxims that we would have liked to see engraved in golden letters on the portals of all the places of worship in the world. What religious university, what al-Azhar, could match the Sage of Bandiagara?[25]

Among those who came to listen to Tierno, not all were from the Tijani order. One day several Qadiri, members of the Qadiriyya brotherhood, one of the most ancient orders in Islam, came to listen to his classes. When the time came to carry out the great *dhikr* (the common

---

[25] *Tierno Bokar, le Sage de Bandiagara,* p. 80.

chanting of the Name of God) one student asked Tierno, "Are those who are not Tijani going to take part in the *dhikr*?"

"Make the *dhikr* without worrying about them," he replied. "If some of them want to participate, you have no right to forbid them. And if they prefer to leave, you have no right to restrain them."

The *dhikr* took place, in the presence of numerous Qadiri. When it had finished, Tierno spoke:

The Rainbow

The rainbow owes its beauty to the variety of its shades and colors. In the same way, we consider the voices of various believers that rise up from all parts of the earth as a symphony of praises addressing God, Who alone can be Unique. We bitterly deplore the scorn that certain religious people heap on the form of divine things, a scorn that often leads them to reject their neighbor's hymn because it contrasts with theirs. To fight against this tendency, brother in God, whatever be the religion or the congregation to which you are affiliated, meditate at length on this verse:

"The creation of the heavens and the earth, and the diversity of your languages and of your colors are many wonders[26] for those who reflect" (Koran 30:22).

There is something here for everyone to meditate upon.

During a certain period, American Protestant missionaries had come to the Soudan. They liked to preach in the areas where the Catholic Church had not been able to establish itself. Because Bandiagara was one of these places, the head of this Protestant mission arrived one day in the town, set himself up on the market square, and began to speak of God in the Bambara language.

Astonished, or at least amused to hear a foreign pastor express himself thus in their language, large numbers of curious people sur-

---

[26] The Arabic word *aya* signifies at once "marvel," "miracle," "sign," and "verse." If the revealed verses are "signs" of God, in an inverse manner one can also say that all the "marvels" that exist in creation are also "signs," therefore another mode of divine Revelation. According to this perspective, everything is Revelation. It is we who do not know how to read.

rounded him. When he started to speak of God with warmth and strength, and above all when he translated the psalms of David into Bambara, people were moved. Muslims are always moved by Biblical language, especially when it is translated into their tongue. But there were a few bigots in the audience who took offense to the scene and who tried to turn the crowd away crying, "It's a Christian! It's a Christian!"

One of Tierno's students had been present at the scene. When he arrived in class, he reported these facts to us, exulting in a malicious way what had happened to the pastor. "Today," he said, "a pastor wanted to talk to us about God. But we made so much fun of him that he was obliged to leave."

Tierno was revolted by this behavior. Wanting to put his students on guard against disrespectful behavior towards men who spoke in the name of God, he launched an out-and-out call for tolerance on that day:

Children of the Same Father

Are children of the same father, although physically different from one another, any less brothers and legitimate sons of he who fathered them? In accordance with this law-truth, we pity those who deny believers from different confessions a spiritual identity and brotherhood under one single God, the unique and immutable Creator.

Although it may not please those attached to the letter,[27] for us one thing alone counts above all others: to profess the existence of God and His unity. So, brother in God who comes to the threshold of our *zāwiya*, which is a center of love and charity, do not harass the follower of Moses. God Himself witnesses that He has said to His people, "Implore God for assistance, and be patient. The earth belongs to God

---

[27] Editor's note: That is, to outward forms, as in "the letter of the law." The exoteric form of a religion will necessarily exclude other possible forms, but here Tierno is suggesting that the central tenet of Islam, God's unity, implies for those with the virtues of love and charity that they must expand these virtues to encompass other children of God, through that very principle of God's unity, which encompasses all.

and He bequeaths it to whom He will among His servants. A blissful end will be for those who fear Him" (Koran 7:128).

Neither should you harass the follower of Jesus. God, in speaking of the miraculous child of Mary, the Virgin Mother, said, "We granted to Jesus, son of Mary, the gift of miracles and We comforted him through the Holy Spirit" (Koran 2:253).[28]

And the other human beings? Let them enter, and even greet them in a brotherly way in honor of that which they have inherited from Adam, of whom God has said, addressing the angels, "When I have perfected him and breathed into him of My Spirit, then fall down before him prostrate as a sign of your veneration" (Koran 38:72).

This verse implies that every descendant of Adam is the repository of a particle of the Spirit of God. How would we therefore dare to scorn a receptacle that contains a particle of God's Spirit?

Moreover, Tierno often said:

You who come to us and whom we esteem, not as a student, but as a brother, reflect! Meditate on this verse from the Book of Guidance:

"There is no compulsion in religion. The Truth distinguishes itself from error. He who rejects false deities in order to believe in God has grasped a handhold that is firm, unbreakable. And God is All-hearing, All-knowing" (Koran 2:256).

Relations with Other Religions

"Tierno," I asked him one day, "is it good to converse with people of another faith to exchange ideas and better understand their god?" He answered:

---

[28] Editor's note: This Koranic passage is usually translated as: "We gave Jesus, the son of Mary, clear signs [or 'proofs'], and strengthened [or 'confirmed,' or 'supported'] him with the Holy Spirit."

Why not? I will tell you: one must speak with foreigners if you can remain polite and courteous. You will gain enormously by knowing about the various forms of religion. Believe me, each one of these forms, however strange it may seem to you, contains that which can strengthen your own faith. Certainly, faith, like fire, must be maintained by means of an appropriate fuel in order for it to blaze up. Otherwise, it will dim and decrease in intensity and volume and turn into embers and then from embers to coals and from coals to ashes.

To believe that one's race or one's religion is the only possessor of the truth is an error. This could not be. Indeed, in its nature, faith is like air. Like air, it is indispensable for human life and one could not find one man who does not believe truly and sincerely in something. Human nature is such that it is incapable of not believing in something, whether that is God or Satan, power or wealth, or good or bad luck.

So, when a man believes in God, he is our brother. Treat him as such and do not be like those who have gone astray. Unless one has the certitude of possessing all knowledge in its entirety, it is necessary to guard oneself against opposing the truth. Certain truths only seem to be beyond our acceptance because, quite simply, our knowledge has not had access to them."

He added:

Avoid confrontations. When something in some religion or belief shocks you, instead seek to understand it. Perhaps God will come to your aid and will enlighten you about what seems strange to you. . .

Not only would Tierno Bokar not prohibit his students from interacting with believers of other faiths, but he also considered this practice an actual therapy for the soul. He asked people to make the necessary mental effort and to struggle against what is holding them back so as to better understand.

Along these same lines, one day he told us about a vision he had had:

In my mind, I saw a gigantic man lying on his back. People of various religions and faiths were bustling about him. Some were speaking into his ear, others were opening his mouth, others were making him breathe in various perfumes, others were applying an eyewash, etc.

"What is this that I am seeing, who is this man?" I cried out to myself.

A voice answered me, "This is the blessed man who reminds himself of the Unity of God and of the brotherhood that should unite His worshipers, wherever they may come from. He is receiving, as you see, all the teachings. The result is better for him. He is porous, like sand. God gave him the power to conserve and to assimilate."

He added:

The religious teaching given by a Prophet or by an authentic spiritual master is like pure water. One can absorb it without danger to one's spiritual or moral health. Such a teaching will be intelligible and of a superior order. Like clear water, it will contain nothing that can change it by modifying its flavor, its odor, or its color. It will mature the mind and purify the heart because it does not contain any external pollutant that could have the effect of obfuscating the soul or hardening the heart. We cannot overemphasize the benefits of studying the teachings of revealed religions. They are, for everyone, like potable water. We advise, however, that they be assimilated slowly, and to avoid murky theology that is likely to contain a spiritual Guinea worm.[29] The saying goes, "When you are sweating, do not take in cold water." We recommend that "When your soul is in mystical fervor, do not read anything."

---

[29] Guinea worm, also called in French "filaire de Medine" (*dracunculus medinensis*). The larvae live in stagnant water. They implant themselves into humans, live in subcutaneous cellular tissues, and develop particularly in the legs, where they appear as enormous abscesses which in fact are made up of the implantation of the female and the accumulation of microfilaria. Upon the slightest contact with water, the sore opens and the female releases the mass of microscopic worms which renew the cycle.

He constantly tried to inculcate into us the spirit of tolerance and make us understand that it was only the intrinsic spiritual quality of a man that mattered:

> Our planet is neither the largest nor the smallest of all those that our Lord has created. Those who inhabit it can therefore not escape this law: we should not believe ourselves to be superior, nor inferior, to other beings in the universe, whatever they be.
>
> The best of created beings amongst us will be those who live in Love and Charity and in respect for their neighbor. Upright and radiant, they will be like a sun that rises and that goes straight up towards the sky.

Being on Guard against One's Own "Dust"

As an attentive spiritual educator, he never neglected to put us on guard against the dangers of complacency towards oneself, which could insidiously accompany the soul all the way to the highest level. He said:

> Whatever a man's race might be, when the Spirit crystallizes in him due to the effect of his worshiping God,[30] his soul becomes like a mystical diamond. The skin color or the circumstances of the birth of such a man have no influence on the quality of his spiritual illumination. Whatever his social standing or the disadvantages of his birth might be, if he has reached this state, no outer element will be powerful enough to make this state slip away from him.
>
> For adepts who have reached this degree, there remains but one recommendation to make: One must be on guard against one's own "dust"; that is, of the admiration of what comes from oneself. The admiration of self, however subtle and hidden it may be, can corrupt the soul of the worshiper, even if he has reached the spiritual degree called "diamond";

---

[30] The Arabic word *'ibādāt* means both worship and service.

from that degree, the colorless and formless Light of the hidden Name of God radiates.

. . . When a soul accedes to true faith, it continues to bow down through modesty, like a horseman on a steed taking off at great speed. A soul filled with God never keeps itself upright and haughty on its tiptoes. Always fearing a possible fall, the soul will bow down, turning quickly at the same time towards the Truth. This bowing down will give the soul the necessary moderation and security to maintain its equilibrium.

There was a perfect simplicity to Tierno's own nature, to which pedantry or self-importance was unknown. Being able to take things in life with humor, he liked to teach while still enjoying himself, and he often repeated to us the warning, "Always being overly serious is something that cannot be taken seriously!"

Religion is One in Its Essence

One can see that for Tierno Bokar there existed but one eternal Religion, unalterable in its fundamental principles but varying in its forms of expression and corresponding to the conditions of time and place of each Revelation. This primordial Religion was, for him, comparable to a trunk from which the known historical religions branch off like the branches of a tree.

It was this eternal Religion which was taught by all the great Messengers of God and which was molded to serve the necessities of each epoch. Too often, however, most people had only understood or retained the outward forms, in the name of which they entered into conflict with each other.

This concept is in conformity with the teachings of the Koran itself, which emphasizes the unity of the divine Revelation throughout time:

Say ye: We believe in God and that which has been revealed unto us and that which was revealed unto Abraham and Ishmael and Isaac and Jacob and unto the tribes; and that which was given unto Moses and Jesus; and unto that which was given unto the Prophets from their Lord. We show no preference between any of them, and unto God we submit ourselves (Koran 2:136).[31]

Lo! Those who believe, those who practice Judaism, those who are Christians or Sabaeans, those who believe in God and the Last Day, those who do right—these are the ones who will find their reward beside their Lord. They will know no fear, nor will they grieve (Koran 2:62).

Set your face to the pure Religion, the religion of the *fitra* (original primordial nature) through/for which God created mankind. There is no changing God's creation. That is the immutable religion, but most men know not (Koran 30:30).

O Messengers of God. . . . This your religion (*dīn*) is One. I am your Lord, fear Me (Koran 23:51-52).[32]

Tierno elaborated on this:

That which varies in the diverse forms of Religion—for there can only be one Religion—are the individual contributions of human beings interpreting the letter with the laudable aim of placing religion within the reach of the men of their time.

As for the source of religion itself, it is a pure and purifying spark that never varies in time or space, a spark which God breathes into the spirit of man at the same time as He bestows speech upon him.

Contrary to what usually happens, one should therefore not be surprised to find spiritual riches in someone from a people considered as backward, but one should instead be

---

[31] Editor's note: The final sentence of this verse is usually translated as "We make no distinction [or, 'difference'] between any of them, and unto Him we surrender."

[32] Editor's note: Other translations would render this section of the two verses as "O Messengers of God. . . . This your community [or 'nation' or 'brotherhood'] is One and I am your Lord, therefore fear [or 'keep your duty unto'] Me." The Arabic word *umma* can imply all these meanings of "religion," "nation," "community," or "brotherhood."

troubled at not finding them in civilized individuals who have long worked on developing their material lives. . . .

In its Essence, Faith is one, whatever the religion that conveys it might be. But in its manifestations, it presents, as we have seen, three fundamental states: solid, liquid, and gaseous. Faith is the essence of religion, which can then be seen as an atmosphere surrounding a universe populated with three categories of men: the believing masses, preachers blinded by parochialism, and finally initiates who have found God and worship Him in truth and in silence.

God, Who Confounds Human Intelligence

If this God must be worshiped in truth and in silence, in one's depths, it is because He cannot be enclosed within any intellectual definition. This is what Tierno made me understand one day when I asked him a question which was as naive as it was audacious.

He was commentating to us on a theological text of Shaykh Ibrahim Laqani. The author was citing different schools: "One says this, another says that. . . ." In the midst of all these formulae, some of which to me seemed contradictory, I got lost. I was incapable of distinguishing between them.

So, mustering all my courage, I turned resolutely towards him and said, "Tierno, may God prolong your days! I want to confess something. Personally, I get lost in the labyrinth of the theologians, whether they are speaking of the attributes of God or of His Essence. Every time I think I understand a theologian, another comes along and tangles me up. I do not know which one to trust, since I don't know them. Also, Tierno, if you do not forbid me from doing so, I would like to completely put aside all those theologians and refer myself to you, since you are my model. I am not saying that I refuse to trust the others, but you I can see and so I know you not through hearsay or through a written text. I would like you to answer my question, according to your own experience: What is God?"

It was as if I had plunged him into the unfathomable depths of an ocean. He remained immobile, his eyes shut, as if he were paralyzed. As it is said in Africa, "he had swallowed himself up." He remained in this state for several minutes, then returned to himself as if arising from mysterious depths.

He opened his eyes and fixed his gaze on me for a long time. Finally he said, firmly stressing each word, "Amadou, Amadou! God . . . God . . . God. . . (*Allāh . . . Allāh . . . Allāh.* . .) He is That which confounds human intelligence."

"Excuse me, Tierno," I responded, "but this hasn't helped me move forward at all. I am telling you that I am lost in the muddle of the theologians. I am asking you for a precise answer and you declare that God is 'That which confounds human intelligence.' This does not remove me from my own bewilderment. Why is He That which confounds human intelligence?"

He answered:

I am very happy that you have formulated your question precisely, because the well-formulated question of a student propels the master, and helps him to find the right answer. For the answer to be precise, the question must also be so.

God is the bewilderment of human intelligence because on one hand, if you affirm His existence, you cannot, in any case, prove it materially or mathematically. On the other hand, if you deny His very existence, you deny your own existence, which is merely the effect of His existence. Of course, you do exist. And even if one cannot prove God materially, it is nonetheless necessary to remember that the non-visibility or non-tangibility of a thing is not absolute proof of its non-existence.

Finally, God is the bewilderment of intelligence because everything that you conceive in your thought and give form to in your speech as being God ceases by this very fact to be God. It becomes no more than *your own way* of conceiving Him. He escapes all definition.

The Turbaned Hypocrite

Tierno Bokar had an aversion to ostentation in all its forms and especially to religious ostentation. One day, I asked him, "Tierno, what sort of behavior do you hate the most?"

He replied:

My friend, I do not like to hate, but the behavior I disapprove of most and that I pity is that of the ridiculous hypocrite. I am speaking of the kind of person who dresses himself up in a turban twisted eight times around his head, conspicuously wearing a rosary around his neck with large beads, walking along and leaning unnecessarily on the shoulder of a disciple and on a stick that is more of a fetish than a pilgrim's cane. This man pronounces the formula of the *Shahāda*[33] with much more volume than fervor, and he preaches with an ardor that is only motivated by the hope of immediate gain. Such a man corrupts the mind and perverts the heart. He is a thousand times more abominable than an assassin who merely attacks a body.

Religious Struggles

He didn't like to hate, and, in his eyes, religious hatred was an unbearable monstrosity. It was toward this religious hatred, and this alone, that he hurled the only "Down with. . . ." phrase that ever came out of his mouth.

Never satisfied with his answers, one day I asked him what he thought of struggles that were ordered in the name of religion.

He said:

Personally, the only struggle that I am enthusiastic about is the one that has as its goal the conquering of our own faults within ourselves. Unfortunately, this kind of struggle plays no part in the wars that the sons of Adam undertake in the name of a God whom they declare to love very much, but whom they love poorly because they destroy part of His work.

Brothers of all religions, let us in God lower the boundaries that separate us. Down with the artificial creations that pit human beings against each other!

---

[33] *Lā ilāha illa 'Llāh* ("There is no god other than God").

We have distanced ourselves from God, we have lost ourselves in the labyrinths of our own disastrous edifice that was built from bricks of lies and with the mortar of calumny. Let us quickly leave this place that was so sadly arranged by our pride and our egoism and by the laxity of our manners and the hardness of our hearts. Let us fly as an eagle with powerful wings towards the union of hearts, towards a religion that is not inclined towards the exclusion of other "credos" but towards the universal union of believers, freed from their own selves and morally liberated from the appetites of this world.

From the height of a heaven of love, we shall, as one, attest piously to the Unity of God, which is the Source of Life that spreads light and which cannot be enclosed within any human definition.

This Religion, which Jesus sought to deliver and which was loved by Muhammad, is that which, like pure air, is in permanent contact with the sun of Truth and Justice, as well as with the Love of the Good and Charity for all.

These words, let us recall, came out of a modest room of dried earth, in the heart of black Africa, in 1933.

Battle Horses

Moreover, for Tierno Bokar, violence is devoid of any moral efficacy. On this subject, he spoke words which still convey all of their power today:

> When will man understand that the panting war horses and the weapons that cause death and destruction to burst forth can only destroy the material man, but never the very source of evil that inhabits minds that are wicked and deprived of charity? Evil is like a mysterious breath. When one uses violence or weapons to kill an evil man, the source of the evil then springs from the body which it can no longer inhabit and it enters into the murderer through his dilated nostrils. The evil takes a new root within him and becomes even more tenacious, its strength now doubled.

Evil should be combated with the weapons of Goodness and Love. When it is Love that destroys an evil, this evil is killed forever.

Brute force only temporarily buries the evil that it wants to combat and destroy. Now, evil is a persistent seed. Once buried, it develops in secret, germinates, and reappears with even greater vigor.

The Bird Fallen from Its Nest

The love that Tierno Bokar had for human beings went far beyond the confines of his religious group; it spread over the whole of the human race. It even went beyond this to embrace all of creation, to the most humble of God's creatures.

One day in that year of 1933 which I spent with him, he was sitting in the small room where he was to die seven years later. Addressing the eldest of his students, he was elaborating on the esoteric meaning of the Tijani rosary. We were all spellbound. Outside, the wind was blowing. It made the sand rise up and was ruffling the feathers of the rooster who was clinging to a pillar. A stronger gust shook the structure. At the shock of this, a swallow's nest, which had been balanced on top of the wall under the awning of the roof, opened up. A chick fell out, chirping. We gave it an indifferent look. The attention of those listening to Tierno did not slack for an instant. Tierno finished his sentence, then was silent. He sat up, passed a sad look over his students, and then extended his long fine fingers towards the small bird:

"Give me this other one's son."

He took it into his cupped hands. His look became brighter.

"Praise to God, Whose anticipatory grace embraces all beings!" he said.

Then he put the little bird down, got up, took a box, and put it under the nest. He went out and soon came back. Between his fingers we saw a large needle and a cotton thread. He climbed up onto the box, put the little swallow at the bottom of the torn nest and repaired it with the same care that he used to use when embroidering *boubous*. Then he got down again and took his place on the matting. We were waiting impatiently for the continuation of the lesson, but instead of taking up his rosary again, which was serving as the basis for his explanations, he left it alone. After a moment of silence, he spoke to us:

> It is necessary that I speak to you again about Charity, because I am pained to see that not one of you has enough of this real goodness of heart. And yet, what grace! . . . If you had a charitable heart, it would have been impossible for you to listen to this lesson, even about God, when a small miserable creature was crying out to you for help. You were not moved by this desperation, your hearts did not hear this call. . .
>
> Well, my friends, in truth, he who learns by heart all the theologies of all the religions, if he does not have charity in his heart, he can consider his knowledge to be like so much worthless baggage. No one will rejoice in the encounter with the divine if he does not have charity in his heart. Without it, the five prayers are but insignificant gestures; without charity, pilgrimage is a worthless pleasure trip.

The scene on that day is etched indelibly on my memory. I can still see him, dressed in his white garment, delicately repairing the home of this "other one's son" whose call we did not answer, so preoccupied were we with ourselves.

In a general way, he taught us never to kill an animal without necessity, even a simple mosquito. For him, all of nature, animals and plants included, should be respected because they are not only our nourishing Mother, but they are, moreover, the great divine Book wherein everything is a living symbol and a source of teaching.

The Little Dog and Paradise

A touching anecdote relating to his little dog illustrates how the slightest circumstance was material for reflection for Tierno. It also shows how he perceived higher realities through everything, even the smallest plant. Here is the anecdote, as he told it to us himself:

> One day I left for the fields, accompanied by my faithful dog, who is a sworn enemy of the monkeys who ravage the plantations. The time of the great April heat had arrived. My dog

and I were so hot we could hardly breathe. I expected that one or the other of us would end up fainting. Finally, thank God, I saw a *tiayki*[34] tree whose dense branches offered a vault of refreshing greenery.

My little dog let out small cries of joy and ran at full speed in the direction of the blessed shade. When he had reached it, instead of staying there, he came back towards me with his mouth open, his tongue hanging out, and his pointed white teeth showing. Seeing his rapid breathing, I understood how exhausted he was.

I walked towards the shade. I could see how pleased my dog was. Then for a moment, I pretended to continue on my way. The poor animal groaned plaintively but followed me anyway, his head low, his tail curled between his legs. He was visibly desperate, but decided to follow me, whatever might happen.

This faithfulness touched me deeply. How could one fully appreciate the gesture of this animal that was prepared to follow me to its death without it being necessary for him to do so, and without his being constrained by anything whatsoever? He is devoted, I said to myself, because he considers me to be his master. He proves his attachment by risking his life, with his sole intention being to follow me and remain at my side.

"Lord," I cried out, "cure my troubled soul! Make my faithfulness like that of this being that I disdainfully call a dog. Give to me, as You have given to him, the strength to master myself when I must carry out Your will, that I may follow, without asking where I am going, the way which You guide me upon!

"I am not the creator of this dog, yet he blindly obeys and quietly follows me, resulting in a thousand sufferings that could cost him his life. It is You, O Lord, who have bestowed this virtue upon him. Give, give, O Lord, to all those who ask

[34] A kind of tree that keeps its leaves even during periods of intense heat, when all the other trees have lost theirs.

it of You, as well as to me, the virtue of Love and the courage of Charity!"

Then I turned around and took refuge in the shade. Thoroughly happy, my little companion came and lay in front of me in such a way that his eyes were turned towards mine, as if to speak to me seriously. His two front legs were stretched out parallel to each other; his head was raised very high. While resting in this way, he kept watching me so that he would not miss any of my movements.

A few minutes later, neither I nor my companion felt the slightest fatigue. Thus protected and refreshed by the blessed shade, I began to reflect. The shade that is provided by a green and living foliage spreads over the entire area that it covers, and is a vivifying element that neutralizes the suffocating element produced by the heat of the sun. I had many times experienced that a tree covered with dead leaves does not provide the same sense of well-being. Therefore, I told myself, there exists in the green of vegetation a necessary source of healing that sustains life in man and animals. This vivifying principle, which comes from green vegetation by the action of heat, made me dream of Paradise, as it is metaphorically described in Koranic verses.

The "green," of Paradise, I thought, is none other than the spiritual Reality of which the green of plants here below is a manifestation on the material plane. Realizing this relationship caused a brilliant flame of understanding to surge from my mind. Paradise, as it is described, is a symbolic garden[35] of which the green is eternal. This eternal green attenuates for us the rays of divine Light, which are too strong for our sight. In this spiritual garden which is always green, the elect can contemplate the Light of the divine Essence and assimilate the emanations of the Source of eternal life. With ears that have been purified of any dullness, they listen to the voice of their Lord. They thus enter the state of beatitude described in verses ten and eleven of Sura 88: "They will have a sublime Paradise (a 'Garden on high') wherein no frivolous word will be heard."

---

[35] The Koran usually uses the term *Janna* ("garden") to signify "Paradise."

Brother in God! While waiting for the chance to enter the celestial Garden tomorrow, respect today the great garden that makes up the plant kingdom. Refrain from destroying the smallest plant without good reason! A plant is a symbol that God causes to spring from the soil for our instruction, our nourishment, and our comfort.

Tierno Bokar was conscious of his duty as an educator to the community which had chosen him as a guide, but his sensitiveness was such that it would be difficult to find in any of his teachings a "do this. . ." or "do not do that. . ." In his mind, only the divine Word had the power to order or to forbid. Only the divine Word could set imperatives of a moral order. However, this moral aspect was blended into all of his teachings. He suggested more than he expressed. He shaped souls, he never bullied them.

Addressing the problem of human passions, he spoke of them as inward impulses which must be guided and not as enemies which must be defeated. His language was never one of an "inquisitor." Above all, his teaching was intended to be constructive and educating.

For Tierno Bokar, passions are shared by all people. They are like a flock that the shepherd must manage to direct and to guide. He said:

When the sheep run away, the shepherd cannot guide them anymore. Then, you will see him moving about to keep his animals from scattering. Each of us is the shepherd of our passions. It is up to each of us to tame them and to prevent them from jumping over our heads and from overwhelming and then leading us into a moral abyss.

He always brought our attention to real and lasting values, unlike the ephemeral nature of the attractions of this world. One day, the meeting turned to the discussion of beauty. He made us understand that there are two sorts of beauty: one outward, illusory, and ephemeral, and the other completely inward and spiritual, saying:

The Two Kinds of Beauty

The magical multicolored clouds which greet the sun when it rises and when it sets disappear a few moments after the dawn or sunset. In the same way, the charms of a virgin soon wilt. Over the years, the maiden becomes plain and has wrinkles appearing in her face. And what about delicious food? As soon as the mouthful of food has gone down the throat it is drowned in the liquids of the body.

O adept, still at the threshold of this *zāwiya* where we hope to see the sacred flame of sound advice shine for all of us, and for all who live, know that purely physical beauty is as ephemeral as the fires of the sunset or the redness of the dawn. Turn your efforts from searching just for this beauty and redirect them towards the acquisition of true and immutable beauty: inner beauty, that which flowers in spiritual meadows.

Search in truth and keep searching! Search within the shadows of material life, and when you have proven worthy of it from God, the shining star which is in the holy Book will guide you into the garden of real and eternal beauty. Then you will be capable of remembering your God[36] Who has said,[37] "Remember your (God), for the remembrance[38] is of use" (Koran 87:9).

Tierno always refrained from judging others. A student had reported the behavior of the young son of a family who claimed to be descendants of al-Hajj Umar. The boy's conduct was not, it appeared,

---

[36] The expression "your God" might seem surprising. What is being addressed here is God in His personal relationship with each individual being. This relationship is personal, unique, and specific. A *hadīth* of the Prophet alludes specifically to this: "He who knows himself (or: 'He who knows his *soul*. . .'), knows his Lord."

[37] Editor's note: The translation of the Koranic verse that follows diverges from all translations known to us. The correct rendering of the verse should be: "Remind (other people), for the reminder is of use." It should be noted, however, that the Arabic verb in the Koran means "to make others remember" (thus "remind"), which amounts to the same point being made by Tierno Bokar: The act of remembering God is beneficial.

[38] The word *dhikr*, translated here by *remembrance*, has multiple meanings: (a) mention, reminder, recollection, commemoration, mindfulness. In the Islamic tradition, the word is used to designate the *mention* of the Name of God, either aloud or silently. This utterance is intended to evoke in us or to remind us of His Presence; put another way, it is intended to remind ourselves of, or recall ourselves to, His Presence. Thus, this is something that is much more active than a simple mental recollection, which is no more than a stage on the path of the *dhikr*. The abundance of possible meanings for this word explains the diversity of translations that have been given for it. All of these meanings, however, center upon a single idea: the relationship between the Name and the Named.

without reproach. The student asked Tierno for advice. He gave this answer:

> Speaking glibly of chastity, uprightness, courage, and wisdom is easier than being chaste, upright, courageous, and wise oneself. Ranting against disorderly conduct, or revealing such conduct by one's neighbor and then condemning him with citations of Koranic verses which are sometimes misdirected or with *hadīth* of doubtful authenticity is easier than correcting one's own faults and easier than forgiving others for the offenses that they commit against one.

White Birds and Black Birds

Not only did he refrain from judging others, but he went further. He tried to make us understand that a good thought is always preferable to a bad one, even when it is about those whom we consider our enemies. It was not always easy to convince us, as shown by the following anecdote in which he spoke to us of white birds and black birds.

On that day, Tierno had been commenting for us on the Koranic verse "And whoso does an atom's weight of good will see it then, and whoso does an atom's weight of ill will see it then" (99:7-8).

As we were questioning him on the subject of good acts, he told us, "The good act that is the most beneficial is that which consists of praying for one's enemies."

"How so?" I exclaimed with surprise. "Generally, people tend to curse their enemies rather than bless them. Wouldn't this make us look a little stupid to pray for our enemies?"

"Perhaps," he replied, "but only in the eyes of those who do not understand. Men certainly have the right to call down curses upon their enemies, but they wrong themselves more by speaking ill of them than by blessing them."

"I do not understand," I replied. "If a man calls down curses on his enemy and if his curses take effect, it could destroy the enemy. Shouldn't this rather put him at ease?"

Tierno responded, "In appearance, perhaps, but this is then only a satisfaction of the egoistical soul (*nafs*, the ego), therefore a satisfaction at a lower material level. From a mystical point of view, the fact of blessing one's enemy is more beneficial. Even if one is thought to be a fool in the eyes of ignorant people, in reality one's spiritual maturity and the degree of one's wisdom become apparent by this."

"Why?" I asked him.

To help me understand, Tierno then spoke of white birds and black birds:

> In relation to one another, men are like walls that face each other. Each wall has in it a multitude of small holes where white birds and black birds are nested. The black birds are bad thoughts and bad words. The white birds are good thoughts and good words. Because of their shape, the white birds can only enter into holes for white birds, and the same holds true for the black birds, who can only nest in holes for black birds. Now, imagine two men who believe they are enemies of each other. Let us call them Yousef and Ali.
>
> One day, Yousef, persuaded that Ali wishes him ill, feels full of anger towards Ali and sends him a very bad thought. In doing this, Yousef releases a black bird and at the same time frees up a corresponding hole. His black bird flies towards Ali and looks for an empty hole to nest in that is adapted to its shape. If from his side Ali has not sent a black bird towards Yousef, that is, if Ali has not sent out any bad thoughts, none of his black holes will be empty. Finding no place to lodge itself, Yousef's black bird will be obliged to return to its original nest, taking with it the evil with which it was burdened, an evil which will end up eroding and destroying Yousef himself.
>
> But let us imagine that Ali has sent out a bad thought, too. In doing this, he frees up a hole in which Yousef's black bird will be able to enter and then deposit part of his evil, thus accomplishing his mission of destruction. During all this, Ali's black bird will fly towards Yousef and will lodge itself in the hole freed up by Yousef's black bird. Thus, the two black birds will have achieved their goal and will have been effective in destroying the men for whom each was destined.
>
> But once their task is accomplished, each black bird will return to its nest of origin because, it is said: "Everything returns to its source." Since the evil they were loaded with has

not been exhausted, this evil will turn against their originators and will end up destroying them. The person who creates a bad thought, or a bad wish, or an ill-spoken word is therefore attacked by both the black bird of his enemy and by his own black bird when this latter returns to him.

The same thing happens with white birds. If we send out only good thoughts towards our enemy, while the enemy only addresses bad thoughts to us, the enemy's black birds will not find any place to lodge themselves with us and will return to their sender. As for the white birds who bear good thoughts that we have sent to him, if they find no free place with our enemy, they will return to us charged with all the beneficial energy which they are carrying.

Thus, if we send out only good thoughts, no evil and no curses can ever reach into our being. That is why one should always ask for blessings on both one's friends and one's enemies. Not only does the benediction go towards its objective in order to accomplish its mission of making peace, but it also comes back to us, sooner or later, with all that it is carrying.

This is what Sufis call "desirable egoism." It is the commendable Love of Self which is tied to respect for oneself and for one's neighbor. This is because every man, good or bad, is the depository of a part of the divine Light. That is why Sufis, in accordance with the teaching of the Prophet, do not want to soil either their mouths or their beings with bad words or bad thoughts, or even with seemingly benign criticisms.

Because of the principle that "everything returns to its source," he urged us to produce only the purest spiritual vibrations by consecrating our thought and tongue to the recitation of the Name of God (*dhikru-Allāh*):

The *Dhikr*

The power of God is like an immense enclosure that surrounds the earth and sky. Everything within this enclosure is moving about and ends up bumping against the eternal inner walls just to return to its point of departure.

Once in movement, our actions, good or bad, develop and end up colliding with this obstacle. The collision increases their strength, but changes their direction and makes them return to their point of departure. Thus, the effects of our acts return to us like a wave which hits the shore and then falls back on itself and returns to the center of the sea from which it came.[39]

O brother in God, you who desire to be an adept of the *zāwiya* of true communion, pronounce the sacred Name of God (*Allāh*) knowing that the effects of our acts return to us. Pronounce it unceasingly, night and day, gently in your heart, inwardly in your mind, or with all your lungs as if by blowing into a bull's horn!

More than any other thing, this Name evokes the Essence of the Divinity. It acts, and causes waves of spiritual well-being to emanate from the heaven of the Divine Attributes.[40] These waves of peace rise up and then flow back towards your spirit, the core from which the invocation emanates. It is thus that both our happiness or our unhappiness depend upon that which we send out.

Like all Sufis, Tierno attached great importance to the *dhikr*, which holds a central place in the spiritual practices of the *turuq*, or brotherhoods.

He urged his students to surrender themselves not only to the outward *dhikr* (the *dhikr* of the tongue), which is an initial approach, but also to the permanent inner *dhikr*, which fills the entire being with

---

[39] As if a stone were thrown in it, for example.

[40] Editor's note: In the original French text, the author had included an Arabic term, the "*hawa'il asfa*," which he translated as "the heaven of the Divine Attributes." The Arabic terminology is obscure and possibly particular to Tierno Bokar. For this reason, we have not included it above. However, Dr. Vincent J. Cornell, a scholar of Islam and Sufism, notes that the author could be referring to a term that means, literally, "the purest air" and which thus might be a reference to the Paradise of the Divine Spirit. Dr. Cornell further suggests that in this context *al-hawa' al-asfa* "recalls the Qur'anic term *al-'Illiyun*, [which] refers to the place of the supernal," meaning, the highest heaven.

the Presence of God and which Sufi tradition calls the *"dhikr* of the heart" or the *"dhikr* of the intimate."[41]

Let us listen to what Tierno had to say about this:

> Brother in God, you who comes to ask for our advice, make your happiness the intimate[42] utterance of the Name of God. Stay away from anyone who uses faith for devious purposes: at the end of the soul's journey, he will be rudely disappointed—he will find himself frustrated by that which he had believed he had gained. . . .
>
> Every believer has noticed that at certain moments the ardor of his worship is very much alive but at other times this ardor is less so, in spite of his best intentions. Know that there is a mystical heat that comes from God as a result of uttering His Name a great number of times. It penetrates the adept and warms his soul. Under the effect of this fire, the soul believes in its own capacity for worship, in the same way as iron increases in volume under the influence of the fire of the forge.
>
> Therefore, our mystical warmth and coolness depend upon us, on the way in which we recite the Name of God (or the Names of His attributes) and of the number of repetitions. Happy are those who, in one day, can recite the great Name of God (*Allāh*) 34,560 times maximum or 960 times minimum![43]
>
> When the Name *Allāh* is uttered, the light which bursts forth from it strengthens the spiritual flame which is deposited by God in each soul at the moment it comes into existence.
>
> The constant repetition of this Name or the formula of the Unity of God (*Lā ilāha illa 'Llāh*) is the surest way to

---

[41] See pp. 220-221.

[42] Editor's note: The original French word *intime,* here translated as "intimate," can also mean "innermost," or "secret." It might be noted that Sufism often speaks of the "secret" of a God-centered person. Also, in Sufism, a saint is called a "friend" to God, meaning someone who is on intimate terms with the divine Presence.

[43] The number of repetitions is linked to the science of numerology, in relation to the simple or deconstructed value of the letters that make up the Name. This is too vast a subject to go into here.

introduce into oneself the breath that will stir up the inner fire. Without this fire, the spiritual ember that has been deposited in us will die down little by little and will end up being black coal, inert, and in which there resides a corrosive acid.

From within his modest compound, Tierno had observed men. No nuance of their souls had escaped him. Splendidly applying the advice of the Prophet, "Speak to people according to their ability to understand," he knew how to adapt his teaching to the understanding of each one.

I had observed his way of doing this, and one day I could not restrain myself from sharing my astonishment with him. I said, "Tierno, when I listen to you speak with the small children in the courtyard, I notice that you ultimately say to them the same thing that you say to us, but in such a way that it becomes a fairy tale. When you speak to my aunts, I see you take on yet another language. Finally, you can even say the same thing to the old marabout Alfa Ali and to Gabouli, the little eight-year-old girl, except that you use a different form and color. Why?"

He answered me:

The Three Types of Clothing

There are three ways of washing clothes. Thick, coarse fabrics are beaten with a small plank, fabric of average thickness is stomped on by the feet, and very fine fabric is wrung out by hand. One would not wash a thick woolen blanket in the same way as a *boubou* made of thin European fabric.

It is the same with human souls. Before they can attain the level in which the mind is constantly occupied by praising the Name of the Lord, all souls must undergo trials that are more or less rigorous depending upon their state.

Tierno, who loved all men, also loved sinners. He did not give himself the right to judge them. Tierno, who would lament the state of Bandiagara before he died, had always thought that he had a duty to fulfill towards those who had strayed from divine paths, but he did not condemn them.

When one of us asked him, "Tierno, what do you say about those who abandon themselves to solely temporal things?" He merely answered, "Those are the souls for whose protection one should pray."

Until the outbreak of the tragedy which was to mark the last years of his life, Tierno Bokar remained the uncontested spiritual guide of the Muslim community of Bandiagara. He was also frequently asked to give his opinion on how to behave in social situations. Whether a question was from an impressionable little boy who had been entrusted to him or from a powerful chief explaining to him a complicated problem of major or minor political significance, his answers were always drawn from a depth of moral health, purity of intention, and perfect detachment which marked all his relations with his peers.

Regardless of their social backgrounds, he used to encourage all the children whom he instructed to live modestly:

The Palace and the Thatched Cottage

In a dream I once saw a monster-like man who cried out with seventy-two tongues, "I am the son of the chief, I am the son of a saint, I am the son of a wise man, I am rich and powerful."

All people of good judgment should pronounce such words in a low voice, even if they are speaking the truth. Do not dig too much around the roots of the illustrious trunk of your origins because beyond several layers of earth you risk discovering that the roots originate in a mass of refuse. Be less proud, because if you search well, from every royal palace you will find an alleyway that leads to the thatched cottage of a poor person.[44] Rather, meditate on the first verse of Sura 4: "O mankind! Fear your Lord Who created you from a single being. . . ."

---

[44] If one goes far back enough, it can be discovered that every royal lineage originates, at a certain point in time, in a family of modest means.

For Tierno, human society, which participates in the divine Reality, forms a whole, like an immense caravan whose members are necessarily united because they face the same dangers and they all are walking towards the same goal. He used to say:

> Everywhere in the bush country where plants interlace thickly, the foliage spreads over the earth in a thick cover which imparts freshness and restores strength. Let us benefit from this lesson to come together spiritually and to unite ourselves one to another in a vast forest (*toggéré*) under which our souls shall find rest in the otherworldly shade.

To those who would rise up against certain abuses committed by important people, he preached calm and patience and recommended that they begin by transforming themselves. He spoke to children as if he hoped to make them brothers forever bonded to each other. He spoke to men, some of whom were already embittered by life, as if they would only be able to find calm in gentleness, simplicity, and tolerance. He said:

> Seeing and criticizing social inequalities, denouncing them with grand gestures and grand words is easier than making oneself humble with regard to those who are less fortunate. Also, the sons of men who once were important[45] now show themselves incapable of bringing themselves to say to the sons of their former subjects, "You are men just like us, we all have the same rights because in the eyes of God we are all identical creatures."

The Responsibility of Leaders (Chiefs)

Although he advised men to be tolerant and patient, he nevertheless condemned the abuses of leaders who failed in their duties. When I asked him, "Tierno, why does one see even the smallest fault in a leader?" he answered, with the smiling humor that he often used:

[45] He was alluding to important secular or religious leaders who at that time—and often still today—thought of themselves as superior to others.

Because, my friend, the seriousness of every fault committed by a secular or religious leader is proportional to the size of his country. This seriousness is multiplied by the density of the inhabitants of his domain or of those who follow his rule, multiplied again by the weightiness of the fault, and increased by the exaggeration of wandering tale-tellers. Added to all of this is the ample weight of the credulity of the masses.

He became more serious as he recounted another image dealing with the same subject:

One day, I dove into the river. Suddenly, I felt that I was falling into an abyss and that a crushing mass of water weighed upon me, as if the spirits inhabiting the heights from which I had leapt were applying their full weight on me. A great effort was needed to get back to the surface. Once I was out of the water, I had to make another effort to find in my moral life something that corresponded to the strange trouble that I had just experienced. Upon reflection, I understood that the consequences of our faults are measured by the stature of our social standing on the one hand and, on the other hand, by our personal situation at the time of the fault. The higher our social rank and the more honored our situation, the deeper the abyss into which we will fall and the more violent our moral or public asphyxiation will be.

Always scrupulous and concerned with justice, he did not condemn the chief when the fault was with his intermediaries or representatives:

One kind of absurdity surprises me more than many others: I wonder why subjects attack the chief when some servant fails in his duties. The chief, the king, cannot reasonably be implicated when their agents do something unscrupulous. As long as a servant remains faithful to his assignment, he should be considered as a servant. But as soon as he departs from his duty, he ceases to be the agent of the one who sent him and the former becomes a victim in the same way as the others.

It was 1933 when Tierno Bokar was addressing these topics—he had yet to suffer personally the action of such intermediaries. But later someone said to him, "France does not like the 'eleven-beaders,' and is ordering them to be pursued and persecuted." He answered:

Are you certain that it is really France that said that? Would it not more likely be our antagonists who, being unable to overcome us through their own power, skill, or prestige, have chosen to carry tales to France about us in order to use France's strength, prestige, and skill against us?

As the proverb says: "They beat the drum to urge on two groups who have nothing against each other, in order that they might exterminate both for their own benefit." We might call this "Fight each other, while I beat the drum for you."

He considered power a strong drug that could be dangerous in inexperienced hands. In this respect he told a humorous parable, which, alas, has lost nothing of its relevance:

The Throne and the Butcher Boy

One day, a volcano began to belch fire to punish men for their iniquity. This fire spread all over a vast country, consumed everything, and caused the last valorous men of this kingdom to perish, leaving only a few survivors. A strange worm bristling with hair that until then had lived in the bowels of the earth now found itself suddenly thrown upon the golden throne of the monarchy, in a room of the palace that miraculously remained intact.

Landing on the royal throne, he found an ugly fly sitting there in the lap of luxury. The fly said to the worm, "Scoundrel, coarse occupant of the dark underworld, what are you doing on this throne? Be off with you, or I will have you sent to the pastures of the occupants of the poultry-yard!"

Without saying a word, the hairy cylindrical thing wriggled towards the disgusting fly. Then, coiling itself up, it said, "You species of the lowest origin, too quickly and too highly placed due to a huge catastrophe, here, take this for your haughtiness and your insolence!"

Unwinding its body like a spring, it swatted the nauseating fly, which then rolled over and, unable to use its wings, was squashed against a wall. Proud of his exploit, the worm left to settle himself as comfortably as possible on the throne.

Then a large black dog which had escaped from the catastrophe came along. Fleeing the flames and beside itself with fright, it jumped on the throne, squashing the worm without even noticing.

After this, a lowly butcher boy who had also escaped the torments rushed into the room.

Finding the dog perched on the throne, he grabbed a large club and without any further comment, chased the dog away with a rain of blows. Furious but helpless, the dog fled and ran through the streets of the town barking wildly, as if to rouse the survivors into mutiny against the usurper.

During this time the butcher boy settled himself on the throne and began to speak to himself, saying, "Better late than never. It was human injustice alone that had condemned me to my subservient profession. Instead of slaving away as a butcher, I feel that I am capable of governing the world!"

Having said this, he put on the royal accessories that were still in the room and grabbed the scepter of command.

The survivors, who had been assembling in the court-yard of the palace, saw the butcher boy appear sumptuously dressed and brandishing the scepter of command. They immediately submitted to him and listened for his orders because, they thought, this man could only be the new king sent by God to their devastated country.

The new king started to give orders. Alas! He only knew the jargon that was spoken in the slaughter houses. So each of his orders was punctuated by this typical phrase:

"Those who resist me will be sliced up like prime-quality meat!"

"This parable," added Tierno, "is as valid for you as it is for myself, O brother in God. It teaches us many things. It warns us that not everyone is right for every task. Our functions are apportioned to us by the intelligence of Providence. When the opportunity to assume the role of a leader comes to a coarse soul, he only knows how to set up a megalomaniac dictatorship. Instead of establishing a reign of peace for all, this will be the beginning of dark terror. Scoundrels will become bankers and rogues will mint money. Morality will toss dangerously about on the raging sea of unleashed passions."

Tierno Bokar had already noticed with complete clarity the threat of disequilibrium which weighed on African society, which was being torn apart by forces that uprooted children from their traditions. The phenomenon of cultural disintegration that had been set into motion before the watchful eyes of the Sage of Bandiagara was infinitely distressing to him. For him, the remedy lay in the cultural essence of the ethnic groups themselves, in this glue that for millennia had been strong enough to assure the cohesion of African society.

It was Tierno Bokar's view that before young Africans give themselves over to the attractions of this or that foreign culture, they should meditate on the treasure inherited from their ancestors instead of, as is all too often done today, ignoring it or keeping it as if it amounted to nothing. His advice could be summed up like this: "Do not go seeking fortune by begging in far off places, you who are seated upon a sack of gold. Make use of this fortune, make it grow by trading in it with others."

Tierno Bokar had a broad background in African cultures. He was Tukulor through his parents, then successively Hausa, Bambara, Fulani, Marka, and Dogon by adoption. From each of these ethnic groups he had drawn a piece, all of which then made up the whole of his experience. He had enriched this harvest thanks to his orthodox religious knowledge. Koranic teaching had made him a master of African Sufism. The men from near and far with whom he had mingled during his eventful youth had transmitted to him the precious teaching of the traditions of many African lands. Ultimately, he did not see any fundamental difference between the two worlds which had shaped him.

Tradition and Change

To a question on traditions, he replied:

> Respect them. They make up the spiritual heritage of those
> who preceded us and who had not broken with God. Tradi-
> tions can be presented in the form of different sorts of tales of
> varying length: stories for children, didactic or initiatic stories.
> Whatever they may be, meditate upon them, try to unlock
> the secret wrapped in them. Dig deeply, as the gold diggers
> would do in the mines of Bourré.[46]
>
> Every story, every riddle, is like a tunnel, and when all of
> these are put together they make up a mine of information
> that the ancients bequeathed to us according to our region,
> race, or family, or often from individual to individual. But it
> goes without saying that to work profitably in this mine and
> to get around it easily, one must see clearly, in other words,
> possess a key or a teacher. . . .
>
> When risky speculations prevail over divine laws and over
> customs instituted by traditional wisdom—customs which
> we do not truly appreciate due to a lack of sufficient knowl-
> edge—then unavoidable hardships beset the world, against
> which contemporary people can do nothing. . . .
>
> All tongues in these times conjugate the phrase "want
> to get" in the first-person present indicative.[47] Acquisition
> becomes an imperative duty. As for the means of acquiring,
> one is little concerned whether it is licit or not.
>
> These are times in which the poor, honest man lives and
> dies in obscurity. Yet, he is happy, unless he is spurned by all,
> even by his own relatives!

Even in the relative isolation of Bandiagara, that town protected
by its cliff, Tierno Bokar had perceived the impatience of the young

[46] A gold-bearing region of Mali.

[47] Editor's note: This means that everyone only seems able to say "I want to get. . . ."
Tierno Bokar is emphasizing people's egotism ("I"), acquisitiveness, and impatience
("want to get"—now) in current times.

people of the area to conjugate the verb "to develop." He had sized up both the nature and necessity of it. He was too sagacious to oppose it. But he corrected the simplistic definition that certain people gave too hastily to this verb, with its almost magical attraction. Develop, yes, but from a solid starting point. He said:

> Some believe that to develop is to break completely with all of one's traditions, often through "snobbism," in order to adopt those of a race whose ways one admires. For us, to develop is to perfect our inheritance, which is not made up merely of our homes and our fields: it is also to improve our thinking, our entire way of being.
>
> That which fits in a country of temperate climate cannot entirely suit a tropical country. We see our Soudanese children copying Arabs or Europeans more or less awkwardly according to their upbringing. They are like those waterfalls that expend themselves in rushing uselessly over slabs of stone without ever flowing into a lake to ease their mad and fruitless course.

This starting point, tradition, should be solid enough in the minds of those who set out, to allow them to retrace their steps and make a new start in case of a fall or a mistake. Tradition is the anchor-point and reference point that permits one to know who one is and to advance boldly on new or far-off roads without thereby losing one's equilibrium and one's identity.

Blind imitation of others (*taqlīd* slips in everywhere. . .) does not make us become them, but it does make us forget ourselves. As the proverb says, "The piece of wood can float on the water all it wants, but it will never become a caiman."[48]

"Sources" is the title that a young African, al-Hajj Abdulwahab Doukouré gave to an article he wrote that was inspired by the teaching of Tierno Bokar and which was published in *Le Soudan français* (issue 96, July 11, 1952). He wrote:

---

[48] Translator's note: A reptile related to the crocodile.

What struck me the most was to notice that [Tierno Bokar] had absorbed the progressive ideas contained in the Koran. He taught them using local material, but did not violate the pure essence of the Revelation, nor did he violate the orthodoxy established by the law of the Imams. Tierno Bokar Salif's teaching was oral. He gave it in Fulfulde, the Fulani language whose richness and poetry are unrivalled. I do not exaggerate in saying that no Arab library (and I have visited many in Morocco, Algeria, and Tunisia) possesses a work that is as synthetic, practical, and alive, accessible to both literate and illiterate people. . . . [Tierno] understood that the mercy of God surpasses His rigor. This all-encompassing mercy permits one to affirm that God opens wide multiple doors to His creatures to order to facilitate their return to Him. . . .

With Tierno, the neophyte begins by becoming conscious of his own existence, and then that of others. The teacher makes him sense the superiority of his own nature and the conditions necessary for the development and the flowering of this nature. There are moral responsibilities that correspond to the exceptional gifts created for man; all of this is supported by Koranic verses and authentic *hadīth*. . . .

I [al-Hajj Abdulwahab Doukouré] know through personal experience how many young Blacks with a thirst for the Divine have gone abroad . . . and returned—I do not deny it—perhaps versed in Arabic literature but completely deprived of their natural simplicity, of their ardent faith, and of the boundless charity that they have seen their elders practice. . . . The Prophet said, "Work for the salvation of your soul as if you were going to die tomorrow [and] work for your material well-being as if you were going to live forever." I conclude that we must, on the one hand, strengthen our traditions and reinforce our faith, and on the other hand we must try to improve our manner of material life by the acquisition of modern science, the sources of which are found in the West.

To close this chapter that is dedicated to the personal "message" of Tierno Bokar, let us listen once more to this call that he addressed to all men in the name of spiritual unity:

With all my heart, I desire the coming of the era of reconciliation amongst all religions of the earth, the era in which these united religions will support each other to form a spiritual and moral canopy, the era in which they will be at peace in God by resting upon three supports: Love, Charity, Brotherhood.

There is only one God, and there can be only one Way that leads towards Him, one Religion of which its various worldly manifestations are like branches spreading out from a single tree. This Religion can only be called Truth, and its dogmas can only be three: Love, Charity, Brotherhood.

Could not this reconciliation that has been so often foretold, prepared for, and awaited, truly be called "a trustworthy Alloy"?

Truly, a meeting of essential truths from within the diverse religions into which the earth is divided could prove itself to be of vast, universal religious use. Perhaps such a meeting would be more in conformity with the Unity of God, the unity of the human spirit, and the unity of all Creation.

Part 3

———— ∽⦾⦾∽ ————

His Teachings

Tierno Bokar was, above all, a master teacher. When he opened his Koranic school at the beginning of this [i.e. the twentieth] century, the community of Bandiagara entrusted their children to him for instruction and education. He taught them as he had been taught in his youth. Over the years he imparted to them the knowledge that constitutes the basis of what can be called Islamic culture, conforming to what was expected of him by the community. This included Arabic language, writing, and grammar, the study of the Koran and its extension, *Tawhīd* (theology[1]), the study of the *Sunna* and the systems derived from it (jurisprudence, rules of religious, moral, and civic life), rhetoric, general Muslim history, etc.

The students of the Koranic school had three days off a week. During these three days, Tierno held gatherings in his home that were dedicated to the teachings of the Tijaniyya and which were open to everyone. All the marabouts of the town came to listen to him. The elderly Alfa Ali, who was the most important Koranic school teacher in Bandiagara at the time, used to read passages from *Jawāhir al-Ma'ānī* (*The Pearl of Meanings*), the principal book about Shaykh Ahmad al-Tijani. Tierno Bokar, who was a *shaykh* of the brotherhood, would then comment upon and interpret these passages. He would first do this according to the teachings of Shaykh Ahmad al-Tijani himself, then according to the book of al-Hajj Umar, *Al-Rimāh* (*The Lances*),[2] and finally according to the fruit of his own meditations, of his *ijtihād* (effort at personal reflection). He owed his reputation as a master teacher to the quality and originality of his *ijtihād*.

As for the more specifically esoteric aspects of the Tijaniyya (the science of numbers, letters, geometric shapes, etc.), he dispensed these individually according to the aptitudes of each adept. In the same way, it was on an individual basis that he guided us along the path of inward perfection.

Indeed, his entire person, his very life, were his teaching. He approached the highest or most subtle truths through the most common events of daily life. He knew how to use the simplest images

---

[1] *Tawhīd*: Oneness (of God). This term covers the study of the qualities and attributes of God and of their relationship with creation, particularly with that of man.

[2] Editor's note: The full title of al-Hajj Umar's book is *Rimāh hizb al-rahīm 'alā nuhur hizb al-rajīm* ("The Lances of the Party of the All-Merciful against the Throats of the Party of the Accursed").

to help us understand things that were unclear to us. It was thus that over the days, little by little, we became imbued with that which radiated from him, through his words as well as through his silences.

When he spoke, he strove to put himself within the reach of his listeners and to find a language that could be understood by all. One day, an elderly, unlettered[3] Dogon who was called Antiamba came looking for him in order to receive instruction in Islam. In order to transmit to him the basic principles of the religion, Tierno began to use a mnemonic method which he continued to use later for other students, particularly for those who did not know any written language.

As he was explaining the principles and developing the reasoning that connected them, with his index finger he would trace in the sand a series of points which, little by little, were organized into a simple diagram that captured the attention and could easily be etched into the memory.

This basic teaching is divided into three essential parts or "lessons," each of which is illustrated by a particular diagram which the reader will find on pages 168, 182, and 193.

The title of the first lesson, "The Primordial Pact," echoes verse 172 of Sura 7 of the Koran. In it, God, in the mysterious world of preexistence (before the descent into time, one could say), poses to the souls of men the question, "Am I not your Lord?" (*alastu bi-Rabbikum?*), to which the men reply, "Yes, we bear witness to this." This "yes," which was the first existential act of the human soul, the original recognition of its belonging (to the Creator), constitutes the very essence of this "profound Intelligence," which is the subject of the first lesson. In the depths of each soul there resides a knowledge—which is often dormant and which seems to be covered with veils—of "who" the soul is and "where" the soul came from. It is this profound Intelligence, this spiritual instinct, which permits the soul to distinguish truth from error and to embark upon and then progress along the path of Return. "Verily we come from God and to Him we return" (Koran 2:156).

---

[3] "Illiterate" only from the point of view of written French and Arabic; this word does not signify ignorance and has nothing pejorative about it here.

After having laid out that which makes up the intrinsic nobility of man in this way, Tierno Bokar straightaway places him in a relationship of solidarity and responsibility towards his peers, beginning with kindred, recalling the *hadīth* of the Prophet: "Every one of you is a shepherd and each shepherd is accountable for his flock."

Then, alluding to the particularly troubled and difficult conditions of our times, he places man where he must face the necessity of a choice which engages his entire being and which is like the echo of the primordial "yes." This is the choice between the ascending path, a path of effort and courage that leads him to the realization of himself in a rediscovered eternity (the path of the abode of the eternal city *Qarārin*), or the downward path, which is very easy and which leads to dissolution and to the loss of oneself (the way of the abode of *Bawārin*, the perishable abode).

In the second lesson, *Mā 'd-dīn* ("What is religion?"), Tierno Bokar lays forth the basic principles of *Islām* (submission to God), of *Īmān* (faith), and of *Ihsān* (perfect conduct). He then states the attributes of God and His Messengers. This is, in a way, the catechism of Islam.

Here, the way of faith is presented as being built upon three pillars. We will again find these three pillars in the third lesson ("the inner law") where they correspond to the three successive degrees that are markers of spiritual progress. Indeed, spiritual progress proceeds from the periphery towards the center or, to use Tierno Bokar's image, it goes from the peel of the fruit (first degree), to the pulp (second degree), then to the kernel (third degree), this latter being the sole bearer of life and renewal.

Of course, these three lessons are only a foundation for his teaching. The lessons lay down the principles, but do not develop them in all their implications. As we will point out later, for Tierno Bokar each point of this teaching could be developed in greater depth and variety to correspond to different levels of understanding, both exoteric and esoteric. Whatever the degree of the students' progress, Tierno often had to return to these first lessons that provided them with necessary points of reference, so that they would not stray from the path.

From the beginning to end of this section, it is Tierno Bokar who speaks through the mouth of Cissé, the religious teacher found throughout the lessons. Tierno had invented the person of Cissé so as not to push himself forward and to avoid using the pronouns "me" and "I," of which in his view we are inclined to make excessive use.

Therefore, let us listen to Cissé.

First Lesson

The Primordial Pact

An elderly Dogon, whose eyes had been opened by long and numerous journeys and by contact with other ethnic groups, returned to his people and said to them:

O, my family! We are in error. Our religious practices have no meaning. I have seen the religions of many countries, but never have I found identical forms of worship in any two places. Every country has its own. One even finds idols for individuals—one for the mother, another for the child—, idols of the tribe, idols of the clan, and special fetishes, some made by shaping a rock or a piece of wood, some in the form of a fish or a snake. Such multiplicity can only indicate error. On the other hand, among the Muslims everything is homogenous—their words and gestures are identical. The times, places, and calls to prayer are similar. When a Muslim healer writes down efficacious signs,[1] all the other initiates can decipher them, whereas with us powders and the elements of potions can only be recognized by those who made them.

[1] Editor's note: Dr. Louis Brenner notes that "This is a reference to the tradition of Muslim healing known as *tibb al-nabī* or 'Prophetic medicine.' These healing practices vary considerably, but most are based on written formulas, usually excerpts from the Koran or other sacred sources, although other symbols and figures are also used. Muslim healers are consulted on a wide range of problems, and the treatments they prescribe might include the wearing of a talisman, or the placing of a protective talisman somewhere in the home; such talismans consist of formulas written on a piece of paper that is usually enclosed in a leather pouch. Another common form of treatment is known as 'Koranic erasures,' in which specially selected verses of the Koran are written on a wooden slate, after which the ink is washed off and the solution is either drunk or used for bathing the body. For further information, see Ismail Abdalla, *Islam, Medicine and Practitioners in Northern Nigeria* (New York: The Edwin Mellen Press, 1997), and Abdullahi Osman El-Tom, 'Drinking the Koran: The Meaning of Koranic Verses in Berti Erasure,' *Africa: Journal of the International African Institute*, Vol. 55, No. 4, Popular Islam (1985), pp. 414-431."

I conclude from all of this that Truth is one, and that its manifestation should not lack harmony. I want to practice Islam.

His listeners were skeptical and much attached to the religion of their ancestors, a religion several thousands of rainy seasons old. They said to him, "If you are convinced of Islam, go to Bandiagara where you will find company."

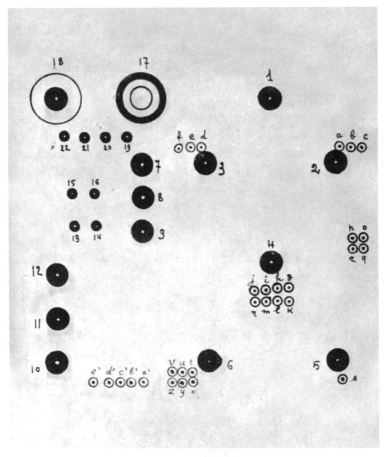

The Primordial Pact

Antiamba—this was the old Dogon's name—therefore came to Bandiagara. He approached a passerby and exchanged the customary greetings with him. He confided to the passerby his desire to be instructed in the Islamic tradition. The other person said to him, "Go to Cissé. His sole occupation is to teach religion. Through him, you will find satisfaction, God willing."

Antiamba went to Cissé's, entered, and said in greeting, "Peace be upon you, you of this place!"

Cissé replied, "We only have peace, only peace.[2] May peace be upon you. Welcome!"

The request having been made, Cissé prepared himself to teach Antiamba, but he came up against a major difficulty: Antiamba did not know how to read or write; he did not speak the ritual language, Arabic; he only knew Dogon and Fulani. Everyone knows the difficulty one has in making oneself understood to someone who is uncultivated, especially when it is a discussion about religion. But Cissé, who knew everything about the Muslim tradition, was not unfamiliar with this maxim from the Prophet of God: "Speak to people according to the level of their understanding."

Cissé said to himself, "This man cannot read a book, but if I use the language he speaks, along with diagrams I trace on the ground, his memory will retain everything, my task will be facilitated, and this man's wish will be fulfilled."

He then thought of these words of Muhammad in relation to spiritual guides: "A portion of the divine Power's secret is sealed within every man of God. By virtue of this portion, he is able to extract the truth from the midst of doubts and lies, as one draws milk from the midst of blood and bodily wastes."[3]

On the advice of Cissé, the old Dogon brought some fine sand and spread it out on the ground. Anyone unfamiliar with this method who might have come upon a man drawing lines and points in the sand and uttering words, would have thought that he was dealing with a geomancer[4] or a demented person. Despite its strangeness, Cissé's

---

[2] A traditional formula of answer to a greeting.

[3] Shepherds and nomads of former times believed that a cow's milk was located between her blood and bodily wastes.

[4] Editor's note: Dr. Louis Brenner's comments on geomancy: "A form of geomancy

method is the only one which is compatible with the intellectual and material conditions of the majority of people. Anyone who wants to instruct those around him according to scholastic rules will only meet with failure. Cissé's method is designed for the illiterate masses, anticipating that death will not wait for anyone and that the divine order will never be rescinded. This method smoothes out all difficulties. Linguistically, it universalizes the teaching and makes it accessible to all ages, all tastes, all capacities, and has the greatest promise of success in the least amount of time.

Cissé began to speak:[5]

1. Neophyte, the Master[6] created you. He made you in the image of Adam, the most honorable and most beautiful of forms. This form was that of our Lord[7] Muhammad (on him blessings and peace!). God took the most precious of His diamonds, conferred it upon you, and said, "Here, take care of it. But remember that I shall take it back from you. In the meantime:

2. Use it.

3. Trade with it.[8]

---

known as 'sand-writing' (*khatt al-raml*) has been practiced in Muslim Africa for centuries. The diviner develops a pattern of signs in a tray of sand from which he 'reads' the response to his client's question or problem. For further information on this practice, its variations, and its extensive influence in Africa, see Louis Brenner, 'Muslim Divination and the History of Religion in Sub-Saharan Africa,' in J. Pemberton (ed.) *Insight and Artistry: A Cross-Cultural Study of Divination in Central and West Africa* (Washington: Smithsonian Institute Press, 2000), pp. 45-59."

[5] As Tierno develops the reasoning of his lesson, he moves his index finger along the diagram in the order which we have represented here by numbers and letters (see p. 168).

[6] A Fulani word which, like the Arabic word *rabb*, means both "Lord" (the Sovereign) and "Master" (he who possesses).

[7] Editor's note: For those unfamiliar with Islamic modes of address, it should be understood that the names of all prophets are typically preceded by the honorific title "Lord." This is still done today in aristocratic systems, such as in England, where the title "Lord" is used to designate nobility.

[8] Editor's note: The reference to 'trading' the "most precious of His diamonds" is very reminiscent of the Parable of the Talents in the New Testament (Matthew 25:14-30).

    a.   If you take good care of it,

    b.   If you serve it well,

    c.   And if you gain from it,

the whole of the gain will be for you. It is of no use to me at all. In addition, I will give you a Kingdom, the likes of which no monarch has ever seen: Paradise after death.

It is written in the Noble Book, 'As for him who has feared appearing before his Lord and restrained his soul from passions, Lo! for him the (enchanting) *Jannah* (Garden) will be his abode' (Koran 79:40-41).

But:

    d.   If you neglect it,

    e.   If you defile it,

    f.   If you tarnish it,

I will overwhelm you with tortures more overwhelming than anyone has ever undergone before: the torments of hell after death."

It is written in the Noble Book: "Then, as for him who has transgressed all bounds, and preferred the life of this world, Lo! For him the inferno of *al-Jahīm* (hell) will be his abode" (Koran 79:37-39).

4.   The diamond in question, is the Intellect[9]

Both there and here, the emphasis is on taking a great thing that one does not own oneself and through effort causing it to increase, much as one creates gain through commerce.

[9] Here it is not a question of a purely intellectual "rationalizing reason," but of this profound Intelligence, the divine particle breathed into man by God; it sometimes remains dormant in certain people, even if they seem intellectually brilliant.

   The Fulani word that is used here (translated as "Intellect"), corresponds to the Arabic word *'aql* and designates at once that which is able to understand (similar to the Arabic word *fahm*, intelligence), to reflect, and to reason.

   Editor's note: The distinction mentioned above by the author is essential. In the original French version, he used the word *Raison*, always with an uppercase "R." In the note above, and in his use of the uppercase term, it is clear that his use of the term "Reason" has a significantly different meaning than the one we typically attach to the word today. The Arabic term *'aql*, referred to by the author, is almost always

g. It is this Intellect which differentiates man from beast.

h. It is this Intellect, among men (people), which differentiates the believer from the unbeliever.

i. It is this Intellect which, among the believers, differentiates the erudite from the ignorant.

j. It is this Intellect which, among erudite believers, differentiates the righteous from the wicked.

From among all the animals of creation, what makes man superior?

k. The Intellect.

From among the totality of men, how can a believer be considered superior to an unbeliever?

l. Through the Intellect.

Of all believers, how does a learned man have an advantage over devotees?

m. Through the Intellect.

Of all learned men, how does the righteous[10] man have an advantage over the (merely) erudite ones?

n. Through the Intellect.

Certainly, it is right to celebrate the worth of all that is bestowed upon you by your Master. He has perfected within you the image of Adam. He has provided you with a diamond more precious than all things. Through this gift, you are differentiated from beasts, from unbelievers, from ignorant people, and finally from wicked men. It is right that you

---

translated in this context into English as "Intellect," and indicates a supra-rational faculty with which only humans are invested at birth and which awaits full activation and unfolding to give access to the divine Truth that evades conventional reason. We believe that current usage and a need for clarity require that we translate the term in this section as "Intellect."

[10] That is, the good, the charitable person.

know the Lord who has done so much for you. Moreover, knowledge of Him is an obligation for you. When you know Him, then your two lives[11] will be full of happiness.

But if you scorn this gift, you will miss the goal of this life, and the next life will not be guaranteed for you.

    o.   It is through the Intellect that one maintains one's religion.

    p.   It is through the Intellect that the world is governed.

    q.   Without the Intellect, there is no religion.

    r.   Without the Intellect, there are no connections.[12]

5. Dedicate your Intellect to religion:

    s.   Material life will be pleasing for you.

6. (But) if you dedicate your Intellect to the material world:

    t.   You will run great risks (and)

    u.   You will bring harm to yourself,

    v.   Because you will be defying the Invincible.

Why?

Because of all that God has created, He prefers the Intellect (the Spirit), and of all that He has created, it is the material world that He most will leave to itself.

Now, He took that which He considers beyond all value and He entrusted it to you, so that you can use it and derive benefit from

---

[11] The life here below and that of the future.

[12] Editor's note: There is little context here to understand what is meant by these "connections." It might be noted, however, that our term "religion" itself derives from a root that means "to bind together." It may be that Tierno Bokar, after referring to the supra-rational Intelligence as the faculty that connects us to God by allowing us to understand formal religion, is now saying that it permits us to perceive and connect to God in other ways as well. It may also mean human "relations," that is, connections with other people.

it; but you, who are disobedient, will dedicate this treasure to that which He holds in the least esteem—to the temporal, to ephemeral acquisition.

    x.   You are therefore reckless.

    y.   You go astray.

    z.   May God help me, and you, too.

It is the Intellect that has led you to know:

7.   The Book (the Koran)

8.   The Tradition (the *Sunna*)

9.   Consensus (*Ijmā'*)

What is commanded by the Book? **7**[13]

It is commanded in the Book:

"O you who believe in God! Safeguard your souls and those of your kin from the fire."

Because of this, it is obligatory for each one to know himself, to behave according to the Divine Law (*Sharī'a*), and to assure that his family does the same.

Our Lord Ali[14] (may God have mercy upon him) said, "Teach your family[15] the precepts of good." This is the meaning of the verse cited above.

---

[13] Editor's note: This, and the following two sections, are numbered in this way to refer back to the main outline, namely to the categories "The Book," "The *Sunna*," and "Consensus."

[14] Son-in-law of the Prophet and ancestor of the *sharīfs*.

[15] This includes all of one's parents, children, and relatives.

Therefore, everyone has the divine mission of teaching his family theology,[16] ritual purification, and prayer. Only then will he be released from his responsibility vis-à-vis his family. There will be no reprimand for him on the day of the final Judgment.

What is commanded by the *Sunna* (Tradition)? **8**

It is written in the *Sunna* that "Each of you is a shepherd, and each shepherd is answerable for his flock."[17]

A head of state, the head of a city, the heads of families, and isolated individuals, all will have to provide an explanation. He who offers a clear and easy reckoning (to God) will receive a recompense which will take into account the number and importance of those who had been entrusted to him. The degree of this recompense will not lessen in any way the remuneration of those others themselves.

God (may He be exalted) will say to him who shepherds badly, "O bad shepherd! You have fed off of the flesh of your own kin, you have sucked out their milk until they can give no more, then you left them at the mercy of the hyenas. I entrusted you with the safeguarding of a few of my servants. You have enjoyed their services and you have not taught them their religion. You left them to Satan, who has led them astray." And the bad shepherd will endure a torment equal to the sum of the torments of all those whom he led astray. But this punishment will not decrease that of the subjects (i.e. those for whom he was responsible) themselves.

What does Consensus command? **9**

Consensus says:

"Insisting that others do good and forbidding them to do evil is an obligation for every believer."

---

[16] *Tawhīd*: everything related to the Oneness of God and His Attributes.

[17] *Hadīth* of the Prophet.

It is necessary, first of all, to insist that we ourselves do good, that we forbid every act of iniquity for ourselves, and then that we persevere in this. Then it is necessary to act in the same way with all our relatives and all those who willingly listen to us. It is clear that the person who orders others to do what he does not do himself will never be obeyed, nor will the person who forbids what he permits for himself be obeyed.

Now that you have heard what the Book, the Tradition, and Consensus have prescribed, look at the behavior of people and consider how well they measure up to these decrees nowadays. You will be forced to admit that our century is one of carelessness, a century in which we witness:

10. A decrease in the number of instructors (guides), and

11. An eclipse of true religious Knowledge.

Due to these things:

12. Religion is neglected.[18]

This makes ours one of the most terrifying of centuries. Wise people of all times have hoped that they would never have to see any such era during which:

13. People are not attracted to the Good,

14. They are not repulsed by evil,

15. The Truth has no impact (upon anyone or anything), and

16. Lies are not considered to be wrong.

---

[18] Literally, "going astray," abandoned, like someone who leaves the path and wanders aimlessly in the forest. This term is used for something which, once its proper station of importance has been lost, can no longer be recognized.

One who lives in such a miserable time lives in sadness and worry. For us who live in these times, may God:

a. Watch over us,
b. Liberate us,
c. Help us,
d. Protect us,
e. And make us triumph over the traps of these times.

Nevertheless, despite all appearances and the corruption of the times, the decrees of the Book, of the Tradition, and of the Consensus remain pure and immutable. Anyone who lets himself be seduced by the attractions of the world will be lost through his own actions, unless he receives secret assistance from God (exalted be He!).

People only have to recall that there were times more depraved than our own which then passed away, in order for them to be comforted by the certainty that only the Divine Truth is permanent. Such people will follow the decrees of the three sources.[19] They will abandon the world to what the Supreme Will has set for it.

In conclusion, there are only two kinds of paths on this earth, leading to two abodes:

17. The abode of *Qarārin* (eternal), or

18. The abode of *Bawārin* (perishable).

The *Qarārin* is an abode of stability and tranquility.
The *Bawārin* is an abode of ruin and eternal perdition.

When God created Paradise, he said to the angels, "Go and look. I have created something."

---

[19] Koran, Tradition, and Consensus.

The angels went to see and then came back jubilant: "O excellent Master! We have contemplated Paradise. Never have we seen such an agreeable abode."

God (may He be exalted!) said to them, "Go back and look."

Before the angels were able to get there, God surrounded Paradise with a circle made up of what the soul dislikes most.

The angels saw the place and were overcome. They came back to God and said, "O excellent Master! We have found Paradise enclosed in a circle of trials impossible to get through without the aid of Thy Magnanimity."

God said to them, "Go, I have created something else."

The angels went back to the place. There they found hell: dark, gloomy, foul, the very manifestation of ultimate punishment. They were very grieved over it. Then they returned.

"O Master!" said the angels, "We have seen hell. Never have we seen such a terrifying place. Whoever sees hell will make sure that he will never enter it."

God said to them, "Go back and look."

The angels went back and found hell encircled by irresistible pleasures. They returned to God and said, "Excellent Master! We have visited hell; but so desirable and attractive are the pleasures along its borders that none will escape this precipice without your Divine assistance."

The Prophet of God said: "Paradise is surrounded by a circle of painful trials and hell by a circle of appealing pleasures."

We can infer from this that the decrees

of the Book, **7**

of the Tradition, **8**

and of Consensus **9**

make up the difficult trials that surround Paradise. The easy pleasures of life are the things that circumscribe hell.

And you, Neophyte, thanks to

your INTELLECT, **4**

you have been able to judge and guide your deductions to these three conclusions:

(1) No matter how rigorous the trials surrounding Paradise may be, the torments of hell (**18**) are more terrifying and longer lasting.

(2) No matter how pleasurable the things surrounding hell may be, Paradise (**17**) is more pleasurable and longer lasting.

(3) Finally, undergoing a momentary trial (**17**) that is compensated with eternal bliss is more advantageous than a momentary joy (**18**)[20] followed by perpetual torment.

So, say to yourself: "From now on I am only interested in my salvation. I act on nobody's behalf but my own. I cannot, nor should I, impose anything on anyone. As for myself, I have decided to put into practice the decrees of the Book, of Tradition, and of Consensus, until my death."

If you agree, then listen, my friend: Do not delude yourself. Know that above all, and this fact is well known, that whoever proposes to live in conformity with the decrees of the Book, of Tradition, and of Consensus, chooses the life of a prisoner.

Why?

---

[20] Whenever Tierno Bokar would mention a word already marked on the diagram, he would go back and place his finger on the corresponding point.

Because the Prophet of God has said, "The life of the world is a prison for the believer and a paradise for the unbeliever."

You are going to undertake the conquest of religious knowledge beginning with the Koran.

19. Learn the first sixtieth (of the Koran). In the absence of this, then the knowledge of the following eleven *sūra*s will, for the most part, be sufficient: 1, and 105-114.

20. Learn the concepts of theology (*Tawhīd*), even if it were only the esoteric meaning of the *Shahāda*.[21] This knowledge is indispensable and it is sufficient, for the most part.

21. Learn about the requirements for the ritual purification, and finally,

22. Get yourself initiated into Sufism.

This initiation will help you understand the true stature of our Lord Muhammad. You will come to know how his remarkable life on earth unfolded, the true meaning of his teaching, and the scope of his social and religious reforms.

As for the material world, our Lord Muhammad compared it to a rubbish heap and a decaying carcass, and those who covet it to dogs.

Therefore, once you are familiar with the example of our Prophet, it will be easy for you to guard yourself against worldly temptations despite your worldly desires.

---

[21] *Shahāda*: literally, bearing witness, the Muslim declaration of faith. The first part is: "I bear witness that there is no god but God, Who is unique and without associate," and the second: "and I bear witness that Muhammad is His servant and His messenger."

Second Lesson

Mā 'd-Dīn[1]

Cissé smoothed out the sand, pressed a point into it, and said, "Ask me questions." Antiamba asked questions and Cissé responded:[2]

9. *What is religion?* Religion is a way (a path).

8. *How many ways have there been?* There have been seventy-three.

7. *What is their standing?* The first seventy-two are ways of error.

6. Only the seventy-third is the path of rectitude,

5. the sole path that leads to God.

4. From our father Adam until our Lord Muhammad, all have followed the same path:

3. It is called ISLĀM.[3]

2. It is the path of deliverance.

1. It is the way of salvation, the way of the *Hanafiyya*.[4]

---

[1] Literally: "What is religion?"

[2] See the diagram on p. 182.

[3] The word *Islām* means literally "submission to God," total acceptance of His will. The word here not only designates the historical religion revealed in Mecca, but also the immutable primordial Religion, the eternal submission to God by all who have been devoted to worshiping Him since Adam.

[4] *Hanīfs* (the pure ones): a name given to certain men of God who lived in the desert before the historical appearance of Islam and who dedicated themselves to the worship of the one God. It is supposed that *Hanīfs* have always existed. In Islam, Abraham is considered one of the greatest of the *Hanīfs*. The *Hanafiyya* is therefore the way of pure, eternal Religion, the way of worshiping God for Himself.

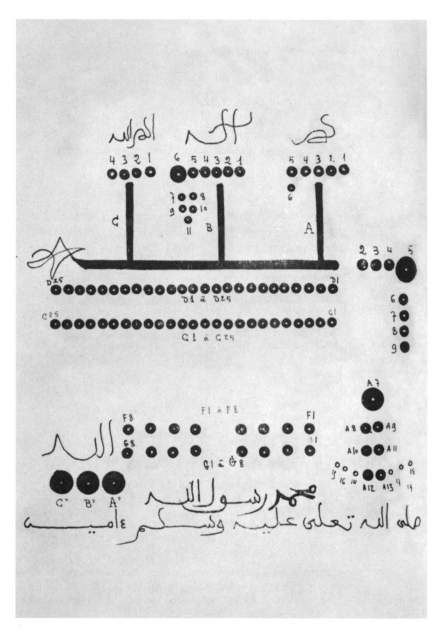

What is Religion (*Mā'd-Dīn*)?

Upon what is this path built? It is built upon three pillars, which are:

A. ISLĀM (submission to God)

B. ĪMĀN (faith)

C. IHSĀN (faultless conduct)

What does Islām ***consist of?***
  Islām includes five obligatory actions. *What are they?*
  They are:
  A1. The articulation of the double formula of faith, without which no act is valid: "I bear witness that there is no god but God, Who is unique and without associate; I bear witness that Muhammad is His servant and His messenger."
  A2. The performance of the five daily prayers.
  A3. The payment of *zakāt* (the annual tithe intended for the poor).
  A4. The fast during the month of Ramadan.
  A5. The pilgrimage to the sacred House, to Mecca.
  A6. As for the pilgrimage, it is required only of those able to accomplish it.[5]
  These are the fundamental dogmas of the degree of *Islām* (resignation, submission to God).

What does Īmān ***consist of?***
  Īmān consists of belief in six principles:
  B1. God,
  B2. the Last Judgment,
  B3. the Angels,
  B4. the revealed Books,[6]
  B5. the Prophets of God,[7]

---

[5] That is, for the person who has the physical and material means to accomplish it.

[6] A Muslim must believe in the books which had been revealed by God before the revelation of the Koran. See pp. 132-134.

[7] A Muslim must also believe in the prophets that God sent to earth before the

B6. and in the decree of God.

B7. Whether this decree brings something pleasing
B8. or painful,
B9. pleasing, such as having a good son,
B10. or painful, such as a union with a bad spouse,
B11. in both cases one must believe that everything comes to us from God.

What does Ihsān *(faultless behavior) consist of?*
C1. worshiping God
C2. as if you see Him,
C3. for even if you do not see Him,
C4. He sees[8] you.[9]

Antiamba continued, "I have asked you about the paths. You told me that there are seventy-three. You have chosen one of them and have affirmed that it is the only true one leading directly to God. You told me that this path is built upon three pillars: *ISLĀM, ĪMĀN* and *IHSĀN*. I have learned that each of these pillars is made up of acts and principles. Of these, *Islām* includes five, *Īmān* six, and *Ihsān* four. Be patient Cissé, I am a novice. It is very important for me to question you so that I can clarify my knowledge."

The ever-obliging Cissé said to him, "Question me as you wish. I will hide from you nothing of what I know."

"What," said Antiamba, "is the esoteric teaching of the double formula of the testimony of faith, the *Shahāda*?"

Prophet Muhammad and must grant them similar respect. Their names are preceded by the same formula, *Sayyidna* (our Lord) and followed by the same salutation: "Upon him blessings and peace."

[8] It is a question of living in the certitude that we are always under His watchful gaze, a certitude which leads to the very real consciousness of God's permanent Presence. These four points regarding *Ihsān* are taken from a *hadīth* of the Prophet.

[9] The perfection of one's *Islām* is, of course, when one reunites these three levels, the last two being contained as potentialities within the first.

Cissé first placed his finger on the point for ISLĀM (A1) and then moved his finger down to make a new point (A7) in order to explain:

A7. The Creator has performed two miracles for you:

A8. He gave you life.

A9. He developed it in you.

Man is obliged to bear witness to this.

Each of these manifestations of the Divine has its appointed time.

A10. God shapes man in his mother's womb and through His power sustains life there for the prescribed term.

A11. Then He causes the infant to see the light of day through birth. And He aids the infant through His actions until the completion of his growth.

A12. At an age chosen by Him, He endows him with a Spirit (Intellect)[10] and imposes duties upon man.

A13. The first act, before any other duty, is the articulation of the formula of the profession of faith (*Shahāda*).

The scholars have affirmed that whoever is unaware of the esoteric teaching of the *Shahāda* will in no way enjoy the (full) privileges attached to *Islām*:

What is the hidden teaching of the Shahāda?

It is knowledge of God.

What can one know of God?

That which one can know of God is not tangible.

One can know THREE STATES of God:

A14. That which is necessary for Him,

A15. That which is impossible for Him,

A16. That which is contingent for Him (i.e. what is possible, or what He may choose to do or not do).

What is necessary for God?

Twenty-five attributes are necessary for God:

D1. existence,

---

[10] Translator's note: We have chosen to translate the French *Esprit* here as "Spirit." The word can also mean "mind." The word in parentheses in the original is *Raison*, which we have once again chosen to translate here as "Intellect."

D2. eternity,

D3. possession,

D4. transcendence,

D5. independence (i.e. self-sufficiency),

D6. oneness,

D7. power,

D8. will,

D9. knowledge,

D10. life,

D11. hearing,

D12. vision,

D13. speech,

D14. to be powerful,

D15. to exercise will,

D16. to be omniscient (all-knowing),

D17. to be living,

D18. to be hearing,

D19. to be seeing,

D20. to be speaking,

D21. to be without need,

D22. to be without obligation to act,

D23. to be free of any obligation,

D24. to be free of any custom (habit),

D25. to be the cause of all creation.[11]

What is impossible for God?

Twenty-five attributes are impossible with respect to God:

E1. non-existence,

E2. [to have a] beginning,

E3. envy,

E4. similarity (to created things),

E5. need [of something other than Himself],

E6. existence of an equal to Him (or anything like Him),

E7. poverty,

E8. necessity (i.e. to act through constraint),

E9. ignorance,

E10. death,

---

[11] These attributes are all taken from the Koran.

E11. deafness,

E12. blindness,

E13. muteness,

E14. insufficiency (that He be impotent or weak),

E15. constraint,

E16. that He be ignorant,

E17. that He be inanimate,

E18. that He be deaf,

E19. that He be blind,

E20. that He be mute,

E21. that He have need of anything,

E22. that He be compelled to act,

E23. that He be constrained by anything,

E24. that He be bound by custom (habit),

E25. that His existence came after that of creation.

What is contingent for God?

For God contingency constitutes a kind of middle way between the necessary and the impossible attributes. The contingent can either exist (like the necessary) or not exist (like the impossible). For example, the decision for God to create or to leave something in nothingness is contingent.[12]

The twenty-five necessary attributes plus the twenty-five impossible attributes make up the fifty articles of the hidden teaching of the first part of the *Shahāda*: "I bear witness that there is no god but God, Who is unique and without associate."

What, therefore, is the esoteric teaching of the second part: "I bear witness that Muhammad is the Servant and the Messenger of God"?

It is the knowledge of the Prophets.[13]

How can one know the Prophets?

---

[12] That is why the "contingent" (or "potential") does not figure in the Table, except in the form of a void that separates the "D" and "E" lines from the attributes. (p.xxx)

[13] The Prophet Muhammad here typifies the entirety of all the other Prophets sent by God.

The Prophets are recognized by THREE STATES:

A17. by what is necessary for them,

A18. by what is impossible for them,

A19. by what is contingent for them.

What is necessary for the Prophets and what is impossible for them?

Necessary for the Prophets are:

F1. Faith,

F2. Truthfulness,

F3. Transmission (making known the message of God).

As a result, what is impossible for them are:

G1. disbelief,

G2. treachery,

G3. deceit.

What is contingent for the Prophets?

F4. Prophets are subject to human contingencies;

G4. it is therefore impossible for them to be above human contingencies.

What does the faith of the Prophets consist of?

It consists of their belief in:

F5. the previous Prophets,

F6. the angels,

F7. the revealed Books,

F8. the Day of Judgment.

Therefore, it is impossible for the Prophets to deny:

G5. the previous Prophets,

G6. the angels,

G7. the revealed Books,

G8. the Day of Judgment.

The sum of what is necessary, impossible, and contingent for the Prophets, added to their articles of faith, makes up the sixteen articles of the esoteric teaching[14] of the second formula of the profession of

---

[14] Throughout this lesson, that which is called "esoteric" in fact merely constitutes "doorways" to esoterism. It is a preliminary approach destined to be subsequently deepened over time both by thorough teaching and experience. Each attribute mentioned can be expanded much further. For example, *wujūd*, which is translated as "being" or "existence" (D1) not only includes the existence of the Supreme, Absolute

faith: "I bear witness that Muhammad is the Servant and the Messenger of God."

We have related the scholars' assertion: "Whoever does not possess knowledge of the hidden teaching of the double formula of the profession of faith, pronounces it to no effect." Now, whoever pronounces it without effect is not a believer, and the unbeliever is not on the path toward salvation.

It is a source of happiness for us to know—and we thank God for it—that the teaching of the *Shahāda* consists of FIFTY articles for the first formula and SIXTEEN for the second, totaling 66.[15]

May God, Who has enabled us to know these sixty-six points, cause us to utter the *Shahāda* at the moment of our death, as the last act of our life, Amen.

Being, but also the existence of contingent beings, their relationships with the Supreme Being, and their relationships among themselves. Each being, in fact, not only exists in itself, but also in relation to other contingent beings and above all through this relation with its Creator. Therefore, the esoteric aspect of *wujūd* includes both the mystery of the communion between the One and the multiple (between the Creator and His creatures) as well as the mystery of the secret communion and interrelatedness of contingent beings among themselves, united by the One that contains all. We plan to go into more depth in future publications on the subject of this teaching that was given to us by Tierno Bokar.

[15] The interest of this number 66 is that it corresponds to the numerical value of the great name of God (ALLĀH), according to so-called "maghrebi" numerology of the Arabic letters: Alif = 1, Lam = 30, Hā = 5. Knowledge of the *Shahāda* is therefore linked to the knowledge of God.

Third Lesson

A Synthesis of the Esoteric Teachings
Sharī'a Bātiniyya (Inner Law) [1]

a. Sufism

The following teachings are those of the Sufis. Indeed, the Prophet of God—upon him be blessings and peace!—came into the Universe with a teaching comprised of three degrees in order to satisfy all types of religious aspiration. They are:

The Law (divine)	(Sharī'a)
The Way	(Tarīqa)
The Truth	(Haqīqa)[2]

At the level of the Law, the religion is built upon three pillars: Islām, Īmān, and Ihsān.

The teaching that has been elaborated at this level is that of the 'ulamā', or doctors of the outer Law (Sharī'a). Above them are the Sufis, caretakers of an inner, initiatic form of worship. Their concept of Religion is vast, rational,[3] and universal.

---

[1] Editor's note: The subtitle in French is Sharī'a bathénienne. Because there is no context to aid in determining the meaning of bathénienne, which is a word borrowed from another language, we assume that it is a transliteration of the Arabic word for "inner" or "hidden," bātin.

[2] The word Haqīqa bears the double meaning of truth and reality. It is real Truth or true Reality. It is not a question here of a simply intellectual concept, but of a spiritual Reality. It is the direct knowledge of "that which is" above all intellectual formulations or representations, however elevated they may be.

[3] "Rational" in the sense that in the Way one can discuss, seek to better understand, and to deepen, whereas in the Sharī'a discussion is not permitted: one submits to the Law or one is excluded by it. In a tarīqa (i.e. a Sufi order) one can disagree with one's shaykh, and even leave him, without that removing anything of one's status as a Muslim. One could define the tarīqa as being the Way of deepening, of comprehension,

The first point to bear in mind is that the representatives of the outer way and the representatives of the inner way do not contradict one another at all. They both recognize each other's orthodoxy. The only difference between them is that the teaching of the *'ulamā'* is suited for the comprehension of the masses of people, while that of the Sufis is addressed to a minority.[4]

In fact, when Muhammad was chosen to transmit and reveal the precepts of Divine Unity, the faithful understood and imitated him in a variety of ways, each according to his own aptitude for understanding, and capacity for assimilation. It is thus that the *'ulamā'* found in the Koranic message a Law that served as a touchstone in their religious quest, and that permitted them to arrive at an encounter with the sublime. However, pursued in this way, the path is long and the pace slow. As for the essence of this Law, the *'ulamā'* and Sufis share the same opinion in respect to it. There are no divergences between them on this subject.

The most perceptive[5] and observant Sufis reflected on our Lord Muhammad's manner of being. They were struck by the scant attention that he gave to the present life. So they viewed the contingent world as being of lesser importance and decided to imitate the great Prophet in renouncing it. They followed his example of self-sacrifice. They acted with the sole objective of pleasing God and not in the calculated hope of recompense, whatever its nature might be.

Thus, the Sufis prepared themselves for struggle and carried out three wars on three overlapping levels:

> They battled against their souls (against themselves: *nafs*).
> They battled against Satan.
> They battled against the world.

---

and of knowledge, while the *Sharī'a* is the Way of faithfulness and obedience. It goes without saying that the two Ways do not exclude one another, but rather complement one another.

[4] The history of Islam has known and continues to know *'ulamā'* who are scholars of both "outer" and "inner" knowledge.

[5] Literally, the most "awakened."

In emerging victorious from this triple battle, they followed in the footsteps of the Prophet, keeping in mind the Koranic verse, "If you love God, follow me. God will love you" (3:31).

It is easy to understand that the spiritual subtlety of a Sufi initiate might not be satisfied by dogmas that are intended to awaken, catechize, and discipline the masses of believers. The Sufis marked out a path whose many levels do not lead to some paradise or other, but to God Himself, the Essence of everything.

The representatives of the outer law teach that *Islām* imposes upon the believer five obligatory acts, that *Īmān* demands six acts of faith, and that *Ihsān* implies four conditions.

The Sufis also acknowledge *Islām*, *Īmān* and *Ihsān*, but they envisage them according to a more profound definition. While accepting that the *'ulamā'* are correct in their interpretations of *Islām*, *Īmān*, and *Ihsān*, the Sufis believe that the entire religion consists of three successive degrees that correspond to the three stages of *Islām*, *Īmān*, and *Ihsān*:[6]

A'. *Taqlīd*: behavior by simple imitation,
B'. *Nazar*: comprehension of the principles (literally, "to see"),
C'. *Dhawq*: experience (literally "to taste," that is, to feel, absorb, assimilate, "become one" with).

Each of these degrees includes three states:

A' 1. Repentance (or "conversion") (*tawba*)
   2. Uprightness (*istiqāma*)
   3. Reverential fear (*taqwā*)
B' 1. Discernment (*ikhlās*)
   2. Sincerity (*siduq*)
   3. Serenity (*tumānina*)

---

[6] See points A', B' and C' on the diagrams on pages 182 and 193.

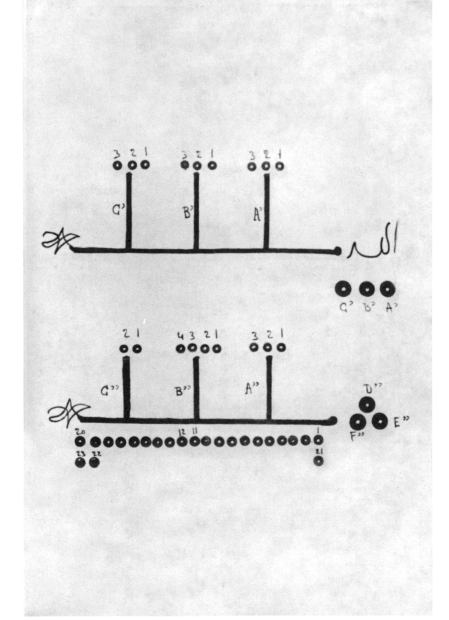

Sharī'a Bātiniyya (Inner Law)

The Canon of the 'Ulamā'	Tierno Bokar's Image	Sufi Initiation		
Islām Submission to the five pillars of faith (see p. 183)	**The Peel** Tangible appearance, Corporality	**Shari'a (Law)** Bestows the faith of obedience	or	**Taqlīd** (behavior through simple imitation) Three degrees: — conversion — rectitude — reverential fear (desire to progress, fear of not being able to; feeling of one's smallness and of one's helplessness before the Divine Majesty)
Īmān Faith in the six points of the dogma (see pp. 183-184)	**The Flesh (Pith)** Vivifying nourishment, Sensation Comprehension	**Tarīqa (Way)** Bestows the faith of knowledge	or	**Nazar** (comprehension of the principles) Three degrees: — discernment (spiritual sensation submitted to the analysis of Intellect-Mind which God has deposited in us, to permit us to discern the successive degrees and not to fall into illusion) (see note 12, pp. 197-198) — sincerity — serenity
Ihsān Supreme goal: perfect behavior: "Worship God as if you saw Him, for if you do not see Him, He sees you." (see p. 184)	**The Kernel** Spirit, Perfect comprehension, Sublimation of faith	**Haqīqa (Truth, essential Reality)** Leads to the faith of certitude	or	**Dhawq (taste)** (inner experience, assimilation) Three degrees: — perceptive meditation (seeing, witnessing) — face-to-face (Presence) — Knowledge/Love

Three Planes of the Spiritual Journey

C'1. Perceptive meditation (*mushāhada*)[7]
  2. Encountering the Presence (*murāqaba*)
  3. Knowledge of God and Love (*ma'rifa*)[8]

These nine states can only be acquired in succession. One is only able to rejoice in the knowledge of God after the encounter (with the Presence). One is only able to rejoice in the Presence after perceptive meditation, in perceptive meditation only after serenity, in serenity only after sincerity, in sincerity only after discernment, in discernment only after reverential fear, in reverential fear (awe) only after uprightness, in uprightness only after repentance.

Thus, everything depends on repentance.[9] It is the first and essential condition for the acquisition of all future states.

The third state of each stage is, at the same time, the upper degree of the first two and the compensation for the effort exerted to accomplish them. For example, the state of "Knowledge of God" is at the highest point of meditation and the direct encounter with the Presence (of God), and, at the same time, the compensation for the effort exerted to get to this state.

From the day of repentance, the adept's objective is the C'3 state: Love-Knowledge.

There are many other stages and degrees, but they are too vast and transcendent to describe here. These stages are reserved for a select few, even for *the elite of the elite*. Anyone familiar with the vastness of the domain of the spirit will not be shocked by this affirmation.

---

[7] *Mushāhadat*: the term means both "truthful vision," and "witnessing," "to witness."

[8] Knowledge and Love are like the front and back of a round straw mat. [Ed: That is, they are indistinguishable because they are made of the same substance.] That is why they are counted as only one point (C'3) and included within the one term, *ma'rifa* (knowledge).

[9] Translator's note: or, turning towards God.

The journey from initial repentance to reaching the knowledge of God is the great mystical journey upon which Sufis embark. The outward symbol of this journey is the pilgrimage to Mecca which every believer should accomplish at least once in his lifetime, if he meets the required conditions.

These are the nine stations of the way towards God; they constitute the all-powerful and benevolent inner Way.

Therefore, we can conclude that:

> *Islām* (submission) corresponds, for the Sufis, to the degree of *Sharī'a* (Law), which brings about a faith based upon acceptance.

> *Īmān* (faith) corresponds, for the Sufis, to the degree of *Tarīqa* (Way) which brings about a faith based upon knowledge.

> *Ihsān* (perfect behavior or character) corresponds, for the Sufis, to the degree of *Haqīqa* (Truth), which allows one to reach, through direct contemplation, a faith based upon certitude.

There is mystery in these three Ways. The great Prophets and the true initiates of all religions know this. Those who are ignorant of it should keep silent. Let us pray for them.

The Prophet said, "For the one who is aware of the limits of his own knowledge, God will facilitate the acquisition of another knowledge, one even more profound, and more divine. . . ."

*　*　*　*　*

It seems opportune for me to step back in[10] and share some reflections relating to the first two lessons.

---

[10] Editor's note: In the following section, the author, Amadou Hampaté Bâ, departs from directly reporting the teachings of Tierno Bokar and now returns to writing his own comments.

In one of his commentaries on the *Mā 'd-dīn*, Tierno said, speaking of the spiritual journey, "The neophyte will discover these riches like one who successively discovers the peel, then the flesh, then the seeds of the fruit." Therefore, this progression is presented in a systematic way in the table on page 194.

The progression ascends naturally. The Sufi stages are considered to be a degree above the corresponding stages in the canon of the *'ulamā'*. It should be understood that this canon is presumably always known and reached before getting to the corresponding Sufi degree.

The three planes of this in-depth search correspond to what was said above about the "three mystical lights" and the "three forms of faith." The initiate who merely touches the peel is only animated by *sulb* (solid) faith; he who bites into the pulp of the mystical fruit attains to the *sa'il* faith (liquid); finally, he whose faith is purified and elevated to the point of becoming *ghāzi*, touches the kernel.

This symbol of the fruit can lead to further insights. As Tierno explained to us, the flesh of the fruit can only be used once. It is eaten and nothing remains of it; one must look for another fruit. The seed should not be eaten but planted in the earth. It then germinates and, producing a plant that has new seeds, it perpetuates itself and multiplies.

Having reached a particular "state" (*hāl*), one often becomes satisfied with the illusion of having reached the goal, of having "arrived" somewhere. In a certain respect, one is nourished by this, one "eats" it as one would eat the flesh of a fruit, forgetting that the flesh is there only to lead to the kernel. It may happen that one touches the kernel. But it is necessary to remember that in order to bear fruit, the kernel must not be eaten, possessed, nor placed in view with other kernels on a shelf. Its sole calling is to be buried deeply in the earth, unseen and impersonal, and to germinate there in secret without any outward sign through which one might seek to gain glory or satisfaction for oneself. So that the seed may bear fruit, it is necessary, in a way, to renounce it.[11]

The way which is then opened up is a way of divestment and renunciation. The *makarou* (illusion, mirage[12]) always lying in waiting,

[11] "If the grain does not die. . . ." (New Testament).

[12] It is the faculty of discernment (*ikhlās*) which allows one to perceive the limits of

suggests[13] to our soul: "You are wasting your time, go back and bite into the flesh of the fruit!" It is at this moment that one must stop listening to one's ego, one's *nafs*, which is always hungry to be more, but to listen instead to one's deepest Intellect, which can become clearer to us through prayer and *ilhām* (inspiration).

Tierno used to say: "Once the seed is put into the earth, with what water should it be watered? With the water of our good works, of our repentances, of our meditations, and of our prayers. When it germinates and produces a tree, we must still be patient[14] until the tree itself bears fruit. Then we will discover that we have gained back everything that we had given up, because not only do we receive fruit but, in this fruit, we find seeds to produce as many trees as there are pieces of fruit."

Did God not say (in the Koran 2:261), in comparing man to a seed, that He would multiply his good actions by seven, then by one hundred, then by two?

The path that corresponds to the kernel is the path of renunciation: total renunciation of the rewards given for our acts or for our good actions. It is renunciation of the "results" of our efforts. It is thus said in all the traditions: "It is the effort that benefits a man, not the result."[15] Moreover, this concept is the basis of *tawakkul* (abandonment to the will of God), which is not at all some passive fatalism, but rather detachment in regard to our effort because the result is actually in the hands of God. It is for man to act, using all of his faculties, but then to keep his heart serene concerning the outcome of his actions.

---

these spiritual "states" when experiencing one of them, and to perform the "letting go," the release, necessary to raise oneself (or to purify oneself) even further. The word *ikhlās* also carries with it the idea of purity. On the other hand, anything that stops one along the way so that one may rejoice in having "attained" something is "the illusion," the mirage (*makarou*) which distracts one from God. [Ed: The author may be referring here to the Arabic word *makr*, whose meaning for some Sufis has been given as "ruse," in the sense of a snare set for an over-inflated ego.]

[13] In the last *Sūra* of the Koran (114) Satan is called the "suggester" (*waswas*), "he who suggests [breathes] evil into the breasts of men [and then furtively steals away]."

[14] God says in the Koran, "I am with those who are patient" (2:153).

[15] From which comes the spiritual danger of a systematic quest for spiritual states, of "results," even for miracles, by means of various techniques which often comfort the ego more than they help it to scrutinize itself.

The sacrifice of the son of Abraham, which is frequently mentioned in the Koran, calls for our reflection here while we are still on the subject of renunciation. Arriving late in Abraham's life, his beloved son was the fruit of the Divine promise and the harbinger of a posterity to come. In spite of all of this, when God asked Abraham in a vision to sacrifice his son, Abraham accepted without hesitation, reckoning that nothing belonged to him. And because Abraham submitted willingly, not only was the child saved but the child became the source of an innumerable posterity.

On the spiritual plane—and perhaps on many other human planes as well—it is active and serene renunciation that presents the fruits, frees up energy, and opens doors in accordance with a process which is not from man, but from God.

This division of the spiritual progression into three fundamental stages, which was adopted by Tierno Bokar, is very common in all Sufi teachings of all times, either in the same form or using other symbols.

Tierno often used another image. He used to say:

There are three ways to know a river: First of all, there is the man who has heard the river spoken about and becomes capable by imitation and repetition to describe it without having seen it himself. This is the first degree of knowledge.

Then there is the man who has undertaken the journey and who has arrived at the banks of the river. Seated on the banks of the river, he contemplates it with his own eyes and is a witness to its majesty. This is the second degree of knowledge.

Finally, there is the man who throws himself into the river and becomes one with it. This is the supreme degree of Knowledge.

The third lesson continues with further detail on the "Tijani Way." Let us return to Cissé.

b. The Tijani Way

There was a secret reason why Muhammad was made the Seal of the Prophets, such that he appeared only after the prophets who were his precursors. Each of these received, in accordance with the places and circumstances of each manifestation, a revealed Law and taught to all beings the existence of the one God.

When it became part of the design of the Creator to close the cycle of prophecy, He delegated this function to Muhammad. He revealed to him the Koran, a hermetic summary of all the previous revelations and religions.

Muhammad summoned people to the Path of rectitude. His reforms accomplished an unprecedented miracle in the history of religions. Among those who followed him were a series of *Imāms* (spiritual guides) who appeared over the passage of time. One of those who received the mission to guide the Muslim community was the Shaykh al-Tijani, who established one of the most eclectic of ways because it represents the summit, or the quintessence, of all the *turuq* (plural of *tarīqa*) which had come before it since the emergence of Islam.[16]

During one of his spiritual retreats, the founder of the Tijani *Tarīqa* was honored in 1196 of the Hijra (1782) with the very holy appari- tion of the Prophet Muhammad. He received from him the secret and mystical gift of being able to comment on the mysterious passages of the Koran, the *Sunna*, and the teachings of the *'ulamā'* and other Sufi *shaykhs*.[17]

---

[16] In fact, before receiving his particular mission, Shaykh al-Tijani had been initiated into all of the *turuq* of his time. In each one, he had received the rank of *shaykh*. There- fore, he thus had the right not only to transmit the initiation of each of these *turuq*, as a *muqaddam* does, but also the right to name *muqaddams*. He thus had within himself the convergence of all the spiritual currents that had been deployed since the time of the Prophet through the various *turuq* (at least for Sunni Islam). During the vision he had of the Prophet, the Prophet had said to him. "From this moment, you are exempt from the authority of all the other *shaykhs*. I am your spiritual master." (See Appendix II on Sufi brotherhoods.)

[17] In effect, the Shaykh had the gift of access to the most profound meanings of sacred texts and also of making them accessible to those who listened to him.

This mission makes Shaykh al-Tijani a Pole, a great figure of Islam. Within Islam, his *tarīqa* plays the role that Islam plays among all religions.[18] This is to say that the founder of the Tijaniyya occupies among the saints the place that Muhammad occupies among the Prophets.

Furthermore, when we speak of "the *Tarīqa*" we mean the *tarīqa* of Shaykh Ahmad al-Tijani. And if we speak about it, it is not because it is ours, but because it presents a perfect analogy with the three pillars of the teaching of the *'ulamā'* and the Sufis.

In fact, the *Tijani Tarīqa*, just as the teachings of the *'ulamā'* and the Sufis, is built upon three pillars:

A". LĀZIM
B". WAZĪFA
C". TAHLĪL[19]

The *Lāzim*[20] is composed of three recitations:
A"1. 100 times the formula *Astaghfiru 'Llāh* ("I ask forgiveness of God"),
A"2. 100 times the *Salāt al-Fātih* (the Opening Prayer):
> O God! Pour out Your grace and peace upon our Lord Muhammad,
> He who opens that which was shut,
> Who seals that which came before,
> Who makes truth triumph through the Truth,
> And who guides on the path of rectitude (the straight path);
> And (pour out Your grace) on his family,
> According to the measure due to them,
> An immense (measure).

---

[18] For Muslims, Islam, which is the last "revealed religion" of our time, recapitulates and contains within it the principles and values of all previous religions. Similarly, for Tijanis, the Tijaniyya (Sufi order) recapitulates the virtues of previous *turuq*. Because it is also the last *tarīqa* to appear, it corresponds to the conditions of our time.

[19] All of these together constitute the *wird* particular to the *Tarīqa Tijaniyya*. See the diagram on p. 193.

[20] The *Lāzim* should be recited twice a day: in the afternoon, and in the morning before the call to the dawn prayer. It represents a first level (or stage).

A"3. 100 times *Lā ilāha illa 'Llāh* ("there is no god but God").

The *Wazīfa*[21] is composed of four recitations:
B"1. 30 times the formula:
Astaghfiru 'Llāh al-azīm, alladhī lā ilāha illa Hu, al-Hayyu al-Qayyūm
"I ask forgiveness of God, the Immense, He beside Whom there is no other god, the Living, the Eternal."[22]
B"2. 50 times the *Salāt al-Fātih* (indicated in A"),
B"3. 100 times the formula: *Lā ilāha illa 'Llāh* ("there is no god but God"),
B"4. 11 or 12 times the prayer *Jawharat al-kamāl* (*The Pearl of Perfection*).[23]

The *Tahlīl*[24] is composed of two recitations which, from an esoteric point of view, are but one:
C"1. 1000 times the formula *Lā ilāha illa 'Llāh*,
C"2. 600 times the sacred Name: *ALLĀH*.[25]

---

[21] The *Wazīfa* represents a second level (or stage). It should be recited along with the *Lāzim*, before the morning prayer, and optionally, after the evening prayer.

[22] This last word, *al-Qayyūm* is extremely difficult to translate. It is a word derived from the Arabic root *qa-'a-ma*, "to stand up," "to remain standing by one's own equilibrium," having the idea of equilibrium between the vertical and the horizontal. *Al-Qayyūm* (a name given only to God), is therefore He who is maintained by Himself, forever, without depending on any cause and by Whom everything is maintained. This explains why it is sometimes translated as "the Eternal" as is done by some Arabists. But it goes without saying that the content of the word is more complex.

[23] See Appendix II.

[24] The *Tahlīl* is only recited on Friday, before sunset, usually in a group; but it can also be recited alone at home. When it is recited in a group, the number of invocations can be unlimited.

[25] The three pillars of the Tijaniyya (*Lāzim, Wazīfa, Tahlīl*) correspond analogically to the three levels on the table on page 194. This table can therefore be completed in the following way:

Canon of the 'Ulamā'	Sufi Teaching	Tijani Way
Islām	*Sharī'a – Taqlīd*	*Lāzim*
Īmān	*Tarīqa – Nazar*	*Wazīfa*
Ihsān	*Haqīqa – Dhawq*	*Tahlīl*

We have seen in the section dealing with *Islām* that the act of pronouncing the double profession of faith is not in itself a sufficient basis for being a Muslim—one must also understand its profound teaching. In the same way, the mere act of reciting litanies and fingering a Tijani rosary does not suffice to make someone a true Tijani follower.

Affiliation to the Tijani order is subject to three conditions:
D". Orthodoxy of the chain,[26]
E". Ordination (initiation),
F". Respect for the regulations.

The 23 requirements which follow must be respected by every Tijani disciple. The first 21 are obligatory. They make up the statutes of the Tijaniyya. He who breaks his obligation in regard to these 21 requirements must renew his affiliation (vows).

A Tijani disciple must know:

1. That a *muqaddam* who bestows the affiliation must be given his function by the founding *shaykh* [i.e. Shaykh Ahmad al-Tijani] or by one of his acknowledged representatives.[27]
2. That the seeker must free himself from having to obey any other *tarīqa*.[28]
3. That it is absolutely forbidden to invoke the intercession of any saint foreign to the *Tarīqa*, living or dead, but that all the saints must be honored and respected.[29]

---

[26] This refers to the chain of transmission that we have spoken of throughout this book, a chain that must go back to the founder of the Tijaniyya and, through him, back to the Prophet himself.

[27] A *muqaddam* can only be designated by a *shaykh*.

[28] This article, which has often been misunderstood, does not at all mean that there can be no salvation outside of the Tijaniyya, or that this way is the only valid one. It is a question of encouraging the novice to concentrate fully on one discipline only, for he who tries to hold too much will lose his grip. [Translator's note: One who disperses himself does nothing well.]

[29] This article has also been much misunderstood. First of all it is necessary to understand the notion of intercession. This word is used for lack of a more appropriate word. In fact, the intercession of saints is not permitted in Islam. One should petition

4. That male disciples must perform the five canonical prayers in congregations and whenever possible at the mosque. Female disciples pray during the first hour of the period corresponding to each prayer. Disciples of both sexes will follow the laws established by the *Shari'a*.

5. That it is necessary to love the *shaykh* with a powerful and ever-growing love.

6. That one must guard oneself from superstition, because this side-tracks the soul by making it place its trust in useless phenomena, often through dreams or demonic fantasies.

7. That disciples must never express blame towards or criticize the *shaykh*.

8. That he risks serious and unpleasant (spiritual) consequences if he abandons the order after being affiliated with it.[30]

9. That it is necessary to have a firm conviction of the efficaciousness of the Way.

10. That he must, in every circumstance, keep himself from everything that can harm the *Tariqa* or discredit it.

God and none other, not even the Prophet. Customarily, intercession consists of asking God something by adding: "For the sake of someone" (meaning: in consideration of the Grace that You have bestowed upon someone, or of Your love for him). But unless one had a deep misunderstanding of what Islam is, one would never ask a saint or a prophet to do something for oneself.

This being said, people often need to support their faith with something tangible, something closer to themselves, and it must be pointed out that the respect and love due to the saints sometimes becomes a veritable "cult." Some people expect "blessings" of all kinds from saints and they go from mausoleum to mausoleum in the hope of reaping a good harvest [Translator's note: i.e. of blessings]. The practices surrounding saints' tombs are not always acceptable. This context must be kept in mind when approaching this article which, like certain other regulations, aims to guard the novice from spiritual dispersion.

Before one has reached a certain level, the adept is considered as a child, the son of his *shaykh*. One should thus turn first towards one's father. However, once one has attained spiritual maturity, not only can one visit all the tombs of other saints of Islam, but this practice will even be recommended.

Moreover, this restriction is not limited to the Tijaniyya. Many other *shaykh*s have also laid down similar rules.

[30] This is to be understood from the same standpoint as above; that is, towards guarding against dispersion.

11. That one who is not affiliated (with the *Tarīqa*) must not recite the orisons without a special authorization from a Tijani *muqaddam* or *shaykh*.

12. That one must attend the recitation of *Wazīfa* every morning, and every Friday evening one must attend the solemn meeting to recite the *Tahlīl*.

13. That one must never recite the *Jawharat al-kamāl* (*The Pearl of Perfection*) without ritual ablutions.

14. That it is forbidden for the adept to be at odds with any human being, and above all it is forbidden to follow one's anger to the point of ceasing to speak to a fellow human being for more than three days.[31]

15. That one must avoid all negligence in ritual observations.

16. That one must not seek intercession except from dignitaries of the *Tarīqa* and more particularly, from those who have acquired through this *Tarīqa* special graces from God.[32]

17. That one must never, without being formally appointed, attribute to oneself the title of *muqaddam*.

18-19. That one must maintain rigorous cleanliness of body, clothes, and home.

20. That during the recitation of the litanies, one must face the Kaaba (the sacred shrine in Mecca), except in exceptional, unexpected cases.[33]

21. That one must never interrupt the recitations with other words except in a case of uncontrollable outside forces [i.e. "acts of God"].

The obligatory requirements stop here.

22. During the recitation it is necessary to concentrate and to try to visualize in one's mind the image of the Shaykh [i.e. Shaykh al-Tijani] or better yet, that of the Prophet (upon him be peace and

---

[31] The adept who ceases speaking to a man through anger or animosity for more than three days, must confess his fault, ask forgiveness, and ask to renew his affiliation (which has been invalidated by his actions). This is an opportunity for him to practice humility and to receive guidance from his master or from his guide.

[32] See the notes related to articles 2 and 3.

[33] For example, if one is traveling on horseback or in a small boat.

blessings!) if one had seen them in a dream or if one had seen a representation of one of them.

23. That it is necessary, if one is able, to grasp the meaning of what one recites. If this is not possible, one must listen with attention so as to listen to the sound of what one recites.[34]

And may the Mercy of God be upon the best of creatures, the last of the Prophets, after whom there is no Prophet!

---

[34] Editor's note: For more information on Tijani rites and prayers, readers should refer to Dr. Louis Brenner's book *West African Sufi: The Religious Heritage and Spiritual Search of Cerno Bokar Saalif Taal* (London: C. Hurst, 1985; second impression, 2005). Brenner's book gives some alternative translations and interpretations of the central Tijani rites and prayers, as well as adding some very helpful context.

APPENDIX I

The Pearl of Perfection[1]

The *Jawharat al-kamāl* is a traditional prayer of benediction on the Prophet. However, in it one addresses the eternal Prophetic Reality (the Logos,[2] as it would be expressed in other contexts) through the Prophet of Islam (whose name does not appear in the text, unlike all other formulas of the same type). In Arabic this Prophetic Reality is called the *Nūr Muhammadiyya*, the Muhammadian Light, the Primordial Intelligence which was created by God before all manifestation. This Primordial Intelligence contains and penetrates all things, and the Prophet Muhammad is the prototype and the final manifestation in time and in history of this Intelligence. For esoteric Islam, it is this eternal Prophetic Light which is expressed through all the Prophets and Messengers of God.

The text of this prayer is untranslatable for two reasons. Firstly, it is written in an especially condensed and synthetic[3] Arabic in which each word contains a richness of meaning. These words do not have exact equivalents in French vocabulary. Rather than attempt to paraphrase, which would draw us away from the text, we have preferred to remain closer to the words (at the risk of not being "literary") and

---

[1] Editor's note: It was the number of repetitions of this prayer (either eleven or twelve times) that came to be the focus of the schism between the Hamallists and other Tijani Sufi initiates.

The use of the word "pearl" in the translated title of this prayer was explained above on p. 80, note 72. The "synthetic" quality of the language of the text applies equally to the name of the prayer itself.

[2] Editor's note: *Logos* is a Greek term used in Christian theology and the Perennial Philosophy. Literally, it means "word" or "reason." It refers to the divine, uncreated Word of God (cf. John 1:1). It is the Principle of all creation and revelation and transcends the limitations of specific forms or manifestations. Thus, the Logos is the Principle which gives birth to the archetype of Prophethood which then, at a lower metaphysical level, is manifested by a specific prophet. Each prophet is different, yet all are united in the archetype that is the origin of their messages.

[3] Editor's note: For an explanation of the author's use of the term "synthetic," as applied to language, see note 5 on p. 112.

to give explanations in notes. Finally, the ostensible meanings of the words correspond to very precise esoteric meanings in the language of Sufi mystics, in which certain tangible realities are symbols of higher realities. Wherever we have been able, we have indicated this in a note.

This work is therefore necessarily imperfect. May the reader consider it as an "approach" to the original text and may knowledgeable Arabists forgive our insufficiencies.

O God, shower Thy Grace[4] and Thy Peace
Upon the source of divine Mercy, sparkling like a diamond,[5]
   certain in its truth,[6]
Encompassing the center of (all) intelligences and meanings[7]
(Upon) the Light of the world,[8] (that) which is and begets
   being,[9]
The (primordial) Light of Adam;[10]

---

[4] *Salli,* the imperative of *salla.* When this verb is applied to man, it is normally translated as "pray" in the sense of "celebrating the canonical prayer" rather than in the meaning of "asking." When the verb is applied to God, it conveys the idea of benediction, of grace, and of the remission of sins.

[5] *Yāqqūt.* Exoterically, this word designates precious stones and all that shines with great brilliance. In the mystical language of the Sufis, it designates the universal Soul, the primordial Soul which is connected to both God and to creation.

[6] *Mutahaqqiqat:* an untranslatable word, taken from the root *haqq:* the True, the real, the correct. It is the True that affirms Itself by Itself, It is Itself Its own proof and the basis of Its right (to be).

[7] *Al-Fuhum:* the intelligences (the act of understanding) and *al-ma'ani:* the ideas, the meanings, significations. In its esoteric sense, *ma'ani* is similar to the "Ideas" of Plato. Here, *Fuhum* and *ma'ani* include on the one hand, he who can understand, and on the other, that which is to be understood.

[8] *Akwān,* the plural of *kawn:* all that exists, therefore all beings, universes, and worlds at every level. It is the Light of all that is, at every degree of existence.

[9] *Al-Mutakawwinat:* an untranslatable word. An intensified and pronominal form of the verb *takwīn,* which means "to bring into existence." It is that which is made to be and causes to be, *par excellence.*

[10] For the Sufis, all that exists, including matter, is in fact made up uniquely of Divine Light; that is, of divine energy. In the hierarchy (as it progresses from God to matter), there are:

(Upon) he who possesses the divine Truth[11]
(Of) the lightning-flashes that light up the rain-clouds and winds[12]
Which fulfill all that present themselves to them,[13]
From the vast oceans to the smallest receptacles;[14]
(Upon) Thy dazzling Light with which Thou fillest Thy Universe,[15]
(Light) which contains all places of places.[16]

1. the Light of God
2. the Light of the primordial Adam (as primordial Soul and not as Adam after the Fall)
3. the Light of all that is, implying that there is only one Light. For the Sufis, the *Nūr Adamiyya* (the Adamic Light) and the *Nūr Muhammadiyya* (the Muhammadian Light) are identical. It is the Primordial Light, the Primordial Intelligence created by God which is the source of *Revelation* throughout history, from Adam until the Prophet Muhammad, passing through all the great Messengers of God.

[Editor's note: In the sentence above, the author stressed in the original text that "the Primordial Intelligence created by God . . . is the source of *THE Revelation* throughout history. . . ." Presumably, he was emphasizing the interesting point that because all individual revelations are derived from one and the same Logos, they can be considered as different aspects of *One Revelation.*]

[11] *Haqq* implies at once the notion of (being) true, real, and upright.

[12] Here rain symbolizes the divine Mercy. The winds (or "breaths") propel these benevolent rains in all directions.

[13] "To present oneself" here carries with it the idea of "facing toward" something. The divine Mercy is said to encompass all things (according to a *hadīth*), but if it is to fill a recipient, that recipient must not turn his back on it, which would be like trying to fill a bottle-gourd (a calabash) that has its mouth facing downward.

[14] For the Sufis, the oceans symbolize the prophets and the great saints. The small receptacles (literally "the vases") symbolize ordinary believers. But whatever the size of the receptacle may be, the verse means that if one opens oneself to divine Mercy, the latter will fill one.

[15] *Kawn* (see note 8): universe, world (literally: existing, that which is).

[16] *Amkinati-l-mākanī:* This phrase refers to the totality of all that is capable of being placed within a "location," either in the material sense (i.e. within "space") or in the spiritual sense (i.e. within the ranks and degrees of the "hierarchy of being"). [Translator's note: This concept is often referred to as "All-Possibility" in metaphysics.]

O God, shower Thy Grace and Thy Peace on the source of the
  Truth[17]
From which the tabernacles[18] *of the (divine) Realities*[19] *are mani-*
  fested;
(Upon) the direct source[20] *of all knowledge,*
Thy most complete and direct way.[21]

O God, shower Thy Grace and Thy Peace
Upon the manifestation[22] *of the Truth by the Truth,*
(Upon) the immeasurable Treasure (of)
Thy emanation of Thee[23] *towards Thee,*[24]
(Upon) the circle[25] *of colorless Light.*[26]

O God, shower Thy Grace and Thy Peace upon him and upon
  his family,[27]
With a grace through which Thou makest him known to us.

---

[17] *Haqq* (see note 11).

[18] *'Urūsh*: literally, bee-hives (indicating a place where honey is concentrated).

[19] *Haqā'iq* (plural of *haqīqa*): divine, essential, truth-reality.

[20] *Aqwam*: straight, not in the "elongated" meaning of the term, but in the sense of verticality and of equilibrium. It is the vertical axis that links the upper (realms) to the lower (realms). The root *qāma* means "to remain standing upright" and by extension, "resuscitate," "bring back to life."

[21] The word here, *'asqam*, which is taken from Maghrebi (i.e. from northwest Africa) dialectical Arabic, means "that which is the straightest."

[22] *Tal'a*: Literally, "face," "aspect." It refers to that through which a reality shows itself, the "face" or aspect through which the reality itself appears (i.e. a theophany).

[23] Literally, "overflowing." The idea of flux and of superabundance. The divine Light, source of life, is considered as a flood gushing forth by the will of the Creator.

[24] A reminder of the Koranic notion according to which everything returns to God: everything comes from Him and returns to Him.

[25] Circle: suggests the concept of encompassing everything, embracing everything.

[26] Literally: "Talismanic light," that is, mysterious, enigmatic, situated above all differentiations (such as colors) which would introduce limitations into it.

[27] This is a recitation of the traditional formula of blessings on the Prophet and his family.

APPENDIX II

Sufism and Brotherhoods (*Turuq*) in Islam

My intention in presenting this book has simply been to introduce the reader both to Tierno Bokar Salif, "the Sage of Bandiagara," and to the treasures of spirituality in black Africa that await those who truly desire to look for them and who set aside all prejudices. Therefore, in what follows I do not intend to present an exhaustive exposition on Islam or on Sufism, but, for the sake of the reader unfamiliar with these concepts, it seemed to me necessary to add some explanation of the significance of the brotherhoods, or *turuq* ("ways," "paths") in Islam, these major vehicles of what is called "Sufism."

First of all, what is the origin of this term? It is agreed upon that the term derives from the Arabic word *sūf* (wool) because of the long robe of rough wool worn by the first saints and ascetics of Islam. These holy men,[1] who lived lives of renunciation and based themselves on Koranic verses and the *hadīth*s of the Prophet, and who called for the burning love of God, came to be known as "Sufis." The term *tasawwuf* (Sufism) refers both to the Sufi way and the inner state that corresponds to it.

Another etymological possibility is that the term is derived from the root S-W-F, which denotes "purity." According to this etymology, the Sufis are those who are "pure," the heirs of those *hanīf*s we discussed above.

The second and third centuries of the Hijra,[2] considered the golden age of *tasawwuf*, witnessed the flowering of great Sufis whose lives and teachings were transmitted through oral tradition and were also recorded in numerous scholarly writings. These great saints (*walī*),[3]

---

[1] Editor's note: It should be noted that the first saints and ascetics of Islam included numerous holy women as well as men, and this is widely recognized in Islam.

[2] Editor's note: That is, approximately the eighth and ninth centuries C.E.

[3] *Walī* (plural: *awliyā'*): Literally, "friend" of God, "near" to God, the "protected" of God. The term includes at one and the same time the notions of love, proximity, and security. *Walāya* is the noun referring to the corresponding state. Through a lack of corresponding terms in French [Ed.: and in English], *walī* is usually translated as "saint"

apart from their own lofty spiritual realizations, were the trustees of an esoteric and initiatic teaching that has been transmitted from them without interruption up to our own times. This chain of transmission (*silsila*) goes all the way back to the Prophet through numerous intermediary links. In almost every case, Ali, the cousin and son-in-law of the Prophet (the fourth caliph of Islam)[4] is at the summit of the transmission and, in a few cases, the transmission passes through Abu Bakr (a very close companion of the Prophet and the first caliph of Islam). Each *tarīqa* very carefully preserves the memory of its chain of transmission, which adds up to its spiritual genealogical tree.

The sixth century of the Hijra (the twelfth century of the Christian era) witnessed the formal organization of Sufism. The first major orders appeared. Followers spontaneously grouped around a master, whether that was the founding master of the *tarīqa* himself or one of his successors, a *khalīfa* (representative, lieutenant). The place of their gatherings was called the *zāwiya*, that is, the place where one gathers to study, receive teaching, and recite the *wird*, a set of prayers and litanies making up the rosary that belongs to the *tarīqa*.

I shall describe, in the order of their appearance, the most well known of these *turuq*:

1. The Qadiriyya, or Qadriyya, from the name of its founder Abdu'l-Qadir al-Jilani, born in Persia in 472 of the Hijra (1078 C.E.) and died in 561 H. (1166 C.E.).[5]

He was a very great saint who left a profound mark on Sufism and whose teachings are still very much alive today. Abdu'l-Qadir al-Jilani was the culmination of a chain of transmission that passed (progressively backward in time) through very prominent Sufis such as ash-Shibli, the great al-Junayd, all the holy Imams (descendants of the Prophet through Ali and Fatima), Ali and, through the latter, to

---

and "holiness."

[4] The younger cousin of the Prophet, Ali ibn Abi Talib, from a very young age remained constantly at the Prophet's side and was one of his strongest supporters. He married the Prophet's daughter Fatima. From their union were born Hassan and Hussein, who were the first in the line of the "eleven Imams" (twelve, including Ali). These elevated and noble spiritual figures of Islam are particularly venerated by the Shiites.

[5] In the remainder of the text, to simplify, the dates of the Hijra calendar will be marked with "H." and that of the Christian calendar with the letters "C.E."

the Prophet himself. Through another branch there were outgrowths beginning with the Imam Jafar as-Sadiq who was linked to the famous saint Abu Yazid al-Bistami and, through another branch, there were links to one of the first known Sufis: Hasan al-Basri.[6]

The Qadiriyya order stretches from Morocco to India. The center of the order is in Baghdad where the tomb of the saint is located.

2.   The Suhrawardiyya, from the name of Umar Ben Abdallah as-Suhrawardi (539-632H./1144-1234 C.E.).[7] The Persian poet Sa'di was one of his students. This order spread throughout Persia and India; its influence is still felt in modern-day Pakistan.

3.   The Shadhiliyya owe their origins to a mystic and scholar of the Maghreb, Abu'l-Hasan ash-Shadhili (593-656 H./1196-1258 C.E.). This order was very successful in North Africa, in Egypt, and in Arabia. The Darqawiyya of Morocco and of Algeria are its heirs. The Shaykh ash-Shadhili was the disciple of the master Ibn-Mashish, the heir to a spiritual line going back to the Prophet through Abdu'l-Qadir al-Jilani and Ali.

4.   Let us not neglect to mention the Mevleviyya order, founded in Turkey by Jalal ad-Din Rumi, called "Maulana" (Our Master), who died in 672 H./1273 C.E. An incomparable spiritual master and great mystical poet in both the Persian and Arabic languages, Jalal ad-Din Rumi introduced the systematic practice of sacred music and dance in Sufi gatherings, notably the whirling dance, hence the name of "whirling dervishes" given to his disciples. The spiritual chain of Jalal

---

[6] On the founder of the Qadiriyya, see Mehmmed Ali Aini, *Un grand saint de l'Islam: Abd al Kadir Guilani* (Libraire Orientale Paul Geuthner, 1967).

[7] Editor's note: According to Annemarie Schimmel in *Mystical Dimensions of Islam* (Chapel Hill: University of North Carolina Press, 1975), the founder of the Suhrawardi-yya order was actually Abd al-Qahir Abu Najib as-Suhrawardi (d. 1168 C.E.). The founder was succeeded by his nephew, the *shaykh* mentioned above, whose name is given in *Mystical Dimensions of Islam* as Shihabuddin Abu Hafs Umar as-Suhrawardi. It has been argued that he was more influential than his uncle, the founder of the or-der, in the early development of the Suhrawardiyya, thus suggesting a possible reason for the confusion over his role in the early history of the order.

ad-Din Rumi goes back to the Prophet through the intermediary of Abu Bakr, the first caliph.[8]

To be accurate, these great saints did not "found" congregations that carry their names as one would found an association today. Attracted by their spiritual radiance, people gathered around them and it is thus that the *turuq* appeared spontaneously, and little by little took the form that we know today. Sometimes the *turuq* were organized during the lifetimes of their masters, sometimes during the lives of their successors. Whatever the case, that which counts is not so much the outward and organized existence of a *tarīqa* as the durability of its "chain," that is, the uninterrupted transmission of the spiritual virtue inherited from the master, and through him, the spiritual virtue inherited from the Prophet himself.

5. The Tijaniyya, one of the last orders to appear, has its source in Shaykh Ahmad al-Tijani, who was born in 1150 H./1737 C.E. in Ain Mahdi in Algeria. He died in 1230 H./1815 C.E. in Fes, Morocco, where his tomb is located.

As mentioned above, in addition to the personal inspiration that he received directly from the Prophet, Shaykh Ahmad al-Tijani was also the heir to the most important *turuq* of his time: the Qadiriyya, the Shadhiliyya, etc.

Besides the basic teachings common to all of Sufism, Shaykh Ahmad al-Tijani's teaching is characterized by a great tolerance ("God also loves the infidel. . .") and an open spirit which, in his time, was not always understood.

*

*   *

Before going on, we should clear up a misunderstanding that still holds sway in certain Western circles with regard to Sufism. Certain orientalists, in the absence of being able to live the Sufi experience

---

[8] On Jalal ad-Din Rumi, see Aflâkî, *Les Saints des derviches tourneurs*, translated from the Persian by Clement Huart (Paris, 1978), and the works of Eva de Vitray-Meyerovitch, *Mystique et Poésie en Islam, Djalâl-ud-Dîn Rûmi* (Paris, 1968) and *Le Livre du dedans* (Paris).

inwardly, are only able to appreciate it through its written expressions. Furthermore, it should be said that these orientalists have sometimes been influenced by preconceived ideas and have been determined to see Sufism as a phenomenon foreign to Islam itself. They claim that Sufism fulfills the role of a mystical dimension which had been lacking in Islam.

Now, not only are the *turuq* which I have just discussed not situated "outside of" Islam, but they represent, on the contrary, the inner sap and spiritual dimension of the religion. It would be completely false to believe that the *turuq* had broken away from the Islamic law and the entire Koranic revelation. In fact, it is from within this Law and this Revelation that the *turuq* draw their inspiration, which is part of a constant effort of deepening and interiorization. Within these *turuq*, the requirements of the *Sharī'a* are respected as they are by others, and sometimes even more, but they are perceived, one might say, from other heights; that is, through their spiritual dimension. Thus, the ritual ablution (*wudū'*), which every Muslim must perform in order to be able to validly accomplish the canonical prayer, would be considered by Sufis as the first stage, on the exterior plane, of the inner purification necessary to approach God. The inner dimension does not exclude the outer dimension. It is a matter of the same reality lived at different levels.

In the same way, the pilgrimage to Mecca symbolizes the inner journey towards God, the supreme Center upon which all of our being should converge, and it aids in accomplishing this. The prohibition of the hoarding of wealth is understood as being linked to an attitude of inner renunciation and of "non-attachment." As for the central words of Islam: *Lā ilāha illa 'Llāh* ("there is no god but God" or "no divinity, if not God"), they are lived implacably and meditated upon, not only as the negation of all divinity outside of God, but also as the negation and dissolution of all of those inner divinities to which we cling and which we worship without realizing it, beginning with our own "me."

In reality, from the first centuries of Islam up to our days, the teachings of the great Sufi masters have constantly and intimately been linked to meditation upon Koranic verses and the *hadīth*s of the

Prophet. As for the precepts of the *Sharī'a*, the Sufis generally observe them precisely and scrupulously in a way few people can.[9]

It is true that in certain *turuq* one has seen the emergence of a progressive abandoning of the basic practices of Islam and a sense of belonging only to the *tarīqa*, since this affiliation is considered as enough to guarantee the expected spiritual benefits. But this is a degeneration that has occurred only over time and is related, more often than not, to a lack of knowledge of the true teachings of the founding masters, or even to a certain ignorance of Islam itself. Undoubtedly, such a phenomenon exists in Africa; the events reported in this book are an illustration of this.

In the Middle East or in the Far East one finds sects or congregations, said to be "extremists," who have, not only through ignorance or laziness but willingly, broken off from the precepts of the *Sharī'a*, thus distancing themselves from the bosom of Islam. But these groups make up an exception and not the rule.[10]

Moreover, certain orientalists have advanced the theory that *tasawwuf* was by nature foreign to the vocation of Islam, that it owes its existence only to the influence of certain pre-existing religious trends, in particular Christianity and Judaism. Here again, this shows a lack of knowledge of the purely Koranic roots of all Sufi teaching, as well as of the constant meditation upon the *hadīths* and verses of the Koran which nourish that teaching.

Certainly, at first glance, Sufism may appear different from Islam as the latter is commonly lived or understood by the masses. But, as we have already explained, this is a difference of level and not of nature. This multiplicity of levels of understanding or of paths of inward seeking within Islam is precisely a proof of its richness and its

---

[9] A very common symbol in Sufi teaching will enable one to better understand the position of the *turuq* in Islam. Islam, with its three fundamental levels, is symbolized by a circle with its radii and its center. The circumference represents the *Sharī'a*, the outer law. The various radii are the *turuq*, each of which is a way to approach the center but which all rest upon the circumference without ever being separated from it. The center is the *Haqīqa*, the One Truth, the essential Reality, the ultimate goal of every authentic spiritual way. It can be seen that the closer the radii are to the center, the closer they are to each other. The few elect who reach the center share the same language—Unity and Love—concerning that which relates to the essential.

[10] I do not intend to pass any judgments against them. I am simply saying that they do not represent a current that is purely Islamic.

vitality. The line of reasoning which explains this diversity as simply the result of external influences is, in truth, a little simplistic and is perhaps not entirely free of patronization.

No one would deny that during a certain period extremely rich exchanges began to take place between Muslims and other religious and philosophical cultures. The Koran itself, which is full of accounts concerning other prophets, inspires such a spirit of searching. One must not neglect to mention the *hadīth* of the Prophet: "Search for knowledge even all the way to China." Rather than speak of "influence," I prefer to use the word "encounter," which seems to me to be much more accurate.

How many great souls there have been who, having reached a very lofty spiritual level, have recognized their counterparts in other religious traditions through the experiences and the expressions of those counterparts! Why should this be surprising, since there is only one Truth and since the ultimate goal, though expressed by various words and human labels, is the same for all men? It would be insulting to these great spiritual masters to distrust the authenticity of their individual religious experiences and to judge all these to be no more than the result of an "influence." One can, however, understand that some of these masters who learned of a spiritual experience of the same or a similar nature to theirs, even if it was outside their own tradition, would find joy and enrichment in this. Moreover, depending upon the times, this phenomenon seems to have worked in both directions.[11]

The similarity of language (between masters of different traditions) can also create confusion for some. Tierno Bokar, for example, had not read the Gospels and did not know about Jesus except for what is recounted of him in the Koran. Moreover, Tierno Bokar did not read French. Yet, we hear numerous "evangelical" echoes in his words which cannot have escaped the reader! Moreover, some researchers have found in the teachings of certain great Sufis surprising similarities with the teachings of Taoism or of Zen. To all evidence, the great Sufi masters in question had never had any knowledge of those traditions. Therefore, it is not a question of influences but of

---

[11] Editor's note: An example of this would be the appreciation of Sufis in India for the spiritual treasures of the Hindu tradition, and then, in the "other direction," Jewish Kabbalists in Andalusia appreciating the riches of Sufism.

encounters.[12] Far beyond the screen of words and mental images, the soul makes its way, through its experience, towards the One Truth, towards the "Circle of Colorless Light" which is spoken of in *The Pearl of Perfection.*

*

* *

But let us come back to the various brotherhoods. They could be compared in a certain way to monastic orders that exist within Christianity, with the main difference being that in Sufism they are lay orders. The "brothers" of the *turuq* are usually married and participate in the life of this world. The *zāwiya* is a place for meeting, often on a daily basis, but it is not a place of extended residence except for certain periods of spiritual retreat (*khalwa*) which are carried out under the direction of a master, after which the disciple returns to his family. Therefore, one could not call it a "monastic" life, strictly speaking.

The researcher (or seeker) who approaches the study of Sufism for the first time can find himself disconcerted by the number of different branches. Let us recall that these branches, for the most part, are but subdivisions that have derived from a common source and that they often differ only in their names.

In fact, it can happen that an extraordinary spiritual master, a Pole (*qutb*), appears within the line of a *tarīqa* and gives it a new impetus and sometimes introduces an innovation into the spiritual exercises. The disciples of this master will henceforth give the name of this master to their *tarīqa*, even though the *tarīqa* remains an emanation of the original *tarīqa*. Only the name changes. Most of the *turuq* have, in some way, emerged from each other, which can be understood from the continuity of the chain of transmission.

---

[12] Do not confuse "encounter," which is the recognition (or acknowledgment) and respect for the other and which leads to a mutual enrichment, with "syncretism," which is the outward mixing of distinctive characteristics (or symbols), and which leads to giving up one's own roots. For more on all such issues, see the books of René Guénon and Frithjof Schuon, notably Schuon's *L'Unité transcendante des religions* (Paris, 1979). [Editor's note: The most current English edition is *The Transcendent Unity of Religions* (Wheaton: Quest Books, 1984).]

Let us take an example. Within the Shadhiliyya, a great spiritual master appeared one day, the Shaykh ad-Darqawi. All those who vowed obedience to him henceforth took the name of "Darqawi." Within the branch of the Darqawiyya, the Shaykh al-Alawi later appeared, who lived in Algeria at the beginning of the twentieth century (he died in 1934). He gave his name to the *zāwiyas* that claimed him,[13] but the Shadhiliyya line still remains intact.[14] The "Hamallists," (a name given by the French administration, one may recall, but kept by the disciples) are in fact part of the Tijaniyya order, and so on. . .

Thus, it is a matter of branches emerging and spreading out from a common trunk which goes back, as we have seen, to the Prophet himself. Apart from a few details, the doctrine which is taught is the same everywhere, since it is basically founded upon meditation upon the Koran and upon the *hadīths* of the Prophet, upon the teachings of the founders, and then upon the teachings of the great masters of Sufi thought such as Ibn Arabi, al-Ghazali, etc.

The objective is always the same: while maintaining respect for the *Sharī'a* (the revealed Law), one embarks upon the spiritual journey (*tarīqa*) which leads to union with God through death to oneself. In this journey one passes through successive and gradual stages of inner renunciation and of purification of the soul (*nafs*). The differences amongst the *turuq* only relate to details of certain modalities of methodology.

Let us now move on to the method. Apart from the study of the teachings of the masters, the method is essentially based upon the repetition of prayers or formulas which make up the *wird* (or rosary) of each *tarīqa*.

---

[13] See the book by Martin Lings, *Un saint musulman du vingtième siècle: le Cheikh Ahmad al-Alawi* (Paris, 1973). [Editor's note: The most current English edition is *A Sufi Saint of the Twentieth Century: Shaikh Ahmad al-Alawi* (Cambridge, UK: Islamic Texts Society, 1993).]

[14] Editor's note: As a shorthand way of referring to a *tarīqa*, it may simply be called, for example, "the 'Alawiyya" (from the name of the Shaykh al-Alawi, as mentioned above), but its full name would actually include all of the major *shaykhs* whose names were added to the initiatic chain in earlier times. Thus, the 'Alawiyya brotherhood would properly be called the ". . . Shadhiliyya-Darqawiyya-'Alawiyya," following the chain (*silsila*) back through however many major *shaykhs* one chooses to mention.

Here also one finds basic elements that are common to all brother-hoods. The *wird* always begins with an asking of forgiveness of God, which corresponds to the level that has to do with the individual; then a prayer of blessing on the Prophet, which corresponds to the level of the universal Man;[15] finally there is the *dhikr*, or the repeated recitation of the formula *Lā ilāha illa 'Llāh* ("no god, if not God"), which corresponds to the divine level. To this litany is added the *dhikr* of the great Name of God, *Allāh*, or of certain of His other names or attributes, all of which are taken from the Koran. Other prayers or formulas that are specific to each *tarīqa* can be added to this founda-tion which all *turuq* have in common.

Of course, the objective of these practices is not to eliminate or replace the basic practices of Islam, namely the five canonical prayers, the fast, the alms, and the pilgrimage to Mecca. The Sufi practices are superimposed upon those basic practices. It is a question of a supple-mentary spiritual effort undertaken at a personal level to intensify and deepen the spiritual life and not to eliminate the basic practices, which would not make any sense. The basic rites of Islam were revealed by God and cannot be abrogated by anyone. Otherwise, there would, strictly speaking, no longer be any Islam, and it is necessary to understand this clearly.

The practice of the *dhikr* responds to a divine injunction which is repeated several times in the Koran, in different forms:

Invoke the Name of your Lord and devote yourself to Him with a perfect devotion (73:8).

. . . Say, "God" (*Allāh*) and leave them (i.e. men) to their vain play (6:91).

---

[15] Editor's note: This is a reference to the Sufi doctrine of *al-Insān al-kāmil*, translated either as "perfect Man" or "universal Man." In his classic book *An Introduction to Sufi Doctrine* (World Wisdom, 2008), Titus Burckhardt defines the term as the "Sufi term for one who has realized all levels of Being; also designates the permanent prototype of man." When offering prayers on the Prophet in this way, the Sufi is also recognizing the supremacy of this prototype itself.

Remember Me, and I will remember you (2:152). (This verse can also be translated, "Mention me, and I will mention you.")

The word *dhikr* is laden with meaning. It means at once "mention," "remembrance," "commemoration," and "reminder." It can therefore be understood either in the outward sense of mentioning the name of God aloud (this is the "*dhikr* of the tongue") or it can be understood in the inward sense of the commemoration of the Name and of the presence of God until the *dhikr* takes possession of the entire being (this is the "*dhikr* of the heart"). In the final stage, the Sufi will find himself immersed in the "Presence without duality" (this is the "*dhikr* of intimacy" related to the state of perfect *ihsān*).

Within the *turuq*, the *dhikr* is carried out both individually and communally. Besides the individual daily recitations, the brothers gather regularly for communal sessions of *dhikr*. It is upon these occasions of communal sessions that one observes differences amongst the *turuq*. In some—notably with the Darqawiyya and certain brotherhoods of the East—the communal *dhikr* is accompanied by a sort of dance, a full rhythmic moving of the body back and forth along with a controlling of the breath. In other *turuq*, it is the head which moves (forward and to the sides), with visualization of the breath within certain points of the body; this is done particularly during the *dhikr* of *Lā ilāha illa 'Llāh*, and is related to the symbolism of the different syllables. Elsewhere, notably with the Tijani, one strives on the other hand for immobility (although the movement of the head is also used). In particular, the prayer of *The Pearl of Perfection* should be recited in a state of total immobility which should not be broken for anything. We should also mention the whirling dance particular to the Mevleviyya, the disciples of Jalal ad-Din Rumi.

As can be seen, it is mostly a matter of outward differences which correspond to different temperaments and sometimes to different cultural heritages. Since the foundations are practically always the same, Muslims have every chance of finding within Islam the *tarīqa* which corresponds best to their affinities or to their type of spiritual fellowship.

The primary virtue of the *dhikr* stems from the fact that it focuses on, as we have said, sacred Names taken from the revealed Word itself, and which therefore carry an intense spiritual energy.[16] This energy is converted, or put into action, by the number of repetitions, this number being related to the numerical value of the letters that make up the Divine Name.[17]

Nevertheless, great danger lies in considering the *dhikr*, by the very reason of its power, as a "recipe" for systematically accessing higher or ecstatic states. This is why the *dhikr* should only be practiced with the express authorization of a *muqaddam* or of a master. When the *dhikr* is communal, therefore more intense, it should be carried out under the direction and attentive control of a master. The objective is not to systematically search for "states" (*hāl*) but to approach God by emptying oneself of everything that is not Him, thanks to the *dhikr*.

"Every act," said the Prophet, "is only valid by its intention" (*niyya*). It is therefore necessary to be extremely vigilant as to the underlying intention when one engages in a spiritual exercise such as the *dhikr*. The latter is a means of realizing the progressive purification of the heart, and of enlivening one's faith, just as the stream of air of the forge enlivens the fire which will melt metal. However, the means cannot be considered as an end in itself. The only end is God, Who should be worshiped for Himself and not for the gifts which He is free to bestow upon us or not.

Moreover, the *dhikr* contains within itself its own antidote. The continual mentioning of the Name of God, which progressively leads to the perception of His real Presence, in fact leads the heart to humble itself and to be abased before the Creator, and finally, as required by *ihsān*, to "live under His gaze."

According to a definition given by the great mystic al-Junayd, *tasawwuf* (Sufism) consists of "God making man die to his 'me' so that

---

[16] Similarly, one of the derivatives of the word *dhikr* means "energy."

[17] Editor's note: Not all *turuq* emphasize the numerological significance of the exact number of repetitions of a litany or of some other type of *dhikr*. There is an aspect of this in Tijani doctrine, and it is thus not entirely surprising from this point of view that a question of eleven or twelve repetitions could cause the furor that erupted in the otherwise non-controversial life of Tierno Bokar.

(man) lives in Him." Another great Sufi, Abu Yazid al-Bistami, said: "I rid myself of my 'me' as a serpent sheds his skin."

This death to oneself is called *fanā'* (literally, "extinction," as the flame of a candle is extinguished), whereas the Way *in* God and *by* God, which is its corollary, is called *baqā'*, "beyond existence" (continuity, permanence).

"The role of the Sufis," said Muhammad Abduh,[18] "is to cure hearts and eliminate everything that veils the inner eye. They strive to establish their abode in the Spirit, before the Countenance of Him who is the highest Truth, until they become, by Him, withdrawn from all that is other (than Him), their essence being extinguished in His Essence, and their qualities in His Qualities."[19]

But what words could better express this state of *fanā'* / *baqā'* (extinction of self/life in God and by God) than this *hadīth qudsī* or "sacred *hadīth*" in which God speaks in the first person through the mouth of the Prophet, a *hadīth* which has been meditated upon by Sufis of all ages:

> My servant does not cease to approach Me with supplementary acts[20] until I love him. And when I love him, I am the hearing by which he hears, the sight by which he sees, the tongue by which he speaks, the hand by which he grasps.

A variant of this *hadīth* adds, "When I love him I slay him, and when I slay him, it is I who am his ransom."[21]

---

[18] A great Muslim thinker and reformer (b. 1849) who was named a mufti of Egypt in 1899. See his celebrated work *Rissalat al Tawhid*, translated by B. Michel and the shaykh Moustapha Abdel Razik (Librairie Orientale Paul Geuthner, 1965). [Editor's note: An English translation is *The Theology of Unity* (Kuala Lumpur: Islamic Book Trust, 2004).]

[19] "Do not say that I am good, only the Father is good," said Jesus.

[20] Supplementary acts are those which are accomplished in addition to the canonic prescriptions, with a view to pleasing God. [Translator's note: The translation from the Arabic of this *hadīth* would read more completely as ". . . supplementary acts of devotion (or piety). . ." since the idea of devotion is implicit in the Arabic.]

[21] Editor's note: The "ransom" here is the blood-money that is given as recompense following a slaying under Muslim law and practice.

One could say that all of Sufism is based on this *hadīth*, both for the method (supplementary acts) as well as for the supreme objective: the divine investiture (*baqā'*) after the death to oneself (*fanā'*).

Of course, before reaching such stages, there are many intermediary stages and many trials along the way where the *makarou*,[22] the "divine illusion," constantly lies in wait for us. That is why the aid of a master is necessary. The limits of each individual will depend upon his own disposition, upon the quality of his effort, and finally, upon unconstrained divine grace.

Through an attitude of *tawakkul* (conscious abandonment to the Divine Will), the sincere believer strives to realize in himself, according to the words of al-Hallaj,[23] a "total conformity to the decrees of God upon him" and to empty his heart of all that is "other than God," so as to offer himself to His Presence.

In another *hadīth qudsī*, God says: "Seventy times a day (or 70,000 times, according to a variant) I look into the heart of My servant to enter into it. Alas, most often, I find it full of himself, and I withdraw."

It would be an error, however, to believe that this death to oneself must necessarily be accompanied by a retreat from the world or a flight from one's responsibilities—although the spiritual retreat can sometimes be necessary at a certain stage. This would be contrary to the very spirit of Islam which demands totality, and which engages one's being in all of its aspects. Islam is not *an escape towards the sacred*, but rather, *a conscious integration of the sacred on all planes of existence*. It is a matter of living in the midst of the world, there where one finds oneself, yet no longer living in the name of one's ego but with God, in God, and by God.

"All of life, of daily life, should be filled with the presence of God and the desire to serve Him" (al-Ghazali). It is necessary to turn inwardly towards God at the very heart of life and of action. This is precisely the supreme objective of Sufism: to make not only the prescribed canonical practices, but, according to the words of Hasan al-

---

[22] See note 12, pp. 197-198.

[23] Another great mystic of Islam. See the works of Louis Massignon, especially *La Passion de Hallaj, martyr mystique de l'Islam* (Paris, 1975). [Editor's note: An abridged English version of this monumental work is *Hallaj: Mystic and Martyr* (Princeton University Press, 1994).]

Basri, "all the motions of daily life" participate in the sacred; "To make one's own life a place of divine manifestation," said Ibn Arabi.

One day a man came to find Tierno Bokar and said to him:

> "Tierno, I am worried about myself. I don't have time to recite the Koran very much, nor to practice long *dhikr*, nor to make many spiritual retreats, nor to fast outside of Ramadan. What will become of my soul?"
>
> "What do you do during the day?" Tierno asked him.
>
> "Every day, I work in the fields from morning to evening to feed my large family," answered the good fellow.
>
> "Be at peace," Tierno told him. "It is your work that is your prayer. If you accomplish your work as perfectly as possible and with the intention of pleasing God who has imposed it upon you, then your work becomes worship, just like the *dhikr* or the fasts of those who have nothing else to do."

For the spiritual life, therefore, there are neither times nor places that are privileged. In the very midst of the most demanding work, it is always possible to accomplish all of one's tasks "in the name of God" (*bismi-Llāh* [24]) and to strive to live each instant in His Presence. Are not the Sufis themselves called the "sons of the moment"?

Life in God, linked to the trusting abandonment (of all) to His Will, is equilibrium between the higher and the lower and between the inner and the outer, which are unified in this life in God. According to the words of the Prophet:

> Work for the life of this world as if you were to live a thousand years, and for the life to come as if you were to die tomorrow.

---

[24] The formula *bismi-Llāh* (In the name of God), which opens every chapter of the Koran, should be pronounced by Muslims before accomplishing any act, whatever it may be, in order to consecrate it to God.

BIOGRAPHICAL NOTES

AMADOU HAMPATÉ BÂ (c. 1900-1991) was a well-known Malian diplomat and author of the second half of the twentieth century. Both his fiction and non-fiction books in French are widely respected as sources of information and insight on West African history, religion, culture, literature, and life.

Bâ was born to an aristocratic family in Bandiagara. He first met his spiritual master, Tierno Bokar, while attending the Koranic school run by Bokar in Bandiagara. In 1942, Bâ was appointed to the Institut Français d'Afrique Noire (IFAN, French Institute of Black Africa) in Dakar. At IFAN, he made ethnological surveys and collected traditions. For fifteen years he devoted himself to research, which would later lead to the publication of his work *L'Empire peul de Macina* (The Peul Empire of Masina). With Mali's independence in 1960, Bâ founded the Institute of Human Sciences in Bamako, and represented his country at the UNESCO general conferences. In 1962, he was elected to UNESCO's executive council, and in 1966 he helped establish a unified system for the transcription of African languages. Bâ's term in the executive council ended in 1970, and he devoted the remaining years of his life to research and writing. Of his books that have been translated into English, the best known is his novel, *The Fortunes of Wangrin*, which won him the prestigious Grand Prix Littéraire de l'Afrique Noire award for excellence in African literature. Amadou Hampaté Bâ's most complete testimonial to his spiritual teacher Tierno Bokar was published as *Vie et enseignement de Tierno Bokar: Le sage de Bandiagara* (The Life and Teachings of Tierno Bokar: The Sage of Bandiagara), which later became the primary source for the play *Tierno Bokar*, written by Marie-Hélène Estienne and directed by Peter Brook. This volume is the first complete English translation of that book.

Amadou Hampaté Bâ died in 1991 in Abidjan, Côte d'Ivoire. He is credited with the famous quotation: "In Africa, when an old person dies, it is as if a library has burned down."

LOUIS BRENNER is Emeritus Professor of the History of Religion in Africa, School of Oriental and African Studies, University of London.

He has published extensively on the history of Islam and of Muslim societies in West Africa, with special emphasis on the dynamics and transmission of Muslim thought and ideas, and on Sufism. Dr. Brenner has spent considerable time in Africa following his research interests: During the mid-1970s, he began to research traditional forms of Muslim education and Muslim thought in Mali, which led ultimately to the publication of *West African Sufi: The Religious Heritage and Spiritual Search of Cerno Bokar Saalif Taal.* Research for his book was greatly enhanced by the generous cooperation of Amadou Hampaté Bâ, who at the time was preparing *Vie et enseignement de Tierno Bokar* (the book of which this volume is a translation) for publication. Over a period of several years, Hampaté Bâ granted Brenner many hours of interviews in Mali, Paris, and Abidjan. Dr. Brenner has also written *Controlling Knowledge: Religion, Power, and Schooling in a West African Muslim Society.*

FATIMA JANE CASEWIT is a writer, translator, and educator who lives in Rabat, Morocco. She has a background in linguistics and education and completed her undergraduate and graduate work in France and the United Kingdom. After many years of teaching, translating, and working on a rural girls' education project in Morocco, she is now part of the USAID/Morocco education team. Mrs. Casewit's interests focus on comparative religion and Traditionalist studies, particularly in the area of West African Islam and Sufism. She has published several articles on gender in the light of tradition, including "Islamic Cosmological Concepts of Femininity," which can be found in *The Betrayal of Tradition: Essays on the Spiritual Crisis of Modernity*, edited by Kenneth (Harry) Oldmeadow. Mrs. Casewit had the privilege of visiting the home and family of Tierno Bokar in Bandiagara, as well as the mosque, which has not changed since Tierno Bokar's time. She also met Tierno Bokar's last living *talibé* (student) and his family, who perpetuate the nobility and wisdom of the Tijani way in West Africa today.

ROGER GAETANI is an editor and educator who lives in Bloomington, Indiana. He is co-editor, with Jean-Louis Michon, of the World Wisdom anthology *Sufism: Love and Wisdom.* Mr. Gaetani also directed and produced the DVD compilation of highlights to the 2006 conference on Traditionalism, entitled *Tradition in the Modern World: Sacred*

Web 2006 Conference, and has most recently edited this book. He was born and received his formal education (at Syracuse University and Indiana University) in the United States, but spent a number of years in Morocco and Saudi Arabia as a teacher. While there, and in travels through other countries in Africa and Asia, he gained an appreciation for traditional cultures, thought, and art. Through these experiences, he became acquainted with the Perennialist school of thought, whose precepts he finds essential in explaining the most fundamental questions in comparative religion, modern civilization, and personal spiritual development. Mr. Gaetani is currently working on translating and editing several books on Sufism from the Perennialist/Traditionalist perspective.

INDEX

For a glossary of all key foreign words used in books published by World Wisdom, including metaphysical terms in English, consult:
www.DictionaryofSpiritualTerms.org.
This on-line Dictionary of Spiritual Terms provides extensive definitions, examples and related terms in other languages.

Titles in the Spiritual Masters: East & West Series by World Wisdom

Titles on Islam by World Wisdom

Art of Islam: Illustrated,
by Titus Burckhardt, 2009

Christianity/Islam: Perspectives on Esoteric Ecumenism,
by Frithjof Schuon, 2008

Introduction to Sufi Doctrine,
by Titus Burckhardt, 2008

Introduction to Traditional Islam: Illustrated,
by Jean-Louis Michon, 2008

Islam, Fundamentalism, and the Betrayal of Tradition:
Essays by Western Muslim Scholars,
edited by Joseph E.B Lumbard, 2004

The Mystics of Islam,
by Reynold A. Nicholson, 2002

The Path of Muhammad: A Book on Islamic Morals
and Ethics by Imam Birgivi,
interpreted by Shaykh Tosun Bayrak, 2005

Paths to the Heart: Sufism and the Christian East,
edited by James S. Cutsinger, 2003

Paths to Transcendence: According to
Shankara, Meister Eckhart, and Ibn Arabi,
by Reza Shah-Kazemi, 2006

The Spirit of Muhammad: From Hadith,
edited by Judith and Michael Oren Fitzgerald, 2009

A Spirit of Tolerance: The Inspiring Life of Tierno Bokar,
by Amadou Hampaté Bâ, 2008

The Sufi Doctrine of Rumi: Illustrated Edition
by William C. Chittick, 2005

Sufism: Love and Wisdom,
edited by Jean-Louis Michon and Roger Gaetani, 2006

Sufism: Veil and Quintessence,
by Frithjof Schuon, 2007

Understanding Islam, by Frithjof Schuon, 1998

Universal Spirit of Islam: From the Koran and Hadith,
edited by Judith and Michael Oren Fitzgerald, 2006